Crusading Doctor

Crusading Doctor

My Fight for Coöperative Medicine

By
MICHAEL A. SHADID, M.D.

Foreword by
RALPH NADER

University of Oklahoma Press
Norman and London

Other Books by Michael A. Shadid

The Self Physician (1912)
How to Live One Hundred Years (1916)
A Doctor for the People (1939)
Doctor of Today and Tomorrow (1946)
Principles of Co-operative Medicine (1946)
Diet in Health and Disease (1936)

Shadid, Michael A. (Michael Abraham), 1882–
    Crusading doctor : my fight for cooperative medicine / by Michael A. Shadid ; foreword by Ralph Nader.
    p. cm.
    Reprint. Originally published: Boston : Meador Pub. Co., 1956.
    Includes index.
    ISBN 0-8061-2344-3
    1. Shadid, Michael A. (Michael Abraham), 1882– .
2. Physicians—Oklahoma—Biography. I. Title.
R154.S366A3   1992
610′.92—dc20
[B]   90-50696
                                                CIP

The paper in this book meets the guidelines for permanence and durability of the Committee on Production Guidelines for Book Longevity of the Council on Library Resources, Inc. ∞

Published by the Oklahoma Press, Norman, Publishing Division of the University. Copyright © 1956 by Michael A. Shadid except for the Foreword by Ralph Nader, copyright © 1992 by Ralph Nader. All rights reserved. Manufactured in the U.S.A. First printing of the University of Oklahoma Press edition.

Dedication

This book is dedicated to those medical practitioners who have dared to break through the barriers of decaying medical tradition and dogma, and have suffered persecution and ostracism so that the way might be cleared to wider opportunities for knowledge, truth, and service, to themselves, to the public, and to the profession.

This edition of Michael A. Shadid's *Crusading Doctor: My Fight for Coöperative Medicine*, which has been out of print for some years, was made possible by a grant from the Maximilian E. and Marion O. Hoffman Foundation.

Contents

Foreword, by Ralph Nader   xi

Part One—A Crusader in the Making

1 Syrian Childhood: *Judaidah, 1882–1893*   3
2 School Days: *Beirut, 1893–1898*   10
3 Peddling My Way to College: *America, 1898–1902*   16
4 M.D. at Last: *St. Louis, 1902–1906*   23
5 Guinea Pigs in Missouri: *Maxville, 1906–1908*   28
6 Starting in Oklahoma: *Stecker and Oklahoma City, 1908–1912*   34
7 A Specialist Doctor: *Carter, 1912–1923*   41
8 Settling in Elk City: *1923–1929*   55

Part Two—The Problem of Health for All

9 Medical Chaos and Ideas on Reform   63

Part Three—The Oklahoma Health Crusade

10 Starting a Medical Coöperative: *1929*   87
11 The Die Is Cast: *1929–1931*   95
12 The Termites Attack: *1931*   104
13 Alfalfa Bill Murray to the Rescue: *1931–1932*   116

14	Running the Medical Blockade	123
15	The Plan in Successful Operation: *1932–1935*	140
16	Success Arouses Greater Hostility: *1935–1936*	154
17	The Courts Rescue My License: *1936–1940*	165
18	The Fight in the Legislature and on the Ballot: *1937–1940*	178
19	Candidate for Congress: *1940*	191
20	Running for Congress Again: *1940–1942*	204
21	Three Extraordinary Episodes	209
	1. The Heitholt Bequest: *1938–1951*	209
	2. The Draft as a Weapon: *1941–1945*	218
	3. Polio in Politics: *1949–1952*	221
22	Happy Ending, for Oklahoma: *1950–1952*	225

PART FOUR—HORIZONS IN COÖPERATIVE MEDICINE

23	Coöperative Medicine Across America	241
24	The Co-operative Health Federation of America	254

Some Notes and Reflections Fifty-five Years Later, by Fred V. Shadid	269
Index	271

Foreword

by Ralph Nader

If Hollywood is looking for both drama and historical significance in the life of one immigrant to this country, the saga of Dr. Michael A. Shadid has to be a leading candidate. The sequence was as improbable as it was heroic. Born in 1882 on the eastern slope of Mount Lebanon, then a part of the Ottoman Empire's province of Syria, he was the last of twelve children living in deep poverty. The first nine of his infant brothers and sisters died from poor sanitation and malnutrition.

Dr. Shadid travelled to the United States alone at the age of fifteen and became an itinerant peddler of jewelry and linens across wide reaches of the eastern half of the United States. He earned enough money to put himself through an accelerated course leading to a college degree and then medical school at Washington University in St. Louis. Soon thereafter he settled in Elk City, Oklahoma, and became a tireless and much-loved surgeon and family doctor in those rural areas. His son, Dr. Fred V. Shadid, said that his father drove his horse and buggy and later his Model T Ford "in dust storms and snow drifts, delivering babies and attending to the illnesses of farmers in the shortgrass country of western Oklahoma." He lived the title of one of his books, *A Doctor for the People*.

When President Jimmy Carter made a campaign visit to Elk City on March 24, 1979, he did not mention its claim to fame in American history. For in that little town in the year of 1929 was organized the first cooperative hospital in the nation, owned by its patients and sustained by a pioneering prepayment plan which provided comprehensive health care benefits through a group practice of physicians on salary. Dr. Michael A. Shadid conceived, established, and directed this hospital. To launch this dream, he had to contend with the relentless drive of organized medical societies and their powerful allies to put him and his hospital out of business year after year.

He was subjected to malicious rumors of self-enrichment, charlatanism, and violation of medical ethics in procuring business. Organized medicine tried to revoke his license; the county medical society dropped him from its lists by disbanding the society and restarting it without him. He fought back. His opponents punished the physicians in the hospital by denying them membership in the local and state medical societies. This exclusion led to serious liabilities; the physicians were stigmatized as quacks, refused malpractice insurance, refused admission to postgraduate courses in medicine and surgery, blocked from attending clinical meetings of the medical societies, prevented from becoming recognized specialists, and denied consultation with fellow practitioners. Laboratory and X-ray technicians were similarly ostracized and denied membership in their respective societies. Dr. Shadid called all these maneuvers "the blockade."

When his enemies failed at one stage, they went to another, the courts; and when they failed in the courts, they went to the legislature. At each stage, they underestimated the man whose practice, service, commitment, and ideals for cooperative medicine they were fiercely bent on destroying. His dedication was unshakable to the goal of providing poor farm families in the midst of depression and drought, with quality health care at reasonable prepayment rates, instead of the budget-busting fee-for-service medicine. Shadid in Arabic means "strong." And, indeed, he was just

FOREWORD

that, seeking out tough lawyers to retain, connecting with the influential Farmers Union and key legislative allies, and even, at one time, with the governor of Oklahoma, "Alfalfa Bill" Murray. It was not until 1952 that final victory came, when the county medical society agreed to an out-of-court settlement with the hospital, ending its opposition and permitting full membership in the medical society for staff physicians. That in turn led to memberships in the state medical society and the American Medical Association.

During this long struggle Dr. Michael Shadid expanded the cooperative hospital (called Community Hospital) to serve thousands of farm families; kept himself up with academic medicine through courses at various medical schools; lectured, advised, and exhorted all over the nation and Canada for prepaid medical practice planned around the consumer-cooperative concept; encouraged preventive medicine; and with his indefatigable and wise wife, Edna, raised six children, two of whom became physicians. He even won a statewide referendum in Oklahoma validating prepaid cooperative medical practice, and then lost it under a quirky rule that those who did not vote either way on the referendum were counted as no votes. He ran for the U.S. House of Representatives in 1940 and was the victim of organized voting fraud that robbed him of the primary election. The falsehoods and slanders he documents were remarkable in their intensity and prejudice. He was called a "Communist Turk," a "peddler of rugs," an "atheist," a "fifth columnist," a "chronic drunkard," a father of a "daughter he drowned because she married an American." Checks were forged to tie him to the Communist Party.

His adversaries could steal elections but, try as they might, they could not break "the strong one." He was experienced in running gauntlets. His son Fred described a daily routine in the early thirties: "At age fourteen and fifteen I was driving as his chauffeur [to farmland speaking engagements where Dr. Shadid would spread the seditious doctrine of prepaid medical care], and due to threats on his life, many occasions I sat on the back seat with my 12-gauge shotgun across my knees (I admit my knees were shaky)."

His adversaries in medicine were possessed of creative strategies. In the early thirties, when the Community Hospital was signing up more and more members, two of the four competing hospitals in the county reorganized into phony cooperative hospitals willing to discount hospital bills and surgical fees. After a little investigative research, Dr. Shadid unmasked these imposters as for-profit corporations. "A true cooperative is owned by its members and no one else," and is non-profit, he wrote.

This phony competition, which soon collapsed, was followed by a change in the Community Hospital prepayment plan, which originally was based on a discount system until the membership was large enough to pay at least the physicians' salaries. In 1932 a prepayment plan was worked out to replace the discount system. Families were entitled to unlimited medical examinations, treatments, surgical operations, and laboratory work at the hospital at the following rates: one person, twelve dollars per year; two persons, eighteen dollars per year; three persons, twenty-two dollars per year; and four or more persons in the family, twenty-five dollars per year. Home visits were one dollar in town, plus ten cents a mile each way in the country. Drugs, anesthetics, and ancillaries were extra.

One of Dr. Shadid's speeches urging farmers to join the Community Hospital prepayment plan provides a frame of reference:

> Two thousand of you can pay twenty-five dollars a year for your families and with the fifty thousand dollars you will collectively have you can hire eight or more doctors and specialists who will provide you with free examinations, free treatments and free surgical operations for a year without any additional charge. . . . Many of you have paid from three hundred to a thousand dollars for one case of illness. Under a prepayment

plan, three hundred dollars will pay your doctor's bill for twelve years, and a thousand dollars would pay for a lifetime of protection. In addition to examinations and treatments when you are sick, under the prepayment plan you can receive the benefits of preventive medicine. . . . a large percentage of illness can be checked in an early stage. But under the present setup, the patient doesn't go to the doctor for a slight illness— he can't afford to. . . . Listen carefully to this: It is estimated that one third of the deaths in the United States every year are preventable. And why this tragic failure? Because under our system, the doctor is a private tradesman with services to sell—and only sick people will buy them.

Cooperative medicine will improve the conditions of the doctors by freeing them from the uncertainties of private practice: the charity cases, the burden of uncollectable debts, the overhead of office and equipment, the waste of time. It will give the doctor a chance for regular hours, the use of all essential facilities, freedom from economic pressures. (Pp. 180–81)

No matter how rational the appeal, repetition and more repetition were required. Dr. Shadid made hundreds of speeches throughout southwestern Oklahoma before farmers' gin and elevator cooperative associations. He rarely missed an opportunity to draw the analogy between these farmer co-ops and the logic of also having a hospital co-op that they belonged to and ran. The logic was reinforced through the monthly Community Hospital *Bulletin*, which kept members informed on the activities of the cooperative hospital and advised them on "matters of health and hygiene." This consumer-health publication was another first in Dr. Shadid's pioneering record. Years later, in 1945, Dr. J. P. Warbasse, former editor of the *American Journal of Surgery* and the New York State *Journal of Medicine*, called the *Bulletin* "the most important medical periodical published in the United States . . . because it is the first and only journal devoted to the interest of the patients and prospective patients owning a hospital."

Like a resolute ship moving forward during a ferocious ocean storm, the hospital kept growing and prospering. In 1934 a third story was added to the original structure. Two years later a three-story wing was added to the east end. In 1938 another wing was added, and in 1940 two more stories added to it. Dr. Alex Shadid and Dr. Fred Shadid joined the hospital in 1939 and 1941, respectively. A nursing home was built in 1946, and a clinic building was completed in 1949 with space for twelve physicians. By 1950, 2,500 families were members. The hospital became a model for emulation with feature articles in *Collier's* magazine and *Reader's Digest* in 1943 helping to give it national publicity.

The *Reader's Digest* article, "Cooperative Health Harvest," was written by Paul de Kruif, a well-known science writer, who had visited the hospital and observed:

> . . . Courageously, resourcefully, Dr. Shadid and these Oklahomans have pioneered a way to beat our shortage of country doctors. They have proved that even a poor farm community can build its hospital, pay for it, and hire a staff of competent physicians and surgeons. For rural America, Dr. Shadid and the Oklahoma farmers have shown the way toward a new level of medical strength and vigor made possible by prepaid group practice—the country medicine of tomorrow.

But the horizons of Dr. Michael Shadid were neither limited to building an example of what could be done nor restricted to country medicine. He was on a crusade for both country and city with his writings, his travels, and his detailed advice to budding prepaid group-practice efforts in California, Kansas, Wisconsin, Washington state (Puget Sound Co-op), Washington, D.C. (Group Health Association), Texas, Minnesota, Saskatchewan, and other localities.

FOREWORD

He worked with private lawyers and those at the Department of Justice, testifying before legislatures and grand juries as well as volunteering his expert knowledge of organized medicine's antitrust violations, which eventually were stopped by both criminal prosecutions and civil suits.

In 1946, Dr. Shadid retired as medical director of the Community Hospital, and the Board of Directors of the Hospital elected his son, Dr. Fred Shadid, as his successor. Though exhausted and not in the best of health, Dr. Michael Shadid helped organize that same year the Co-operative Health Federation of America (CHFA) and was elected its first president. By this time cooperative health societies were sprouting up all over North America. Although they varied in approaches and methods of operation, these societies agreed to CHFA's five governing principles, to wit: (1) prepayment, budgeting the cost of medical care; (2) comprehensive medical and health care, both preventive and curative; (3) group medical practice; (4) ownership and management of facilities by prepayment-plan members; and (5) no interference by lay people with the professional practice of medicine by those licensed to do so.

The 1940s witnessed more attacks by the American Medical Association and state and local medical societies against the growth of cooperative health associations. Many such health associations organized by Dr. Shadid in Texas and other states were destroyed because local medical associations blocked licenses, denied membership in local medical societies, and denied hospital privileges to co-op doctors.

The tide began to turn against the AMA and its cohorts in the late 1940s and early 1950s as the AMA turned its attention against President Truman's national health insurance proposal, and Blue Cross expanded in ways that satisfied organized medicine. Indeed, health insurance, employer plans, and later Medicare, Medicaid, and health maintenance organizations (HMOs), became the mix that today's Americans, especially the 70 million of them with no health insurance or grossly inadequate coverage, are finding increasingly unsatisfactory, judged by standards of accessibility, quality, and cost control.

The consumer-sponsored plans with genuine consumer participation are rare, having been overtaken by prepaid plans that are part of collective bargaining agreements, or by insurance plans that offer high profits or higher salaries than consumer-cooperative health societies. It appears that the latter require a higher degree of altruism and loyalty than do their commercial competitors. This higher degree of commitment eventually proved too much for the successors of the Shadid physicians. It did not take long. In 1949, Dr. Michael Shadid described the hospital as "solvent, well staffed, and secure in the esteem of the people." In the summer of 1953, due to overwork and a long-postponed desire to spend time with his family, Dr. Fred Shadid moved from Elk City to Oklahoma City and a less-demanding solo practice. Four months later, frictions developed between the doctors and the Community Hospital board over the division of income between the hospital-clinic and the staff. The staff wanted the annual dues of members increased, arguing that members were being subsidized by hospital income from non-member patients. During the next two stormy years, physicians started resigning, their patients stopped paying dues and joined Blue Cross plans, and a downward spiral began, and with it an ever weaker financial situation and the resignation of the remaining medical staff.

In 1955 the Community Hospital closed its doors. Dr. Fred Shadid summed up the effort this way:

> Community Hospital was born during drought and dust bowl days and the Great Depression in western Oklahoma. In spite of all the opposition and obstacles, it grew and prospered. It served its purpose for over 25 years, filling the need for good health care, at affordable prices, to the farmers of western Oklahoma. It furthered the growth of more prepayment medical plans across the nation. Co-op Hospital and Dr. Michael Shadid

have rightfully taken their place in the medical history of the United States. . . . Why did the Co-op cease to exist? I believe it was due to lack of proper leadership, lack of dedication and sincere beliefs in the fundamental concepts of the cooperative ideas by members of the staff.

What did the remarkable Dr. Michael Shadid do after he left the presidency of the Co-operative Health Federation of America in 1949, following a heart attack? He raised funds in the United States and Brazil for a charity hospital in the Lebanese village of his birth, Judedeit-Merj-ayoun, where nine of his siblings had perished as infants; he returned to his roots to help build this health facility. Small wonder that the University of Oklahoma requested the papers of Dr. Shadid and the Community Hospital for its Western History Collections. Small wonder that a stage play, *Oracle Junction*, on the struggle for Co-op Hospital, was performed in Dallas, Texas, in 1954. And, small wonder that the University of Oklahoma Press, with financial assistance of the Maximilian E. and Marion O. Hoffman Foundation, is placing *Crusading Doctor* back in print for consumers, health care practitioners and officials, medical students, and other Americans to draw inspiration from, as this country moves to another climatic juncture in the quest for comprehensive health care coverage.

The idealism of the past can help nourish the motivation of the future. No better example of service can be recounted than that rendered, amidst a maelstrom, by Dr. Michael Shadid and his sons. They practiced medicine as if only people mattered.

Washington, D.C.
June 1991

Part One

A Crusader in the Making

Chapter 1

Syrian Childhood

Judaidah, 1882–1893

Judaidah, where I was born, is a town of about three thousand people on the eastern slope of Mount Lebanon, in the country of Lebanon, at that time part of the Turkish province of Syria. It is known in the Old Testament as Ijon, and appears on modern maps as Merdjiyoun, from its full Arabic name Judaidat Marj 'Uyun. It is twenty-five miles east of the city of Tyre from which came Hiram, the widow's son who built King Solomon's temple, and twenty miles southeast of Sidon.

I was the twelfth child, and was born a few months after my father died, in just what year I am not sure. There was as little regard for vital statistics as for sanitation in Judaidah, and since my mother could neither read nor write, there was no record of the year of my birth. Later when I had to give a definite date, I arbitrarily chose January first, 1882, for my mother, to whom the seasons rather than the calendar were a guide, had told me that I was born in the winter and that I was eleven years old when we moved to Beirut in 1893.

There was but one old-time doctor in Judaidah. His resources consisted of mustard poultices, and quinine, and calomel, and when the first nine of my infant brothers and sisters fell ill with "summer complaint," that combination of filth and improper feeding, they died.

As a posthumous child, I of course knew nothing of my

father, but my mother used to tell me that he was a good husband and a successful trader. Not a great and rich trader but one who plied his calling with wares strapped on the backs of two strong mules, carrying out products of the village or countryside—dried figs, butter, olive oil, hides—and bringing back grains, mostly wheat from the southern valleys, and bolts of foreign cloth from Beirut. Since burdened mules move slowly and the only roads were rough trails, this was an occupation that often kept him away from home for weeks at a time.

Mother, named Kushfa, was one of a family of five sisters and three brothers, one of whom was, like her father, a priest in the Greek Orthodox Church. She was very devout and I had to go to mass each Sunday morning. Once each month I would go to the confessional with two eggs in payment for the privilege. Priests were not salaried and are not to this day. They live from fees received for performing a marriage ceremony, conducting a funeral, or finding a suitable bride or groom. Twice each year the three Greek Orthodox priests would visit the home of each parishioner, and would, of course, expect to be "tipped." Once at Easter and again on the day commemorating the baptism of Jesus in the river Jordan, a priest would carry a pail of water that had been blessed and would sprinkle it on the walls of the house. Once my mother, embarrassed by not having ready cash to give them, ran to a neighbor's house to borrow. The majority of the people could neither read nor write, but the priests, though uneducated, could do both.

As I look back to my childhood days sixty years ago, I can see that the most divisive element in the life of the people in the Near East was religion. Instead of promoting peace and harmony, religion was a source of strife and hatred, and yet religious forms and language abounded. The salutations, ejaculations, and imprecations of the people were full of the name of God—"Allah". The most sacred words and expressions were constantly on the lips of all, the learned and the ignorant—men, women, and children. Whatever

SYRIAN CHILDHOOD

the subject might be, religion in some form or other had a share in it.

When father died he left mother a one-room house, two mules, and twenty thousand piasters, a sum equivalent to one thousand dollars. Mother was no weakling, but was strong of body and mind, of resolute character, and very religious. I never knew her to fail in burning incense before icons and in kneeling and praying every evening. She had borne with fortitude, and usually with resignation, whatever life had brought to her. Her tiny inheritance had to last indefinitely, and so she had to supplement it by baking, washing, and scrubbing for a meager living. Our fare, like that of most of our neighbors, was of the simplest, consisting chiefly of rice, cracked wheat, dried figs, olives, bread, and molasses; meat and eggs rarely. And it was only once a year—at Easter time—that we had pastry.

Our clothing was even simpler than our diet. We wore no shoes, and went hatless, or rather fezless, even in winter. Mother made our shirts and rompers from calico and muslin sent by her brothers in Beirut.

My brother and sister and I lived with our mother in a home that differed from those of biblical times only in the kerosene lamp that had replaced the ancient olive-oil lamp of our fathers. The house was made of rough-hewn stone, and consisted of one room with a stable attached, where my father had kept his mules when he was alive and active as a trader with the Arabs to the south.

The roof was flat and made of earth which had to be pressed with a heavy roller every day in the winter, to keep the surface hard enough to shed water. The floor was of red clay, kept smooth by rubbing with a stone. Since there was no chimney, smoke from the fire of dried cow-dung hung about the room darkening the white-washed wall and burning our eyes until it drifted out of the door. There was no furniture—no chairs, no table, no bedsteads. We worked, ate, and slept on the earthen floor, with only a cushion, a quilt, and a pillow for our bedding.

And in our home another odor mingled with the usual ones, for we lived near the village cemetery, where the graves were so shallow that the smell of decaying corpses permeated the air. If I were asked to sum up in a phrase the most striking distinction between the East and the West I would answer, "the smells." Very few cities could boast of a sewer system, and certainly not our village. Filth was universal. Every house had its dunghill.

The twenty thousand piasters my father left were placed in the keeping of the head of the Shadid clan, an honest and upright man. I clearly remember occasional visits to him with my mother when she drew out small sums, and each time she would ask the old man how much remained. And each time she would weep bitterly as she realized that our little fortune was dwindling away. But she was frugal and hard-working, and by supplementing the small legacy with what she and my only surviving sister, Deeba, who was ten years older than I, could earn by washing, baking, and scrubbing for our more prosperous neighbors, she made it last ten years.

But no matter how sharply the pennies were otherwise watched, the few dollars necessary for school were promptly paid. The tuition for each child, in addition to the lump of coal required on every winter day, was about two dollars a year. This did not include the cost of books, however, so my brother and I worked during the summer breaking rocks for road-making, for which we were paid ten cents a day.

Mother was sternly determined to see to it that I had an education. One summer she rented a small fig orchard at a place called Tel (the hill) where some of the wealthier families of the village had a large acreage of figs, and where they rented out plots of these figs when ripe to the poorer families of the village. It was necessary that my mother remain with her plot of figs day and night during the ripening season. During the daytime she picked and dried the figs, while at night she protected the crops from robbers. One day I ran away from school and went two miles out to Tel, but when

SYRIAN CHILDHOOD

my mother saw me coming, she met me with strong reproaches and a switch from a fig tree and drove me back to school.

There were three schools in Judaidah: the Greek Orthodox, which I attended, the Roman Catholic, and a Protestant one supported largely with American missionary funds and considered "heretical." In one of the homes along the narrow street, on the way to school, I used to see a violently insane woman chained. She cursed and threatened all who passed by. One morning I was greatly frightened as she seemed to be running towards me, so for a whole week thereafter, my mother took me past that house to school. My teacher was a martinet who thought nothing of whipping a boy for being five minutes late in the morning, or for forgetting to bring with him the lump of coal that was every pupils' tribute to the stove that warmed the room. At the beginning of the school year, my mother delivered me to this tyrant with the conventional maxim "the flesh is yours, the bones are mine." But our teacher needed no urging. His fingers seemed to itch for the rattan, and I can still feel its cruel cut across my flesh.

A name that I often heard during my boyhood in Judaidah was that of Dr. George Post, an American from Pennsylvania. He was the chief surgeon of the Syrian Protestant College, now the American University of Beirut. His name was a household word throughout the villages of Lebanon. He made many trips into the hill villages to perform operations upon people too poor or too incapacitated to make the journey to the city—a matter of fifty or sixty miles but two days' journey on mule-back over rough trails. Dr. Post came to Judaidah more than once. He was a great character as well as a remarkable surgeon, and the success of his operations was narrated widely and was magnified greatly among the simple mountain folk until he became a legendary saint.

Among my earliest memories, as I recall them now after an interval of 60 or more years, are many that have to do with poverty, and the feeling of resentment I experienced in the face of poverty. Why was I barefooted and fezless? Why were my clothes shabby and my lunch at school meager compared with that of other children? Why was my mother a menial? The contrast between the homes of the well-to-do in the village and my own impressed me forcibly—the many rooms, the rich furnishings, the varied and better foods, the more spacious enclosures.

I remember distinctly a tragedy that overtook a neighbor. He was a trader and his only possession and means of livelihood was a mule. I can still recall the death from colic of the mule; the rearing and rolling of the poor beast in its pain; the attempts of the owner and neighbors to give relief in order to save it; the anguished suspense of family and friends as they awaited the outcome; the death of the mule; and with the full realization that their one source of livelihood had been lost, the tears, the wailing, and the agony of the owning family; yes, and of the sympathetic neighbors, too, for this was a real tragedy among the poor. This experience made such a vivid impression upon me that the scenes are deeply etched in my memory to this day.

But our lives weren't all hardship and drudgery, by any means. We accepted what now appears to be our hard lot because we were not aware that any life radically different from ours was possible. After all, we were children, and children manage to play and have a good deal of fun almost anywhere.

Our favorite game was played with a pebble or ball and an astragalus. This last was my introduction to anatomy, as an astragalus is a bone in the ankle of a goat or a sheep that we boys used to beg from the local butcher.

Sundays were red-letter days, for not only did we sometimes have meat to eat, but we enjoyed a combined bath and swim in the village pool. Judaidah's only water supply was a spring on the outskirts of the town, from which a little stream ran through the village, giving water for the fountain. Just below the village an enterprising resident had dammed the brook to form a pool of sorts, and he charged about

SYRIAN CHILDHOOD

two cents for admission. This pool, of course, became the rendezvous of all the village children; it was here that we had the greatest fun and here that we taught each other the rudiments of sex. And, perhaps even more important, it was here that we occasionally achieved some degree of cleanliness.

I way playing joyously at the pool one day when my mother came and called me away. She said I had to go with her to the hut of a friend in the center of the village. As we came near the house, I heard the piercing screams of a woman in agony. Anxious women were gathered about the doorway and crowded into the tiny room.

My mother elbowed her way through the crowd, pulling me behind her. I stood with her beside a large chair and witnessed for the first time the birth of a child. When it was all over, I was presented to the baby, a tiny girl whom they named Adeeba. Then and there this baby and I were formally betrothed by a simple ceremony.

In the Near East, this was in keeping with the common custom. Such a ceremony was not considered absolutely binding, but betrothals were seldom broken when the parties remained in the village together. However, it was most assuredly not the ceremony performed when I was ten years old that caused me to marry, many years later and in faraway St. Louis, this same girl, Adeeba.

At the time, my engagement made little impression on me. And in less than a year it went from my mind entirely when we moved from Judaidah. The last of the piasters left by my father were gone, and my mother appealed for help to her three brothers in Beirut. They advised us to come there, for the city was large and work could be found for my mother and the older children. So our few possessions were tied up in bundles and fastened on the back of the mule, and my brother and I were perched on top of them all. With the others walking alongside, we set off for Beirut, two days' ride away. That night we slept in Sidon, and late the next day we reached our destination.

Chapter 2

School Days

Beirut, 1893–1898

When I went to Beirut, I found not only the largest and most prosperous city along the eastern coast of the Mediterranean, but also a part of America. Here in this Near Eastern city of two hundred thousand people was an outpost of American civilization, a typical middle-western college with a campus of forty acres and twelve fine buildings: the American University of Beirut. And here, too, was Dr. George Post, famed throughout Syria for his skill and his almost miraculous surgery, the man who became my ideal, inspiring me with a burning determination to become a doctor, to go out to little villages like Judaidah and heal the sick.

Those who had started the first steam printing press in Syria and the first boys' and girls' boarding-school were also the first to initiate what took form as the Syrian Protestant College—now known as the American University of Beirut. These were Dr. DeForest, Simeon H. Calhoun, "The Saint of Lebanon," and Cornelius Van Alan Van Dyck.

No man in the Arab lands was more revered and loved than was Cornelius Van Dyck, a missionary of Hollandic origin. During his seventeen years in Syria, he had mastered not only Arabic but also Syrian, Hebrew, Greek, French, Italian, and German. He had a genius for languages, a phenomenal memory, and a clear intellect, and he excelled in medicine, astronomy, and higher mathematics. His knowledge of Arabic, both classical and vulgar, was a wonder to

SCHOOL DAYS

both natives and foreigners. In collaboration with Dr. Eli Smith, another missionary, and assisted by two Arabic scholars—Butrus al-Bustani and Nasif al-Yaziji—he translated the Bible into Arabic.

In the fall of 1866, the college was opened with 16 pupils. The faculty of the college at the outset were Rev. Daniel Bliss, president; Rev. Cornelius V. A. Van Dyck, professor of the theory and practice of medicine, astronomy, and chemistry; Rev. George E. Post, professor of surgery and botany; and afterwards Mr. Harvey Porter, professor of history, with Mr. Asad Shidoody, tutor in Arabic.

In 1953, the student body consisted of 3,108 students and the faculty numbered 713. Of the students, 2,788 came from the Arab countries, 113 were from other countries of the Near East, and 207 were distributed among 34 other nationalities.

This University has been a God-send to the people of the Near East. Its alumni occupy prominent positions in the governments of the countries of the area, where it has been and is a potent force for enlightenment and tolerance. Its excellent schools of medicine, dentistry, and nursing have turned out thousands of well trained men and women to replace the superstitious healers who relied on charms and incantations.

The three happiest years of my life were spent in the preparatory school of the American University, but before that there were two difficult years in Beirut, spent with my family in a one-room house no larger than the one in Judaidah but far more expensive, years of fearful slinking through the streets of a city teeming with reputedly hostile Moslems where I, a despised Christian, believed I might be insulted, beaten, or even murdered at any time.

My uncles warned me, when we first arrived, that I must always conduct myself humbly in the presence of Moslems, for Christians were considered deadly enemies of their faith. And I must avoid as I would the plague all Jews, the other despised minority of the city. I was told that the Jews feasted on the blood of Christian children. Many specific instances were recounted of children stolen by Jews, taken into a chamber with seven doors, stripped naked, placed in a cradle lined with sharp needles, and bled to death so the blood could be used for the Passover bread.

I shuddered with dread at the gruesome details, but never thought to ask how people had learned them, since no child had ever come back from such an ordeal to tell of his tortures. Such tales had been handed down from generation to generation and, living as we did in a world of calculated oppression and sadism, they seemed perfectly credible. Surely religious bigotry, based on such fanciful stories, and implanted firmly in the credulous minds of children, is responsible in large part for the continual persecution and oppression of the Jews.

Fortunately for me, the horror of these stories and the fears of my first two years in Beirut were wiped away by the free and democratic spirit I found in the American University. And I was even more fortunate in having the rest of my family determine that I, as the youngest, should receive a good education. My sister Deeba found work as a servant, my brother Elias was apprenticed to a shoemaker, and I was sent to the primary school in Beirut.

After two years I entered, as a charity student, the preparatory department of the American University, which gave a four-year course equivalent to that of an American high school. Here I was given much more than instruction—I was introduced to the American way of life. Everything about the institution was thoroughly American—the professors, the textbooks, the furniture, the sports, and even the college cheer.

The classes in the preparatory division were termed D, C, B, and A, in ascending order, so I entered the D class. After the monthly examinations, the names of the five students in each class with the highest grades were read aloud in assembly. Naturally my eagerness for learning was stimulated even more when, during the first semester, my name was called out at the head of my class each month. And to my great delight I was promoted to class C at the end of the semester, thus being able to finish the first two years of study in one.

I did more than study, however; I went in for the school games and learned to play football, to take hard knocks philosophically, to be a "good sport." Both in sports and in the classroom I subconsciously absorbed something of the give and take of a democracy, something of the tolerance that makes it possible for people of diverse origins and creeds to live together as one nation.

During the summer vacation, I worked in a foundry at hard physical labor, for wages of about a dollar a week, which enabled me to pay for my textbooks. In the fall, when I entered class B, I was determined to repeat my previous performance and finish the last two years of study in one year. I was anxious to get on to college and my medical studies. There were grave doubts whether there would be enough money for me to carry on through college—it might be necessary for me to get a job and earn my living—but I was going to make sure that at least my grades would not hold me back.

I felt confident that I could make the two years in one, for all through the first semester I was among the first five in the class. So I was tremendously disappointed when the other top students were promoted and I was left to finish the year in class B. I could not understand the reason, so, after considerable hesitation, I went to Dr. Erdman, the principal. He explained sympathetically that it was a school policy not to let anyone do the four-year course in two years. He added, too, that I was still young and would gain far more from my studies, apart from grades, if I did not try to cram too quickly.

Reluctantly I accepted his decision, but I continued to work just as hard even when I took things more slowly. During the summer after I finished class B, I again worked in the foundry, and in the fall began my senior preparatory year with eagerness, as I felt the time approaching when I could start my premedical studies.

Near the end of the term, however, I realized that my family would never be able to keep me in college through the years necessary to get a medical degree. I steeled myself to the thought of giving up my dream of becoming a doctor, and to the necessity of learning a trade and getting a job. Even this would prove difficult, I knew, for opportunities in Syria were few.

It was natural that my thoughts should turn to America, the Land of Opportunity, the land I had come to know and love through my association with its outpost in Beirut. And so, when a distant relative returned from New York for a visit in Beirut, this idea again came to mind, and many a family conclave was held to discuss the possibilities of emigration. My mother finally consulted our American kinsman, telling him of my ambitions, my studies, my desire to make something of myself in this world. She felt that in America I could reach my goal more easily than I could in Syria. After asking a few questions, and learning that I could already speak English, the relative agreed, and said that I might accompany him—and so could my sister—when he returned to New York.

Next my mother persuaded my uncle Gabriel to lend us enough for two steerage fares, to be repaid as soon as we were earning some money in America. Suddenly everything was settled, and I realized with dismay that I would have to leave the American University a month before I should have received my diploma from the preparatory division. I went sadly to Dr. Erdman, to tell him that not only must I give up thoughts of going on to college and medical school but must leave without even my high school diploma after my years of hard study. The principal, who had always been so good a friend, did what he could to console me. The matter of the diploma he disposed of at once, telling me that my scholastic record had been such that he would not let a month's absence prevent my receiving it; when the diplomas were issued to the other members of the class he would mail mine to me in New York.

I said goodbye to my instructors and to my friends. It was not easy to leave a school where I had been so happy and had learned so much more than one can ever get from textbooks.

Before we left for America, one of my uncles, a priest, came to see us and gave me some good advice. "America," he said, "is a new country, a free country. You will find many persons doing things we have been taught are wrong. Do not follow them, but remember the training you have received and go in the way of Our Lord. In America you can be a force for either good or evil, as you choose." It was with this in mind that I set out for America, at the mature age of sixteen.

Chapter 3

Peddling My Way to College

America, 1898–1902

Stepping off the boat in Marseilles, we found ourselves in a new world. Everything Turkish had vanished. All the things we saw were new and marvelous—the electric lights, the trains, the streetcars, the tall buildings. And as the first step in my emancipation from Turkish rule and custom I discarded my fez and bought a hat.

There was one thrill after another for us—our first ride on a railroad train, Paris with its wide avenues, well dressed men and women, another train ride to Le Havre, and then the great ship that was to take us across the Atlantic to America. The voyage itself was not pleasant, however. With hundreds of other passengers, we were herded into the steerage like cattle. The sea was rough, and I, along with many fellow-sufferers, was seasick for days. The cold, greasy unappetizing food was rationed to us in buckets and large pans from which we filled our tin cups and plates.

But the twenty-one miserable days of the crossing were forgotten in the first sight of the Statue of Liberty, my first glimpse of America. It seemed to us, as it must to almost all immigrants, to be a prophecy and a promise of everything we had dreamed about—freedom from oppression, opportunity to earn one's living decently, perhaps even to grow wealthy, at any rate to study and learn—perhaps even to become a doctor.

I put this last hope far back in my mind. I had to work,

earn my living, save money to repay my uncle, bring my mother and brother to America. Luckily I would have some help in getting started from my three cousins in New York, two of whom were importers of French novelties and cheap jewelry which they sold wholesale to peddlers. They welcomed my sister and me into their homes, and made us rest for a week to recover from our voyage.

During this time I saw something of New York, and my wonderment at Marseilles and Paris faded when I looked at skyscrapers, elevated trains, lovely parks—and Broadway. I never got over this first impression, and though I have since been in many European capitals, New York still seems to me incomparable.

Vast and crowded as this city was, it did not seem to have many jobs to offer. Each morning I turned to the newspapers, the front pages of which were filled with exciting stories of the Spanish-American war. I studied the columns of want ads, noting every store that advertised for a clerk, every opening that I thought I might be able to fill. My cousin took me around in answer to the ads, but everywhere we received the same answer—the job was already filled. We started earlier, arrived to wait in line before the stores opened, but still without success. Although my relatives kept reassuring me, I was beginning to despair of ever gaining a foothold in my new country.

I jumped at the chance, therefore, when one of my cousins suggested that I accompany his wife one day on her peddling trip. So, carrying two bags of trinkets, I went with her to Montclair, New Jersey. For a few days I watched and listened as she went from door to door selling hatpins, stickpins, brooches, buckles, bracelets, and belts. I felt sure that I could sell the jewelry easily and, after observing for another few days, this time with one of my cousins, I asked him to let me try. To his surprise I sold more than he did.

I was promptly outfitted with a satchel full of jewelry and started off on my own, full of hope and determination. Thanks to my study at the American University in Beirut,

I spoke a very passable English—better than most of my countrymen who had been here for years. And I was so eager that I was not nervous.

At the first door, I sold a few pieces of jewelry. Jubilantly I went on my way, succeeding far beyond my expectations. In those days, it must be remembered, housewives lacked the ready shopping facilities of today, and the door-to-door peddler was not an unwelcome interruption but rather a necessary link between the store, or producer, and the consumer. I'm sure I would find peddling a much more difficult and hazardous occupation today.

I covered all the towns around New York and went farther away, stopping at cheap boarding houses, selling my trinkets in one village after another. My cousins sent fresh supplies to me regularly, and just as regularly I sent money back to them, to pay for the jewelry sold and to add to my savings that they were keeping for me. The profits were disproportionately large on these cheap imported pieces, and my earnings grew rapidly.

Early in my peddling career I hit upon a plan that helped me greatly, above all in the small towns of the East and Middle West. Since in the Orient personal introductions are the rule, it was natural that I should think of asking Dr. Erdman, the principal, and Mr. Swain, one of the instructors at the American University of Beirut, to give me letters of recommendation. They gladly sent me what proved extremely valuable, letters of introduction stating that I had been a student with them and that I was working so that I might go on with my studies.

When I arrived in a new town, I first visited the clergymen and showed them my credentials. Most were very kind, a few were a little cautious or mistrustful, but from nearly all of them I succeeded in getting some help in the form of letters to their parishioners. Many of these ministers took a genuine interest in me, and some of them asked me to address the Sunday School or preach a sermon. And so I often found myself addressing a congregation with either a sermon on charity or a talk on the Holy Land and the Near East, both of which proved very popular.

The letters from my kind friends at the American University were much more than aids in my selling; they were reminders of my never-to-be-forgotten desire to become a doctor, to go on with my studies. During my years of traveling about the country I read and studied in my spare time, preparing myself for that day when I might once again be able to attend classes, go to college.

But first came money-making. At the end of two years in America I was able to repay the loan Uncle Gabriel had made for our passage, and to send a thousand dollars to my mother and brother for their trip to this country, and in addition, I had savings of two thousand dollars in the keeping of my New York cousins. It was not only successful selling but also the most frugal living that built up my funds so quickly. From birth I had been accustomed to a bare subsistence. Food in America was abundant and cheap, and with meat every day, pastries whenever I wanted any, fresh fruits and vegetables at all times, it seemed to me that I was living on the fat of the land even though I spent little on food.

When my mother and brother arrived in New York in 1900 I felt happy that I had been able to do a little toward repaying them for their earlier sacrifices to give me an education. They went at once to Bloomington, Illinois, where my sister, who had married six months before, was living. My brother faced the difficulty of learning English, but he was able to find work at once as a cobbler.

Before leaving New York he told me that he thought I ought to put my two thousand dollars in a bank rather than keep it with my cousins. When I asked my relatives for the money, however, I was shocked to learn that they had invested it in a store in Brooklyn and had lost it all; they could repay me only in merchandise. Once more my studies had to be postponed, while I worked trying to recoup my fortune.

In an effort to do this quickly I opened a store in Asbury

Park, New Jersey, for the summer, stocking it with my supply of jewelry. But the venture was a failure and in the fall I again had to turn to the road, peddling from door to door, from town to town. I was still young—only eighteen—and there was still time for me to accomplish what I wanted.

There was only one unpleasant encounter that I can recall. In a small town in Virginia, I had just completed a sale and was walking down the drowsy main street when a man approached me. He asked me if I had a license to peddle. In all my travels I had never heard of such a thing, and told him so.

So he led me off at once to the village jail and put me into a cell. I was overcome with shame and begged to be allowed to go free, protesting that I knew nothing about the requirement of a license. Ignorance of the law was no excuse, I was told, and so I had to spend the night in jail, unable to sleep because of my humiliation at being considered a criminal.

The next morning when the jailer brought a breakfast of bread, cold beans, and coffee, I asked him to send for the local minister, who had given me a letter of recommendation. At noon the minister's daughter appeared with a delicious meal and the encouraging word that her father was seeing about my release. In the afternoon I was set free, and after thanking the minister I hurriedly left town.

I continued my travels and my selling, and once more the amount of my savings grew to substantial proportions. One day early in 1902, I found myself in a little town in Texas, looking at a crowd of young people on a college campus. My heart leaped as I gazed about and saw the campus square, the boys and girls with books under their arms. Here again was the America I had first known in far-off Beirut—the American University seemed transplanted back to its original soil.

My mind was made up at once. I asked the way to the dean's office and, with my satchel of jewelry in one hand and my hat in the other, I went in to see him. I told him of my life, my previous studies in Beirut, my constant reading during the last few years, my burning ambition to become a doctor. I asked if I could be admitted then and there to John Tarleton College to prepare myself for medical school. He welcomed me warmly, and for the three remaining months of the semester I was the happiest of students.

I was glad that I had kept on with my reading and studying alone, for I found I was able to take many advances courses rather than start as a freshman. One of my teachers, Lily Pearl Ponder, took a particular interest in me, encouraging me in my determination to study medicine. At the commencement exercises, my Americanization was seemingly complete; I won a gold medal for my talk on "Ambition" in the oratory competition, and in the sports contests I won a four-dollar shirt by throwing a Texas boy two falls out of three in a wrestling match. But most important by far, my grades were such that my pre-medical study was now completed by this short stay in college, and I decided to enter medical school in the fall, choosing Washington University in St. Louis.

During that summer it seemed that one thing after another turned up to complicate my plans. This time it was not financial difficulties, for I had managed to save five thousand dollars, more than enough to give me security while I studied.

On a visit to my family in Illinois, I found that my brother was doing badly in the shoe shop he had started, and having heard about the new land opened up for settlers in the Oklahoma Territory, had decided he wanted to become a farmer. My mother, my sister, and her husband were all enthusiastic about the idea and wanted to go with him. I gave them a thousand dollars to pay for a relinquishment on a hundred and sixty acres in Greer County, Oklahoma, and they all left for the new country.

The second problem that arose was that of Adeeba, who had called herself Edna since her arrival in America with her father some time before. She was a lovely girl, and when I saw her I was not sorry for that betrothal ceremony of ten years before. She was still very young, but not too young for marriage according to the customs of the Near East. The thought of marriage to this delightful girl, of a home and a family, was tempting to me. I had enough money to marry, and I had learned that I could earn a comfortable income in business.

My family urged me to marry, to go into business and forget my idea of becoming a doctor. And right at this time a particularly good opportunity presented itself, as if fate were conspiring against my ambition. I had stopped off in Wichita, Kansas, to visit two school mates from Beirut, the Samara brothers, who had become prosperous merchants. They urged me to go into partnership with them. It was a good chance, since they were doing well and were very shrewd businessmen; later they came to New York and became millionaire importers and wholesalers.

But I put aside all these temptations and held to my resolution. I told the Samara brothers that I was sick of business, that I didn't like to make money just for the sake of making money, that I wanted to be a doctor and intended to be one. And to Edna I said that I must continue with my studies and that, though I hoped she would wait for me, I could not in fairness ask her to do this and so she could consider herself released from our betrothal.

With a heavy heart, but with determination, I boarded the train for St. Louis to begin the study of medicine.

Chapter 4

M.D. At Last

St. Louis, 1902–1906

The School of Medicine of Washington University accepted my application for admission on the condition that, besides the regular medical studies, I take courses in Latin and zoology during my first year. It is obvious that the standards of medical training were considerably lower in those days, for I was admitted to a school with a class A rating despite my very haphazard college preparation.

When I registered at the Dean's office, I signed my name Michael A. Shade—Shade instead of Shadid—thinking that by Americanizing it I would mitigate the prejudices I met with in my travels over the country.

My teacher of Latin and zoology was a fine man, named Spooner. The first time I attended his lectures, he looked at me quizzically, and asked me: "Mr. Shade, you are a Syrian, are you not?"

"Yes," I said. "I am."

"Well then," he said, "Shade is not a Syrian name. What is your real name?"

"Shadid," I said.

"Then why did you change your name from Shadid to Shade?"

"To mitigate the prejudices against a foreigner that I have met with in many parts of the country."

"That is a mistake," said he, "you will find out that many

people prefer to go to a foreign doctor instead of a native; go back and re-register your name correctly."

And forthwith I re-registered: Michael A. Shadid.

At that time the American Medical Association was making a determined effort to drive out of existence the so-called "diploma mills" by grading all medical schools. But even the grade A schools required little in the way of pre-medical training. And internships after graduation were a matter of choice, not of necessity. It is small wonder that among the medical students there were many who had neither the ability nor the devotion which are essential to the making of a good doctor.

These were the students who led in the hazing of freshmen by the upperclassmen. My experiences at the American University in Beirut had in no way prepared me for this American sport, and I resented it strongly. I did not want to be a sissy or a poor sport, but I had come to this school for serious work and not for "horseplay." I must have appeared a strange sight, carrying with me wherever I went, during my entire freshman year, that largest of bones, the femur. Apparently the sight of it was sufficiently persuasive, for I went unhazed to the end of the year.

From the first I plunged into my work with all the energy that I possessed. I had been held back by economic necessity for many years and now that I was free to go ahead in my chosen field I could not restrain my eagerness. This increased my consternation when the results of the first monthly quizzes were announced and I learned that I had failed in anatomy. I felt as though the ground had dropped from under my feet, and I ran to Dr. Coughlin, my anatomy instructor, for advice.

My tragic voice made him smile, but he was understanding, as always, and his sympathetic attitude helped me to regain some composure. Telling me that several other students had failed too, he assured me it was merely a question of learning how to organize my studies properly. With this encouragement, I threw myself into my work with renewed vigor and had no further difficulties for the rest of the four years.

In my first summer vacation I turned to peddling jewelry again, for it was the one way I was certain of earning money. I was finding the cost of medical school higher than I had anticipated, and needed to replenish my dwindling funds as much as possible.

During my second year of school I became more and more absorbed in my work. During the days I attended classes and at night I studied late. However, I did manage to find occasion for some relaxation, and I made several good friends with whom I had enjoyable and stimulating times. We were all interested in social and political movements, in efforts to liberalize and improve the country. We read books and magazines that dealt with the coöperative movement, socialism, trade unions—all the many new ideas and plans that were arousing enthusiastic hope throughout the world. Although my concern with new social movements may seem at first glance to be far removed from my interest in medicine, it really sprang from the same source: a desire to help in improving the condition—social as well as physical—of the common people. It was during this period that I took out my American citizenship papers.

In the summer of 1904, I was able to vary the routine of peddling by acting as a guide in the Jerusalem exhibit at the St. Louis World's Fair. I would lead a group of sightseers from the entrance at the South Gate past the Tower of David, the Wailing Wall, the misnamed "Mosque of Omar," and the Holy Sepulcher, describing according to a stereotyped formula each point of interest, and at the end of the tour I would take up a collection from the members of the party.

Once a middle-aged man, wearing a black suit and a reversed collar, remained behind, and as the others walked off, he asked me in a low tone where the "girls" were.

"What girls?" I asked.

"The love girls," he said. "Where do they stay?"

I was taken aback. "But aren't you a clergyman?" I asked.

"I am in Canada," he said, "but not in the States."

This was the first time, but not the last, that I encountered the point of view that morals are a matter of geography. Later, as a doctor, I was frequently called upon to treat married men who were models of sobriety in their own communities, but who felt that when in St. Louis, New Orleans, or some other large city on business trips, they were exempted from the Seventh Commandment.

Despite my work at the Fair, my peddling, and my reserve fund, my money seemed to be melting away. In addition to tuition, board, and room, there were expensive books to buy, breakage fees in chemical courses, a microscope to rent—on and on it went until at the beginning of my senior year I was broke. So I thought I was very lucky when I found a job in the Skin and Cancer Hospital in exchange for my board. But the food served there was so inadequate that even with the additional bread and fruit I occasionally bought, I felt hungry most of the time. The superintendent of the hospital prided herself on being an efficient executive and used to boast of the low cost of maintenance during her administration—particularly in the reduction of grocery bills.

What with my classes, my studying, my job, and the poor food, I soon found my weight going down. I began to feel weak and lethargic. Becoming alarmed, I visited Dr. Coughlin, to whom I felt I could go with any problem. He percussed my chest and back, and made a thorough examination. When he finished, he said, "You're starving, Shadid."

That was no real news to me, but there was not a great deal I could do about it. I got all the rest I could and supplemented my regular diet as much as possible. By the time the end of the year arrived I hadn't a cent, and I had no idea of what I was to do after commencement.

I had finished medical school and had my degree. But I could not go on with further studies as I really wanted to and I could not get an appointment as an interne in a St.

M.D. AT LAST

Louis hospital because, as I learned, such appointments were then purely political. I was faced with the problem that confronts many young doctors today when their training is completed—earning a living, getting a start.

Luckily, my brother had done well with his cotton farm in Oklahoma and he was able to lend me two hundred and fifty dollars to tide me over until I found something. I was beginning to think that I would have to go back to peddling for a while to earn sufficient capital with which to start practice, when I saw in the want ads a notice inserted by a doctor who needed an assistant.

I rushed to his hotel only to find, as I half expected, a dozen physicians ahead of me waiting for interviews. I sat down dejectedly and in turn was interviewed by the doctor. When I picked up my hat to leave, I was overjoyed to hear him say, "I'd like you to come back tomorrow for another talk."

The next day, he told me I could work for him as his assistant, at a salary of two hundred dollars a month. As was the custom at the time, we had a contract for one year's services drawn up by a lawyer friend of mine. I was not sure just what my duties would be, and at the prospect of handling patients I suddenly doubted my ability. Still, it was with a great deal of pleasure that I set out for the doctor's home in Maxville, Missouri, fifteen miles southwest of St. Louis.

Chapter 5

Guinea Pigs in Missouri

Maxville, 1906–1908

Maxville was a typical crossroads village with two saloons, two stores, a blacksmith shop, and a Catholic church—a typical German-American village of about a hundred and fifty people. The health of these villagers and the surrounding farmers was now given into the hands of a young man just out of medical college. I realized only too well that my knowledge of medicine was purely theoretical and had to support it not one single experience in the examination of patients and the treatment of disease.

We now know that it was absurd to permit a student just out of medical college to start practice without serving an internship in a hospital, but at that time it was the usual thing. I was fully aware that I should have been gaining valuable experience treating patients under the watchful eye of a good hospital staff doctor. Instead I was to learn, single-handed without guidance, by practicing on the trusting inhabitants of Maxville.

The doctor who had employed me remained with me only one week, explaining my duties and introducing me to the patients who came to the office. He did not seem a bit worried by the fact that I had never treated a human being for even the simplest ailment, and assured me, when I expressed my doubts and fears, that I would make out all right. These bland assurances did not quell my misgivings.

"Just phone me when you need me," was all that he said

when he drove off to a somewhat larger town six miles away. I watched him go out of sight, and then went back to my office wondering how on earth I could face patients alone. When the first one arrived asking for a bottle of "diarrhea medicine" for her child, I did my best to act calm and look confident. But I felt like an actor making his first public appearance. I was struck dumb with fright, and for the life of me I could not remember any medicine for diarrhea. Finally, in desperation, I ducked behind the counter and looked up a prescription in my college textbook in therapeutics.

When I had compounded the prescription and the woman had left, I sank down into a chair, relieved that my first test had involved only so simple a complaint. But I worried about the next one. What would the patient bring? What if it were a compound fracture or some obscure disease? But I did not have to face another patient for three whole days. This led me to worry about the lack of patients. But I kept myself busy reviewing my textbooks, reading the medical journals that were on hand, and testing myself on all sorts of questions involving possible diseases of possible patients. Alone in my office, I learned and knew all the answers perfectly, but would I be able to overcome my stage fright if and when any more patients came in?

I began to worry as to why they did not come in. Had the diarrhea medicine not been compounded correctly? What if it had been incorrect, and the woman had already told the townspeople that I was no good? Or could they see, without being told, that I lacked self-confidence? I tortured myself with such self-questioning.

Finally, the waiting got on my nerves to such an extent that I called my employer on the phone. "They do not come, doctor," I said. "Is there anything I can do about it?"

"No," he answered, "when someone is dying they will send for you."

No sooner had I put down the receiver than I was called to the bedside of a child who seemed about to breathe her last. The priest had been called and had already administered extreme unction. The parents were stunned as they saw what was happening.

In the face of this really serious emergency, all of my doubts and fears seemed to vanish. In the urgency of the crisis I was not even aware that they had left me, nor did I fully realize that this was my first major test. Here was a child about to die, and I was the doctor who must save her life. I was not conscious of any tenseness; rather, I felt quite calm.

At first glance, the symptoms suggested laryngismus stridulus, a convulsive attack of the larynx, so I quickly administered a small dose of apomorphine. The child quickly vomited, then relaxed and fell peacefully asleep.

Everyone present was astonished, and as I left the priest shook my hand.

"That was splendid work, splendid work," he said.

I could not have a more fortunate introduction to Maxville so far as making a favorable impression on the inhabitants of town and country was concerned. Nor could there have arisen a better experience to give me confidence in my own ability. Now I knew that I really could be a doctor.

I was very glad, however, that my second case was not my first, for it would not have had such salutary effects. It turned out all right in the end, but for a while I was extremely worried. The patient was a girl suffering from severe abdominal pains. Some officious old woman of the village had prepared a poultice, which had failed to give any relief, but its presence was enough to mislead me. I diagnosed the ailment as simple colic and gave the girl a dose of castor oil and something to ease her pain.

When I went to see her again the next day, the pains were more severe, and the symptoms clearly indicated appendicitis. I immediately advised an operation but the girl's parents refused to consider it. Two days later the girl's appendix ruptured and again I urged an immediate operation, prognosticating death unless it was performed without loss of time. The parents, now badly frightened, rushed their child to a St. Louis hospital where she was operated on by one of my former teachers. Because of the delay the girl had a very difficult six weeks in the hospital, but luckily she managed to pull through.

Since such emergencies were few and the villagers and country folks rarely called on me for slight indispositions, I had a great deal of time on my hands and missed the diversity of interests and the friends I had made in St. Louis. The people in and around Maxville—in the main farmers who raised strawberries and garden truck for the St. Louis market—were simple folk, conservative, lacking the advantages of higher education and doubtful of all strangers. When I tried, ever so cautiously, to talk with some of them about current affairs, I was answered with cold monosyllabic replies that did not encourage me to continue. The only person in the town with whom I became at all friendly was the priest, and I spent many happy hours with him sipping a glass of wine, smoking a cigar, and chatting about the simple events of the village.

At the end of two months, my employer suddenly reappeared and announced that he had not been able to make a go of it in the other town and was coming back to Maxville to practice. I then realized why I had been hired. He had wanted someone, anyone, to hold down his practice in Maxville while he was having a try in a new locality.

"Since there's not enough work here for both of us," he said very casually, "why don't you find a good up-and-coming town for yourself somewhere?"

I reminded him that he had signed a contract employing me for a full year. I was not going to give up my only source of livelihood so easily and told him that I would leave only if he paid me at least six months' wages. He refused flatly; in fact, he said that he would not pay me even for the second month I had worked for him and gave me two days to clear out. I went at once to St. Louis to consult the lawyer friend who had drawn up the contract. The lawyer agreed to begin suit for the two hundred dollars due, saying that there was not much use in suing for more as it could not be collected even if judgment were obtained. I gave him instructions to go ahead and went back to Maxville the same day, thinking he would advise my employer of his intention to sue and thus give him an opportunity to reconsider. When I found my trunk standing on the porch of his house, I knew that he was in no mood to reconsider. There was nothing for me to do but go across the street, rent a room for my office, drug shop, and sleeping quarters, and then hang out my shingle. The drug shop was essential in those days as there were no drugstores in such small communities and each doctor compounded his own prescriptions.

Gradually, largely because of the good impression I had made in my two months in the village, I acquired a small practice. When my case came up before a local jury, I was awarded a month's salary and, although I was never able to collect even this amount, my practice increased as a result of that victory.

I made my country calls on horseback. In a way that was an advantage in those days of unpaved roads, as it was easier to make calls on horseback in the deep mud during the winter and spring rains. Once I narrowly missed being crushed to death when my horse slipped on the ice. But in good weather, I enjoyed riding to the outlying farms. Life in Maxville was lonely and monotonous and I welcomed all diversions, even in the way of work. While I continued to study and to read widely in my spare time, too much of that often left me feeling stale.

It was not any wonder, then, that I eagerly greeted the young lady who stepped from a buggy at my gate one day. As she walked toward my door I stared unbelievingly. It was Adeeba, or Edna, the betrothed of my childhood, to whom I had bid a sad and, I thought, final farewell five years before.

"Good afternoon," she said, blushing, as I opened the

door, "I-I-I am on my way to St. Louis and just thought that I would stop by to see you."

Obviously, this was not the whole truth. One look at her glowing face told me that she was still waiting for me even though I had given her a complete release, and that my five years of absence had not killed her affection for me. Nor mine for her, as I realized at once. During my lonely months of exile in Maxville I had often thought of her and now as she stood before me, blushing and eager, I knew at once that I needed her. She radiated cheerfulness and good spirits and, being Syrian, she would unquestionably be a devoted wife.

It did not take long for us to establish the new relationship. Early the very next morning we drove to St. Louis to obtain a license and were then married by a Unitarian minister. We could not afford a wedding trip as I was still a struggling and comparatively moneyless practitioner, but in a burst of extravagance I bought a buggy so that my bride could at least accompany me on my rounds.

I was no longer lonely. When our daughter Ruth was born, the last trace of monotony vanished. But, as a family man, I had to find a more likely town than little Maxville in which to establish a practice.

Chapter 6

Starting in Oklahoma

Stecker and Oklahoma City, 1908–1912

My mother, Kushfa, out in western Oklahoma, naturally wanted to see the baby, and I decided it would be wise to settle near the other members of my family anyway. I would take the Oklahoma State Medical Board examination and try to establish a practice somewhere in that western country. Ruth was three months old when we set out with all our possessions packed in two barrels tied to the back of the buggy.

The wooded Ozarks were lovely that summer and early fall as we drove at a leisurely pace day after day to the southwest. As we came down out of the hills in the neighborhood of Tulsa, we saw many tall, painted structures in the open fields and even in the yards of homes in towns and villages. They were oil-well derricks, then only recently erected, pumping wealth out of the ground. As we drove westward through the flat countryside of Oklahoma, we came again and again upon oil fields or drillings. Everywhere we heard talk of oil and the oil boom, of sudden riches and rushing business coming to sun-steeped, sleepy villages with the discovery of some new oil field. I decided that it would be a good idea to settle in such a newly rich town if one could be found in which there were no, or few, doctors. I had not yet learned that where there is little or no competition there is usually nothing worth competing for.

But it was not the quick success alone, that might come

from lack of competition, which impelled me to think of choosing a town without doctors. In such a place, also, I would be doing the most good by bringing medical care to people who were without it and hence most needed it.

I settled down at Stecker, in Caddo County, a town of about four hundred people which was at the beginning of what everyone there hoped would be a big oil boom. I was still a young man, only twenty-six, and I thought that I would grow in age and in practice with this town. Apparently, however, the people of Stecker had concluded that no good doctor would ever settle there, for they continued to hurry to the physician of the nearest large town in the case of any serious illness. But they did condescend to visit me for minor ailments and gradually my practice increased.

In Stecker there was a striking and deplorable example of the need of preventive medicine. The town was so new that there were a great many open water wells, mostly poorly located and unsanitary. As a result, typhoid fever reached almost epidemic proportions shortly after I arrived there. I was kept busy treating typhoid patients when someone should have been changing the town's water supply system and educating the people as to the cause of their sickness. I did all I could along that line, but naturally I could accomplish little alone. I did what any sincere doctor does under such circumstances; I kept rushing from patient to patient, tried in my spare time to get health conditions improved, and scaled my fees according to ability to pay.

In Maxville, I had not encountered the necessity of adjusting the regular fees. When I treated poor patients for nothing in Stecker I gave them the same care, naturally, as I gave to patients who could pay. My chief incentives, to do more work, to learn more, to make myself a better doctor, involved not making more money but the satisfaction of achieving results, of making sick people well. True, I had to earn money to support myself and my family, but I knew that I could do my best work and get the greatest pleasure from it if I could work for the sake of the work alone and forget all about the money. The need to work in this manner for the sake of society as well as for my own sake came often into my mind in those days of epidemic in Stecker. I began thinking of how medical care might be put on some such basis. If only the town of Stecker, I thought, could arrange for me to receive a salary sufficient to maintain my family, in return for which I would look after the health of all the townspeople, what could not be done for the community in the way of prevention as well as of cure of disease!

But of course such a plan was not feasible—no doctor had ever worked on such a basis, to the best of my knowledge. So I kept on adjusting fees, working for nothing, or almost nothing, when I found families such as one on a farm eight miles out, where there were the father, the mother, and nine children, who one after another all came down with typhoid fever.

For six months I went out to that farm from three to five times a week, and every time I entered the house the father would anxiously tell me that he did not know when he would be able to pay me. Naturally, I kept assuring this farmer that his bill would be small and that he could take as long as he needed to pay it. But the farmer continued to worry and the effects of this worry suddenly became evident when he recovered from his own siege of the fever. He lost his mind temporarily, compensating for his anxiety over money matters with delusions of grandeur and untold wealth. It was six months before his sanity returned and he was once more normal.

I was shocked that the effect of the farmer's worry about paying had been so serious despite all my assurances. This was another flaw in the system of medical practice—that decent, hard-working honest people could not receive good medical care without the fear of financial ruin. The farmer knew that my regular bill for all those trips, if I charged the usual rates, would be enough to force him to sell his farm and livestock. Even my "small bill" might have been sufficient to compel him to put a heavy mortgage on his place, with the customary exorbitant interest rates prevailing at that time in

Oklahoma. It was no wonder that his worry had brought on a mental derangement following his fever.

This farmer and his family were fine people, hard-working, conscientious, and honest. Such people, I thought, should have some way of knowing that their medical needs would be cared for. Their gratitude to me was deep and of course that gave me real satisfaction, but they should never, in my opinion, have been put in the position of having to feel grateful for something they should receive as a right.

I was rapidly learning about the many problems of medical care, just as I was rapidly learning about the handling of difficult and unusual individual cases. It was in Stecker that I first lost a patient due to an oversight on my part.

She was a child with laryngeal diphtheria who, when I was called in, seemed to be already near death. The only thing I could think of to suggest was the use of the O'Dwyer tube, and though I had one on hand, I hesitated to use it because I had never used the method before. The parents sent for another doctor from a nearby town and then they stood beside me, watching the struggling child, hoping the doctor would arrive in time. They could see that the child was growing steadily worse.

"Please do something," they begged. "Don't let her die."

I knew that it would be at least a half hour before my colleague could get there, and, gathering my courage, I succeeded in introducing the tube into the child's larynx. Her dusky blue face turned to its natural pink and she fell into a deep sleep, breathing easily and regularly.

When the other doctor arrived he congratulated me heartily. "Good work," he said, "splendid." Then he collected a big fee and left the patient to me.

For three days the little girl improved and I was planning to remove the tube the following morning. But in the middle of the night I was roused from sleep by an anxious call from the parents. When I arrived there, the child was dead.

"She just lay there coughing and fighting for her breath," the child's mother sobbed.

I said nothing for I was horrified, as only a doctor can be when he loses a patient and knows that it has been his fault. The tube had become clogged with thick, tenacious mucus, and no one had thought to pull it out by the silk thread attached to it, the end of which was plastered to the child's cheek.

As I drove wearily home I reproached myself bitterly for my failure to warn the parents of the chance of such an emergency. The parents never discovered that, unwittingly, I had probably been the cause of their little girl's death. They were good Baptists and gave me credit for almost saving their child's life, but they felt that "God's will be done."

Edna tried to comfort me by pointing out that my colleague was even more to blame, for he was the specialist in nose and throat diseases and should have warned the parents. Although this was true, it was small comfort to me. This incident served to make me more determined than ever to be a better doctor. Gradually the people of Stecker began to have greater confidence in my judgment and ability, though many of them continued to insist on a second doctor for consultation when the illness was serious.

Usually they turned, for this second doctor, to one who lived about ten miles from Stecker and who before my arrival had enjoyed the entire practice of the district. He was not at all pleased with my cutting in on his preserve, and, patronizingly, would assure me that in another ten years I might be a good doctor, and that a big city was the best place to spend that time. My experience with him, together with several similar experiences, made me begin to doubt the ability and honesty of many physicians. He was unscrupulous and, judging from some of the diagnoses he made, seemed to me little better than a quack.

One afternoon I was called urgently by a woman who had just been to see him and who was very much upset. After examining her, this doctor had announced that she was suffering from aneurism of the abdominal aorta and had recommended an operation. As this is a serious operation, the woman had good reason to be worried. On examination, I could find nothing wrong. It is difficult to diagnose aneurism of the aorta without the use of X-ray, but as he had reached his decision by palpation, I felt justified in using the same method.

"There is nothing wrong," I said. "Better forget the whole thing."

But she refused to be convinced and guided by fingers over the pit of her stomach to call my attention to the pulsation which had been diagnosed as aneurism. As a last resort, I called in her daughter and directed the mother to place her fingers on the daughter's stomach. It was only when she felt the same steady pulsation that she was persuaded that she had nothing to fear.

That was one of his more happy diagnoses, for it resulted in neither injury nor death to the patient. Other persons who consulted him were less fortunate. I was called to the bedside of a robust young man who had gone to bed immediately after eating a hearty meal. He was vomiting and had severe abdominal pains. Diagnosing this as a case of intestinal obstruction, I recommended immediate operation. His alarmed family called in the same physician, who soothed him with a simple prescription of castor oil and enemas. The patient died four days later.

At another time when a patient of mine was recovering from typhoid fever, he became so weak that he was unable to urinate. I called in a "surgeon" from a nearby city, as I had no training in urology and lacked the necessary instruments. The specialist tried to introduce a round steel catheter to empty the bladder and finally succeeded in forcing it through but, apparently, made a false passage and punctured the rectum instead, for all that passed was a little blood. That night the patient died of the shock.

After eighteen months at Stecker, I felt like a real doctor rather than a novice. I had learned as much from my contacts with blundering physicians as I had from my own experience. I felt, however, that I must look for an opening in some other town that offered me more of the opportunities I wanted. The oil boom at Stecker had failed to materialize and the town was not growing. Although I had saved something over two thousand dollars during my stay there, I felt the responsibilities of a growing family since my second child, Bessie, had been born in Stecker.

So in 1911 I moved to Oklahoma City. It was already a fairly large city and was full of doctors. But it was enjoying an oil boom. The many patients I expected, however, did not materialize. There was no flocking to my office.

About this time I realized that my foreign birth mitigated against my success. In Stecker and in Oklahoma City I met with prejudice. I could not, if I wanted to, deny my foreign birth, as my swarthy complexion and my physiognomy plainly enough betrayed my origin. What could I do about it? I had two choices: I could go to some city in the North or East where my foreign birth would not count against me, or I could go to some medical center and learn to do things that the average country doctor could not do, and then locate in a small town. The first choice would take me too far away from my mother, brother, and sister who lived on a farm in southwestern Oklahoma; and furthermore, my finances were too low to buck the severe competition I would meet within a city. I chose the latter course.

I went to Chicago for three months of post-graduate study. I spent six weeks at the Chicago Eye, Ear, Nose, and Throat College, and six weeks at another clinic. There I learned to treat eye, ear, nose, and throat diseases, to refract for glasses, to remove tonsils, to treat hemorrhoids by injection, and other techniques.

On my return from Chicago, I moved once more; this time with a third daughter, Ethel, added to the family, and four hundred dollars, to a village named Carter, twenty miles north of where my mother lived.

Chapter 7

A Specialist Doctor

Carter, 1912–1923

On my return from Chicago, I had gone to see Otto Branstetter, state secretary of the Socialist Party. I told him that I would like to go out speaking on socialism and wanted him to arrange a long list of speaking dates. My purpose, I said, was to find a suitable town in which to practice medicine, and I asked him to send me to a part of the state where socialists were plentiful. Wherever I had formerly practiced medicine I had met with some prejudice on account of my foreign birth; I wanted a location, therefore, where prejudice would be minimal.

Branstetter understood me perfectly, and said he would have my speaking tour arranged in two weeks time.

Like most southern states, Oklahoma had been swept by Populism, but, unlike those of other states, Oklahoma's Populists had not fused with the Democrats when in 1896 the "boy orator of the Platte" steered the farmers into the swamps of "16 to 1." They joined the Socialist Party. At the height of the movement, the Socialist Party commanded close to one-third of the total vote of Oklahoma, and elected six members of the state legislature and a number of county officers. All this was in strictly agricultural districts in which the percentage of foreign born was practically zero.

At the end of two weeks Branstetter handed me a long list of speaking dates and gave me names of comrades whom I was to interview before each meeting. After each speech the comrades would take up a collection to defray my expenses and one of them would take me home for the night, supply my breakfast, and then transport me to my next speaking engagement.

Meetings were held at the local schoolhouses. For light, we had a stable lantern or coal oil lamp. Breakfast consisted mostly of sow-belly and molasses, corn bread or biscuits, and one or two eggs and coffee. Lodging for the night was nearly always in a dugout.

As indicated by the name, a dugout was actually dug out of a hillside. Its walls were that part of the hillside which had not been removed. The roof was made of sod slabs laid over cedar poles and branches hauled from the nearest canyon, which in many instances was miles away. Frequently the common earth was the floor; in better-class ones, the floor was a composite of gypsum, salt, and wood ashes. Ventilation and illumination were secured by leaving the door open. Some had a glass window or a glass door. The size of the dugout was usually 14 by 14 feet.

At the end of a week, I arrived at a town where it was rumored that the "hundred per centers" were going to lynch the first Socialist agitator who came to that neck of the woods. But the rifle men had come from far and near to protect their comrade speaker, and I was not lynched.

My last speaking date was in a little village on Sunday night. I was tired and took a nap in the afternoon. At eight o'clock, I was awakened by a knock at the door. I hurried to the schoolhouse to find a large audience awaiting me. At the conclusion of my address an old man, a Dr. Laird, came forward to shake hands and congratulate me. "Dr. Shadid," said he, "you should go down to Carter and practice medicine, for every other man there is a Socialist."

The next day I telephoned Comrade Branstetter and got the names of two leading comrades at Carter, E. C. Woods, who worked at a local cotton gin, and Charley Hindman, a farmer.

Arriving at Carter I went to see Comrade Woods, and

told him I was looking for a location to practice medicine and that someone had advised me to locate at Carter. Woods told me that the town was the personal bailiwick of a Dr. Danby, an affable man who had been living there for years and who was extremely popular. The women particularly were devoted to him because of his pleasant manner, and the children loved him for his generosity with pennies and chewing gum. It was going to be difficult to start a practice in a town of only a thousand people who were all patients of the established doctor.

I felt discouraged but I drove out a few miles to see Comrade Hindman, and gave him my story. "What Comrade Woods told you is largely true, but if you know your business there are enough Socialists here that will support you." I felt encouraged and rented a house.

The next day I returned to Oklahoma City. I told my wife that I was going to try one more location to practice medicine, and that if I did not succeed there, I was going to quit.

At Carter, I established my office in two rooms with a side entrance, behind a real estate firm. To my great surprise, patients began coming to see me almost at once. Many were eager to try the "foreign" doctor, as Professor Spooner had prophesied, thinking I might be different from an American doctor.

My first case in Carter was a call from a farmer's home where I found the elderly owner writhing with the pain of gallstone colic. I gave him thirty drops of chlorodyne in hot water and waited. After thirty minutes I gave a second dose. "That hit the spot," said the patient. "How much do I owe you, Doc?"

My second patient was a tall, gaunt farmer who walked into my office and asked me to treat a carbuncle that was developing on his right arm. I gave him an injection of staphylococcus vaccine in his left arm. When the farmer rolled down his sleeve, he asked, with evident astonishment, "Doc, how can that fix a boil on the other arm?" I took time to explain to him carefully the principle of the vaccine's action through the bloodstream and then told him to come back in two days. When he returned the carbuncle was going down rapidly, and after another injection of the vaccine, it disappeared completely.

When the farmer reported to his friends the successful and painless treatment of a carbuncle he had expected to be cut open, quite a stir was created in the town and country about. Those who thought that "foreign" doctors were smarter and better considered their beliefs confirmed. People began to call me the "specialist" doctor. Actually my knowledge of special technique was so slight as to make me smile when I first heard the term "specialist" applied to me. Still, what special knowledge and skills I had were far more than the majority of small town practitioners possessed. Dr. Danby for instance, thought it foolish to keep on studying. "It is not what you know that matters so much," he would say, "it's pleasing the folks that counts."

Perhaps, in a way, he was right, but he and I had different ideas about the best way to please the folks. He did it with a little medical treatment and a great deal of friendliness; and I, by becoming a better and better doctor. But this was not easy, as perhaps he had learned. Under medical practice as then organized, a doctor must act two roles simultaneously: he must cure the sick and be able to earn a living at it. To do the former well, he must frequently take months away from his practice—his livelihood—to study. If he does not continually increase his knowledge and keep abreast of medical progress he will soon deteriorate into a second-rate physician.

In the end, I discovered, the money and time spent on such post-graduate work comes back in greater practice, better work, and more money. I was a better doctor for my graduate work and people soon found that out. Though I welcomed the increased income, with my growing family and larger expenses, my chief incentive was a desire to do better work. The more experience I had, as all wise men find out, the more I realized how little I knew. And, more and more, I saw what a vast amount there was to learn—far beyond the capabilities of any one man, even if he could spend all of his time in study. Succeeding issues of medical journals revealed more and more discoveries in every line of medical practice. No one doctor could ever keep up with it all.

After I felt myself sufficiently established in Carter, I went off to New York City for a further two months of study in internal medicine. Two years later I went to Chicago. Later I took post-graduate courses in general surgery, urology, dermatology, X-ray, and radium. Only by this additional study as frequently as possible could I feel that I was even approaching the practice of medicine as it should be practiced.

In spite of all this, my local practice, while steadily increasing, was small. Most local people remained faithful to Dr. Danby, but as time went on more and more patients came from considerable distances to see me. One of my most earnest endorsers was a man from Hereford, Texas, who had traveled nearly two hundred miles to consult me for chronic diarrhea. He had from ten to fifteen stools a day, and as he stood before me for the first time he was literally nothing but skin and bones. He was suffering from amoebic dysentery and I gave him a daily injection of emetine hydrochloride. At the end of two weeks his diarrhea had stopped and he had regained fifteen pounds.

Ironically enough, this man was a sort of competitor of mine, for he was a peddler of patent medicine. But thereafter he invariably sang the praises of the "specialist" doctor who had cured him, recommending me, in his traveling about the region, almost as highly as he did his own nostrums. His word-of-mouth "advertising" or "norating," as the transplanted hillbillies call it, was responsible for a great many of my patients from Texas.

One of them was bedridden and wrote me to come to Hereford to see him. I wrote the local hotel in advance to reserve a room. When I arrived and registered, the proprietor greeted me enthusiastically. "So you're Doc Shadid," he exclaimed. "Twenty people have phoned so far this afternoon to see if you are here yet."

"Well, you can tell them that I will be here tomorrow," I replied, for that evening I had to see my bedridden patient. The next day I saw twenty other patients who had come to the hotel, and I found that I had to stay two more days, treating about sixty patients in all. Many of them had to come to Carter for further treatment. That trip to Hereford resulted in my earning a good deal of money. Those were prosperous days, after the beginning of World War I. Crops were good and everybody was earning; money flowed freely and everyone paid his bills promptly. The first thing I did on my return from Hereford to Carter was to buy something that I had needed badly for a long time, a Ford.

Since many of my patients lived far from Carter, a car was really a necessity. Once I drove a hundred miles—quite a drive over the roads in those days—to Quanah, Texas, to see an old fellow suffering from hemorrhoids, whose doctor was insisting on an operation. I treated him and asked him to call at my office in ten days. When he found he had been cured without an operation he sent another patient similarly afflicted, and within a short time I had treated ten persons from Quanah for the same ailment. I charged each of them fifty dollars, which meant a saving of over two hundred dollars apiece, to say nothing of the pain and inconvenience an operation would have involved.

One of the patients who came to see me as a result of the Hereford and Quanah successes was the wife of a millionaire oil man who lived in Wichita Falls. She was suffering from bronchial asthma and had visited doctors in Boston, New York, Chicago, and the Mayo Clinic without relief. I kept her at Carter two weeks and gave her intramuscular injections of an iodine preparation every other day. This treatment was succeeding well and I advised her to have her tonsils out, for they were large and infected. After their removal, I renewed the intramuscular injections for a while. She recovered completely and later sent me many patients from Texas.

The patients from a distance impressed the people of Carter. The increased practice required larger quarters. I moved into another building where I had much more space and where I put in a few beds for emergencies. It was fortunate that I was thus prepared for a woman patient on whom I had to use heroic measures to relieve her suffering. Her own doctor had brought her to me when her temperature was one hundred and five degrees, and she was suffering with severe chills, and had been expectorating a quart of pus and mucus daily. I found that she had a large tubercular cavity in her right lung but that she was wasting away chiefly as a result of a secondary infection which was causing chills and fever. If I could just clear up the secondary infection, I thought, it might be possible to handle the pulmonary tuberculosis.

I put the patient to bed and gave her an intravenous injection consisting of one ounce of a proprietary preparation of guiacol and sodium salicylate in eight ounces of water. Then I discovered that I had given her eight times the dose indicated, as I should have used one dram rather than one ounce of the compound. I watched fearfully as the patient developed a convulsive chill; her temperature rose to one hundred and six and she broke out in a profuse sweat, heavier than any I had ever seen. Her bowels moved and her bladder emptied involuntarily ten or twelve times; her eyeballs rolled back; she was unconscious.

Despite the violent reactions, she did not die. On the contrary, she improved, and on the following day she had no chill for the first time in almost two weeks. Twenty-four hours later her expectoration was reduced to a minimum and her temperature fell to ninety-nine. At the end of the week she had another chill and was given a second injection, this time using half an ounce of the compound in eight ounces of water. There followed a mild chill and more profuse sweating but no other reactions. In the next ten days she improved rapidly; her chills and fever vanished, her appetite returned, and she gained weight. I prescribed some medicine and sent her home, advising a complete rest. When she returned three months later the cavity in her right lung had closed, her weight was normal, and she felt strong and well.

Let it be emphasized that this treatment is not in any sense a cure for tuberculosis. It has a curative effect on the suppurative secondary infection, such as this woman had, which sometimes speeds a tuberculosis victim toward his death. It was able to clear up the secondary infection while subsequent rest and good food built up the woman's resistance to tuberculosis until the disease was arrested. The people of Carter, however, felt that I had proved myself a "specialist" in consumption. Word spread rapidly of this remarkable cure, for in a small town such news spreads quickly. From then on, I had many tuberculosis patients, once being called as far as Tucumcari, New Mexico, to treat one.

All during these early years at Carter, as my practice grew and I prospered financially, my mind still dwelt on the problems of the poor families who could not, they thought, afford medical care. I had more than my share of people whom I treated without pay. I kept up my interest in the economics and sociology of my profession as well as in general economic and political problems. I saw and encouraged the local farmers to organize and build coöperative cotton gins. At one time some of the local townspeople proposed to install a coöperative grocery store. They came to me to buy shares. I not only bought shares but gave them my check book with instructions to use it to pay for the shares of families who wanted to join but did not have the means at hand. In that way I loaned over eight hundred dollars to the venture. It failed later and I never recovered one cent of the money advanced. But that did not discourage me. The people were trying to find ways of helping themselves as consumers. The experience was worth it, not only

A SPECIALIST DOCTOR

to me, but to them all, so I believed. Coöperation was working in many places in many countries. I read and thought much about coöperation.

In Carter, my practice was largely among the farmers. Some of the town friends of Dr. Danby called me "The Jew Doctor" to emphasize the fact that I was a foreigner, though they did not know enough to distinguish between a Hebrew and a Syrian. Dr. Danby did all he could surreptitiously to discredit me. He knew a number of old women, notorious gossips, in various parts of the surrounding community, to whom he whispered items which he knew they would soon spread. For example, it was rumored by these old women that I exposed the women unnecessarily in child-birth.

The report that I was a Jew led one of the doctors of nearby Sayre to visit me. When I explained patiently that I was not a Jew but a Christian, the doctor exclaimed, "Well, if you are not a Jew, your mother certainly must have had a good look at one."

To the farmers interested in coöperation, it made no difference that I was of foreign birth and a Syrian. These groups were much more widely read than their neighbors. The periodicals and books they read and circulated had broadened their outlook not only in economics and politics but along all sociological lines. These farmers and their families were tolerant and progressive. And this tolerance of my clients made it possible for me to continue my interests actively in political and economic movements.

In 1918, I encountered many problems in diseases of the respiratory system, for it was in that year that the first wave of influenza swept the country. During the fall and winter I worked harder than ever before; I saw more than five hundred cases of the "flu." Scarcely a family was spared. I was very fortunate for I lost only six patients, and those because of complicating pneumonia.

When the epidemic struck again the following year, thanks to an experiment I ventured on one of my patients, I did not lose a single case. The woman had been sick for several days when I was called in. On my second visit, she showed the usual symptoms of dying flu victims; her lungs were filling up and her face and fingernails were turning blue. I spent a sleepless night trying to think of some way to save her. Suddenly I recalled an article I had read some months before which described an apparently successful method of treating acute rheumatism, typhoid fever, and psoriasis by means of typhoid vaccine injections. The authors of the article had come to the conclusion that their treatment stimulated the body's natural defense mechanism to a greater resistance against some types of pyogenic infection. Might not the vaccine also increase the body's resistance to the infection of influenza?

I debated with myself about the propriety of trying the experiment on this patient who appeared to be dying, and who would die according to all my previous experience with flu patients. It might work, but, on the other hand, the severe reactions which could be expected might be more than she could stand. The decision was too important for me to make alone, I thought, so I asked that Dr. Danby be called in for consultation. After he had examined the patient, we walked out to the barn together, stamping our feet to keep warm, to discuss the case.

"What's your prognosis?" I asked.

"She is going fast," he replied. "With that shallow breathing and bluish color it's only a matter of time."

I then briefly outlined to my colleague the article that I had read and told him that I thought the treatment might be effective in this case.

"I didn't read the article," Dr. Danby said, "but I don't see why you shouldn't try it. She is going to die anyway."

Armed with this pessimistic consent, I went back to my patient and prepared the injection. I wanted to inject it into her arm but it was so fat that I had to choose a vein in the back of her hand to receive the dose of sixty million bacilli of typhoid vaccine. I then returned to my office and waited. About an hour later my phone rang and I lifted the receiver with my heart in my throat, half convinced that I would hear that the patient was dead. With a relief difficult to describe, I heard the woman's husband say that she was having a severe chill and asked me what to do. Happily, I told him to give her a nip of whiskey, put a hot water bottle at her feet, and cover her well.

When I visited her the next day, I found her color returning, her temperature down, and more air in her lungs. But I felt shaky when I repeated the dose of the day before, as I had no idea what the second reaction would be. Fortunately, it was the same as the first, and by the third day, she was so much improved that I decided to skip the injection. But on the fourth day a relapse followed, and I prepared another dose.

"Are you going to give me another chill, Doctor?" the patient asked as she watched the preparations.

"Yes," I replied, "and I hope this will be the last one."

It was. The next day she was free from fever, her pulse was almost normal, her color was good, and she had some appetite. She made an uneventful recovery without further treatment, and from that time on, I used typhoid vaccine for pneumonia and influenza-pneumonia cases with complete success. I submitted a paper on my experience to the Oklahoma State Journal of Medicine, citing only a few of the cases I had successfully treated, but the editor returned it with the statement that I lacked sufficient evidence on which to base a conclusion and that he, the editor, considered the treatment a "dangerous" one to place in the hands of doctors generally.

Nevertheless, I kept on using this treatment successfully, even with children. I injected ten million bacilli in a three-year-old child with pneumonia whose fever was a hundred and five degrees. His temperature rose one degree that night, giving him convulsions, the equivalent of chills in an adult. After a severe sweat, his fever broke and a short convalescence followed. Another time I gave sixty million bacilli to a young man suffering a relapse of typhoid after being up for ten days. His chill came two hours later and was followed by two whole days of sweating. But the relapse was aborted.

As I grew more familiar with the action of the typhoid vaccine, I extended its use in my own practice to other diseases caused by pyogenic infection and in most instances the results were excellent. By 1928 I had a sufficient array of cases so that this time the paper I wrote was published in *Clinical Medicine* issued in Chicago.

One of the most amazing cases of my entire career brought home to me forcibly the influence of the mind over the body. I was called to a farm house to deliver a baby, but, on examining the woman in labor, I found that she was not even pregnant. About nine months before Dr. Danby had told her that she was pregnant, and since she wanted a child badly she had responded to the suggestion physically as well as mentally. Her abdomen was enlarged and she had developed other symptoms of pregnancy, even to the extent of labor pains toward the end. Naturally, it never occurred to her that the physician might be mistaken. She had sent for her mother from California to be with her during her confinement. It was a dreadful shock to learn the truth, but all her symptoms disappeared and she soon regained her former figure.

A doctor's life is colored by recurring humor and pathos. In the building where I had my office there was a real estate man who was quite a philanderer. Once an angry husband spotted him while he was being shaved on a barber's chair and went in and slashed his throat. Luckily his jugular vein and carotid arteries were intact and all I had to do was to put about twenty-five stitches in his skin.

On the same day a man and his wife brought an unmarried daughter in for treatment for vomiting. On examination I discovered that the young woman was pregnant. When I told the father and mother of her condition, the father fainted, and his head hit the cement floor causing a brain concussion.

My eleven years in Carter brought me a widely varied

medical experience that added greatly to my store of knowledge. But it brought me more than medical experience, however. My practice was increasingly successful financially but not so astonishingly as my one flyer in the oil boom. I had not been much given to speculation as I had had to work hard for my money. I now had a wife and six children to support and I could not afford to take chances that might involve their welfare. But the constant talk of oil leases and of rich stakes finally got under my skin and into my blood. When oil was discovered at Sayre, only ten miles away, and I heard that one well was flowing a thousand barrels a day, I decided to investigate. Together with Dr. Danby, who was an old hand at oil speculation, I went to Sayre and looked up a local doctor who knew something of the situation, asking him if there were any leases around that he knew of that could be purchased. He gave us the name of a farmer and we drove over to the man's place to look over the fields. Dr. Danby made some show of inspecting the land, but as he really did not know any more about it than I did, any decision we reached was sure to be a matter of pure chance. He was all for flipping a coin to decide whether the lease was worth taking. "Heads we lease, tails we don't," he said and tossed the coin, which landed tails up.

"Let's make it two out of three," he then suggested. Tails the second time; tails the third. He looked unhappy.

"Well, you can do it that way if you like," I said. "I'm going to take the lease."

The farmer drove us to the abstract office and drew up a lease on forty acres at seven and a half dollars an acre. As the farmer was signing the document, Dr. Danby said that he would like to take half the lease after all, if I were still willing. I agreed. Three months passed before we had any more excitement about oil in Sayre and then we heard that a second well was being drilled within a mile and a half of our lease. Dr. Danby and I drove over to Sayre where we met a representative of one of the big oil companies who bought our lease for twenty-four thousand dollars. We sold just in time. The wells that had first caused all the excitement dried up and the new well hardly flowed at all. In the next ten years, many wells were dug in that area but the rich field expected never materialized. I was perfectly content with my gain of twelve thousand dollars on an outlay of one hundred and fifty, but I did not tempt my luck with another flyer in oil for many years.

After eleven years at Carter my health began to fail. The long trips over rough roads in all kinds of weather were wearing; I was now past 40 and lacked the endurance of former days. Country practice often required great strength and stamina, especially for the distant calls in winter. Often at night I was called upon to travel over rutted roads, making long detours around bridges swept away by floods only to find an expected child already born and doing well. I performed unnumbered operations by candlelight or by flickering stable lanterns while the north wind whistled through the cracks in the flimsy shacks.

I had been alarmed occasionally at my weakness after difficult calls such as these but had neglected to investigate the state of my own health, as do so many doctors. Finally, however, I discovered that I had been suffering from a mild form of diabetes. Because of this I now had to take life more easily and give up a country practice that took so much out of me. I decided to move to a city, and gave careful consideration to those nearest my Carter base.

Chapter 8

Settling in Elk City

1928–1929

There were two fair-sized cities not far from Carter, Mangum to the south and Elk City to the north, and for a long time I could not make up my mind between them. Finally I decided on Mangum, because it was only ten miles from the farm where my mother, Kushfa, still lived with my brother Elias and my sister Deeba.

Life in Mangum promised at first to benefit my health. I gave up the long out-of-town drives and confined my practice largely to office hours and to surgical cases in the hospital.

But in Mangum I found a difficult situation among the doctors. Since there were no public hospitals in such a small city, each doctor wanted to establish his own private institution. In Mangum there were two of these private hospitals and the feud between the doctor owners was intense. The other physicians in the city were divided into two camps, those who sent their patients to the one or to the other. I could not see much difference between the two and tried to be impartial, leaving the decision to my patients.

This only caused both doctors to regard me with suspicion. Each was continually sniping at the other, but they were both always glad to take time out to concentrate their fire on someone walking in no-man's-land. I endured this situation for nine months but the constant bickering and backbiting were repulsive to me. I reversed my decision and went to Elk City.

At Elk City I found a situation identical with the one at Mangum—two hospitals owned by two warring doctors with the town divided into factions. I concluded that this condition was one I would have to put up with in any small city practice, and since I liked Elk City in all respects far better than Mangum, I decided to settle there with the hope that here, despite medical factionalism, I would find opportunity and happiness.

At Elk City my practice developed far more quickly than I had expected or hoped. I had more patients than ever before and my annual income, which had been about ten thousand dollars for several years, approached twenty thousand.

Economically, therefore, I was quite content; but I still felt the need for more medical knowledge and so I went to Philadelphia for a course in surgery on the cadaver. I was anxious to become still more proficient in surgery, so I soon took another short leave from my practice to take another course on the cadaver in Chicago.

But the only real way to learn surgery, I realized, was to assist a master surgeon for a period of from one to three years, although the opportunity to work with a really good man was hard to find. In an effort to get this experience, I stopped at St. Louis on my return from Chicago to visit Dr. Coughlin, under whom I had studied at medical school and who was now the chief surgeon at St. John's Hospital. I asked to be allowed to assist him, if only for three months.

Dr. Coughlin said that he would like to help me get the training I wanted, but that he had a long waiting list for such work and couldn't possibly take me on for three years. When I offered to pay for the privilege, Dr. Coughlin brushed aside that aspect of the matter. He insisted that all I needed to be a good surgeon was confidence, since I knew anatomy and had been performing minor operations for many years, and insisted that I go ahead and extend my practice to include major surgery. It was a disappointment not to get the training I wanted, but heartened by such assurances, I returned to Elk City to follow his advice.

Renting the second floor of a business building, I converted it into "Elk Sanitarium." I put eight beds in four of the rooms, purchased the necessary equipment, and started my own career as a general surgeon. I encountered few difficulties in my work and found that my regular patients preferred to have me perform any necessary surgery. The little hospital did well, but one spring day in 1928 I drew up a balance sheet, not primarily a financial one, but of my life as a whole. As far as money was concerned, I had done well. I was worth around a hundred thousand dollars. But I was not really satisfied. I had started out in life as a doctor with high ideals and with the ambition to do my share in improving social conditions. I had thought much about the lack of adequate medical care among the poor people of America. But I did not yet see what could be done about it. And what of a dream I had once of returning to my native land as a great healer and surgeon? I had worked hard; I had been as good a doctor as I knew how; and I had raised a large family. But was that enough? Since I could not see any way as yet to increase and improve medical care for the poor in America, why not go back to Syria, where Lebanon was now a separate state under French mandate, and devote the rest of my life to bringing to my native land some of the medical knowledge and help I knew it needed? I had enough money for myself and my family, and I would be content with a modest way of life.

The result of this stock-taking was that I closed my office, packed my bags, and with my oldest daughter, Ruth, set off for Lebanon. Ruth, I decided, would be my barometer, for from her reactions I would know how her brothers and sisters would take to a transplanting to the land of their parents' birth. She was excited by the prospect of the trip, and in New York we enjoyed buying presents for all the relatives we could think of. As I went up the gang-plank, the memory of my trip to American thirty years before was so vivid that for a moment I was again that half-starved seasick boy. As the boat made its way through the Mediterranean I became completely absorbed in my thoughts of Lebanon and Syria. I was sure that the condition of the people must have improved immeasurably; the French had been among their most ardent champions during the nineteenth century, and there was no doubt in my mind that the oppression Syria and Lebanon had suffered throughout the centuries of Turkish rule was now, under French mandate, no more than a fading memory.

When we came into the harbor of Beirut after two weeks at sea, we received our first shock. The port was much smaller than I remembered it as a boy, and infinitely filthy. By the time the ship had anchored, we were completely surrounded by a horde of small boats with crumpled and dirty sails, whose Moslem sailors were fiercely and vociferously fighting among themselves for the chance to take the waiting passengers and baggage ashore.

Ruth was visibly shocked and frightened. She didn't even want to land, and asked me if we could not return to the United States at once. I was considerably disturbed, and each succeeding event served only to deepen my disillusionment. Many irritations were petty matters, but their cumulative effect was strong. The seamen who took us ashore with our baggage agreed to a price of two dollars before we started, but demanded five when we arrived at the dock. Next, the customs inspector made us pay duties on our clothes and cigarettes, and assessed a tax on the six phonographs we had brought along as presents that was equal to their original cost. I told him to keep them, but the guide informed me that the inspector merely wanted a bribe to deal with us fairly, and he arranged matters satisfactorily.

Beirut, and indeed the whole country, seemed as primitive as when I had left it thirty years before. Ruth and I visited Jerusalem, Baalbek, Damascus, Haifa, and, of course, Judaidat Marj 'Uyun. But in all my travels in Lebanon and Syria,

I found only one place that had grown and improved, and only one place that made me feel that living there might be possible. This was the American University in Beirut. It had new buildings, a larger faculty, and many new courses.

For myself, I thought, I might return to my native land. But my daughter's reactions toward living in the Near East were almost violent and I knew that her five brothers and sisters would feel as she did. We remained in the country a month, and then started on a leisurely return trip back to Oklahoma.

We stopped for ten days of sightseeing in Egypt, visiting Cairo and Alexandria. We then went to Vienna for six weeks so that I could continue my work in surgery. There were two or three hundred American physicians taking post-graduate courses, for at that time the opportunities in Vienna for good training were unmatched anywhere. We learned to love the city, as almost all visitors did in those days, and hated to leave it after such an enjoyable and profitable stay. After short stops at Geneva, Paris, and London, we took a boat for home.

Yes, home was the right word. I had now given up all thought of returning to Lebanon, and had decided to spend the rest of my days in the United States. On the boat back I spent many quiet hours on the deck thinking, in view of that decision, how I could best use my talents in Elk City to improve medical care for all the people.

When I had left the United States in the spring, I had been weak, nervous, diabetic. When I arrived in Vienna, three months later, the diabetes specialist declared that I was no longer suffering from the disease and, indeed, had never had it in its usual form; it must have been a functional type not commonly found. The sea trip, freedom from practice, and mental relaxation had caused a great improvement in my health. When I arrived in Elk City I was fit as a fiddle, physically and mentally, and anxious to plunge into my work once more.

I had no inkling that the next fifteen years were to be the

most strenuous, the most creative, and the most significant of my life.

I prepared to reopen my little second-floor hospital as well as my office rooms, but before I could do that, a doctor who was already operating a hospital in Elk City suggested that we make some arrangement to work together in the use of his hospital. It was agreed that I would teach pediatrics and ethics to the nurses in training, hospitalize my patients at his hospital, and operate on my own patients when that proved necessary. He was to assist me in my operations and I was to reciprocate by assisting him in his operations. Within a very few weeks, however, he found some excuse for breaking this arrangement.

I then reverted to my original intention and reopened my own hospital. My earlier practice returned to me at once and grew to be much larger than before I had taken my trip. Not only had the trip abroad enabled me to recover my health, but my six weeks in the clinics and operating rooms of Vienna had made me a better doctor and surgeon, as I had acquired the latest techniques. My income in 1928 and 1929 rose to its highest level.

In Elk City, as in Carter, my practice was largely among farm families. Many of my former patients in Carter and surrounding communities, now that they had cars and good roads, came to me at Elk City with their ailments.

And at Elk City, as at Carter, my interest in the coöperative movement continued, and I belonged to three different coöperative associations: The Co-Operative Cotton Gin, The Wheat Elevator, and The Coal and Lumber Yard. They were the germ from which a wholly new phase of my career was to commence.

Part Two

The Problem of Health for All

Chapter 9

Medical Chaos and Ideas on Reform

By 1929 I had been in medical practice for 22 years, but it had not taken me that long to learn that the prevailing system of medical care had many defects and shortcomings. During that whole period I had cogitated upon the problem of better medical care. As a poor and struggling country practitioner there was nothing I could do about those defects and shortcomings—the high cost of illness, the neglect of prevention, the inadequacy of the "solo" practice of medicine, the performing of unnecessary surgical operations, fee splitting, and many others.

It should be remembered that in 1929 when I started out upon this crusade, this program of medical reform, there was no Blue Cross Plan, no Blue Shield Plan, or any other plan to make better medical care available to the common man.

What are these shortcomings? and what are the possible programs of medical reform?

1. The High Cost of Illness

As at present organized, scientific medical care is a costly business and none but the well-to-do can avail themselves of its benefits. The fee-for-service system—the system of charging for each visit, each examination, each laboratory procedure, each surgical operation, each day of hospital care—is no longer tenable but outmoded, because it is beyond the reach of the common man. When the practice of medicine was a simple affair, when it consisted solely of the services of a family doctor and the use of the thermometer and the stethoscope, the cost was negligible. It was not a problem. Clinics, specialists, laboratories, physiotherapy, the X-ray, and other instruments of precision and complicated procedures were unknown. Those were the days of the horse-and-buggy doctor. Today the practice of medicine is no longer a simple affair, but a technical and a scientific problem. A sick person may need the services of technicians, surgeons, specialists, hospitals, laboratories, and other scientific paraphernalia and the cost has become prohibitive, but yet the method of payment, the system of fee-for-service, the system of paying for every examination, every treatment, every surgical operation, laboratory procedure, or hospital day, this still remains the same, and as a result, people do not sufficiently avail themselves of the services of scientific medicine.

It is not unusual for an ordinary citizen to have to spend a whole year's income, or go into debt for years to come, to pay the costs of one case of illness requiring a major surgical operation and long-time hospitalization. Many are the farmers who, to my knowledge, mortgaged their farms, and sometimes even lost them, to meet doctor and hospital bills. The exorbitant fees charged by many specialists are a disgrace to the tradition of our guild. They indicate an attitude akin to that of the highwayman who demands your money or your life.

In an earlier time, the practice of medicine consisted in ministering to the sick in a spirit of kindness, sympathy, and helpfulness, and for the satisfaction of relieving pain and suffering, without excessive regard to material compensation, but today it has too commonly become a sordid business.

A recent study made by a committee of the United States Senate showed that nearly 16 million families, including 6 million one-person families, in the United States received money incomes under $2,000 a year and 8 million of these received less than $1,000. Contrast this with the study made by the Bureau of Economics of the American Medical Association in 1939 which showed that families with incomes below $3,000 could not meet the cost of serious illness without assistance or charity. Considering the rise in living costs since that date, we find today that families with incomes below $5,000 are now facing the same problem.

According to Oscar Ewing, formerly Federal Security administrator: "A scant 20% of our people are able to afford all the medical care they need. About half our families—those with incomes of $3,000 or less—find it hard, if not impossible, to pay for even routine medical care. Another 30% of American families with incomes between $3,000 and $5,000 would have to make great sacrifices or go into debt to meet the cost of a severe or chronic illness."

The technology of medicine has outrun its sociology. The people can no longer afford the fee-for-service system since the cost of modern diagnosis, treatment, surgical operations, hospitalization, and specialist consultation has become prohibitive and beyond their means.

The sliding scale of fees—charging people according to their ability to pay—is also outmoded and no longer applicable. It is obviously both morally wrong and economically unsound.

2. *The Neglect of Prevention*

Competitive medicine makes no frontal attack for the prevention of disease.

We all know it is easier and cheaper to prevent fire than to fight fire. We all know it is easier to prevent ill health than to cure disease. And yet competitive medicine is occupied mostly in treating illness. In the United States only 2¢ of each medical dollar is spent for prevention.

The patient usually comes to the doctor when the disease

is well established and has already inflicted irreparable damage to the organism.

For instance, a patient coming to the doctor with a headache and albumin in the urine has had kidney trouble for a long time and should have been seen long before for earlier symptoms. A patient coming to the doctor with general wasting, with fever and cough, is in the last stages of consumption. A patient coming to the doctor with shortness of breath and high blood pressure has had arterial disease for a long time.

An attack of glaucoma ending in blindness is the end result of eye trouble existing over a long period of months or years during which blindness could have been prevented.

Cancer is curable before it metastasizes or is disseminated into the organism, and yet one in every ten deaths is due to cancer. And one out of every seven persons over 45 years of age dies of cancer. It is estimated that about one-third of the deaths occurring in the United States each year are preventable.

The reason for this tragic failure is that the medical profession busies itself with treating the 2 per cent of the population who are sick and neglect the 98 per cent who appear well. The doctor under the profit system finds himself in the same position as a private tradesman. He has services to sell. Only sick people will buy them. The apparently well do not visit the doctor except for business reasons.

As a result, we have a large amount of preventable sickness and preventable death.

Consider also such facts as these:

Of the first two million of our young men examined for the army in 1940–1941, nearly one million were rejected because of physical disabilities.

Most of the people of this country do not enjoy perfect health or even good health. It is estimated that at least 40 per cent of the men of military age are unfit for military service. And these young men are of the age group where illnesses and defects are at a minimum. In World War II the armed services were compelled to patch up as many of these for service as possible. After all doubtful cases had been reexamined, in terms of revised army and navy physical and mental tests, over four and a half million men were rejected and put in class IV-F. They could not pass even the greatly lowered physical and mental standards. Over one and a half million men with major defects were inducted and rendered fit for duty. In the army rehabilitation program there were fourteen and a half million dental cases alone. Nearly 1,500,000 bridges and plates were supplied; 6,000,000 teeth were replaced, and over 31,000,000 fillings were provided. In World War I about 25 per cent were rejected as unfit for military duty. In World War II the rejections had increased to about 33 per cent. When from 40 to 50 per cent of our men in the prime of life are physically disordered or unfit we may assume that much more than half of the whole population need medical attention or are suffering with diseases or disease conditions which at one time might have been prevented. It behooves a people or a nation of which such things can be said to give more attention to problems of health and to be concerned with the related problems of adequate clinical and hospital facilities and the supply of competent physicians.

In 1939, the report of the Technical Committee on Medical Care stated that the gross sickness and mortality rates for the poor in the large cities were as high as they had been for the nation as a whole fifty years before.

Because of the fee-for-service system, with its needlessly high cost, many people do not visit a doctor except as a last resort. When they call a doctor it is because of pain or fear of death. A statistical study extending over a period of five years and at a cost of $1,000,000 conducted by fifty physicians, social workers, and economists, revealed that half of the illnesses of people whose income was less than $1,200 received no medical attention; while one-third of the illnesses of people whose income ranged between $3,000 and $5,000 went without medical attention. The average was 38 per cent.

Many people simply do not patronize the doctors because they do not have the money. They find it difficult to pay for groceries, for clothing, and for rent. They find it hard to educate their children. They have no surplus money for doctors and dentists.

The majority of people who cannot afford to pay for high grade medical care and hospitalization on a fee-for-service basis can afford to pay for it if permitted to pay a given sum periodically when well. They can afford to pay so much a month or so much a year for medical care, but they cannot afford to pay for every office visit, every examination, every surgical operation, and each hospitalization. In other words, they can afford the wholesale price but not the retail price, especially when they have no voice as to what a legitimate price is to be.

As Doctor James P. Warbasse has written:

> The fee-for-service system has been assailed. What does the coöperative health association plan offer as a better form of payment for medical care? It offers as the best solution of this problem the principle of periodic payment. It is the division of this total cost into separate charges for individuals and families.
>
> It guarantees the payment of adequate salaries arranged in advance, to complete medical staffs from physician and surgeon to laboratory technician and hospital orderly. It guarantees to all members of a coöperative health association complete medical service, both preventive and curative.
>
> Individual or single families cannot budget medical costs by themselves. An individual or family can budget rent and food. These expenses are regular, while medical expenses are not. But the cost of giving medical care to a group of people can be determined. Taking the

principle of various types of insurance, coöperative health associations can estimate the costs of complete expert medical care on a sound economic basis. Plans now in operation require advance payment, usually on a monthly basis. The amount of this payment depends upon the scope of the service, and the number of subscribers. This plan of medical service takes down an economic barrier now standing between the doctor and patient. Without fear of high bills, people seek preventive care, and no longer wait until home remedies have failed, until illness is acute, and then call the doctor. Thus periodic payment and preventive medicine tie together.

The prevention of disease is more interesting than its treatment, and has vaster possibilities. The treatment of disease is a deferred undertaking and a confession of failure. Treatment is like an autopsy. The physician feels he has arrived late upon the scene and is always saying "If only I had been called sooner."

3. *The Inadequacy of Solo Medical Practice*

The third count against competitive medical practice is its inadequacy, its incompetency, its inability, inherent in its lack of organization, to bring to the care of the sick the best professional knowledge and skill available.

The practice of medicine is no longer a one-man affair. No two or three physicians can adequately practice scientific medicine. The practice of medicine has become complex. It requires the service of physicians, specialists, technicians, laboratories. It involves many technical procedures for proper diagnosis and treatment. It takes a large group of trained personnel organized around a hospital to diagnose and treat sick people properly. The family doctor is no longer the undisputed medical authority in the household.

Rather he has become a signpost pointing the way to different specialists.

And yet, in spite of this development, this progress in medical practice, 95 per cent of medical care is given by individual physicians practicing alone. Each physician, each specialist, has his own office, his own receptionist, his own bookkeeping system, his own collector of good and bad debts. He feels your pulse, takes your blood pressure, looks at your tongue, and writes a prescription. This is not scientific medicine. It is guesswork. If the patient requires the services of a urologist, an ophthalmologist, a dermatologist, or some other "ologist," he has to visit the offices of these physicians perhaps in different buildings or even in different towns separately, and as each of these is practicing medicine on a fee-for-service basis, each hands him a separate bill for service rendered. And even if the patient can afford the expense, the specialists often disagree and the patient is left in a quandary. He then has the choice of resorting to quackery or else to the Mayo Clinic or some other clinic. The success of these clinics is based on the lack of coördination in ordinary medical practice.

A hundred years ago medical education was in the apprentice stage. It consisted of a year's course of lectures covering the elementary principles of physics, chemistry, anatomy, and so forth, followed by didactic presentation of the accepted doctrine of diagnosis and treatment. This was followed by apprenticeship to an active practitioner. Few students had any college training. What was known about medicine in those days was very little and could easily be grasped by any individual. There were no specialists then. Diagnosis was largely based on the use of the hands, the thermometer, and the stethoscope in addition to the use of all the senses.

The practice of medicine of today is a totally different thing from what it was 75 years ago. Indeed progress during the last 50 years has given us more new knowledge than did the whole previous period of recorded history. Fifty years ago the physician could keep himself relatively abreast of increasing knowledge if he had at his disposal a medical monthly publication. Today if a physician were to undertake to be really familiar with all the new knowledge which might become applicable to the treatment of disease he would have to spend his entire time reading current publications and would not have the time even to digest this knowledge, much less to make application of it.

The modern physician will require a very different and much larger amount of equipment, both physical and intellectual, than was properly required 75 years ago. Today, of necessity, the physician needs to be a person of broad basic education and must therefore spend 4 years in college before entering upon his medical education. To this pre-medical preparation must be added 4 years of medical schooling and 2 years of hospital experience before engaging in general practice. This means that something like 10 years must be spent after graduation from high school before the physician is equipped to practice, and those who would properly term themselves specialists would have to spend from one to five more years depending on the field covered by the particular specialty. Among the physical equipment that the physician must have at his disposal for diagnosis and treatment, if he is to give patients proper diagnosis and treatment, one may mention laboratories, X-ray machines, electrocardiograph, metabolism machine, physiotherapy apparatus, and hundreds of other instruments of precision which as a matter of fact he does not have at his disposal, unless he is within reach of well equipped hospitals and his patients could afford to make use of them, and which he would not know how to use even if he had them and wouldn't have the time to use if he did know how.

The examination of a patient may require the services of several specialists: an eye, ear, nose, and throat specialist, a urologist, a neurologist, a gynecologist, and so forth. The physician is not always in a position to say what line of investigation should be carried out, yet if some are not available because of financial or other reasons than modern medical diagnosis falls to the ground, and the physician's opinion retrogrades toward that given by his predecessor one or two generations ago. And what is said in regard to diagnosis applies with equal force to medical and surgical treatment. In fact, the general physician should be a signpost pointing the way to the appropriate one of many different specialists, for a considerable number of the cases that come to him, if he is to give them really adequate medical care.

In a previous book, I have told how, early in my medical career, I witnessed in one night three operations, which resulted in three deaths, and how the memory of that dreadful night made me determine to work for a better system of medical care.

The majority of those who are plying the surgeon's trade are no more fit to practice that sacred art than a boatswain is competent to guide a ship through a hurricane.

Now it is well known that an apprentice in a given trade or art begins to learn by spoiling material. The cook spoils the broth; the shoemaker spoils the leather; the printer gets the type mixed in the fonts; and all are restrained in proportion to the value of the materials. An apprentice at sea having served as a midshipman or a seaman for a number of years enters upon the higher duties of navigation as a junior officer, where he is under the careful supervision of his superior for years. Otherwise he might sink a ship and ships are too valuable for a tyro.

But a recent graduate from a medical college, or a practitioner who suddenly turns specialist, but who knows less about surgical technique than the printers' devil knows about operating a linotype machine, may settle down and pose as a surgical specialist without hindrance and let his patients pay for his mistakes. And the material he wastes? Only human limbs and organs and, of course, human life itself.

If the Directory of the American Medical Association is to be believed 30 to 40 per cent of the doctors in this country

MEDICAL CHAOS AND IDEAS ON REFORM

are specialists of one kind or other. But most of these are self-appointed and self-anointed.

Until recent years the specialist was a veteran general practitioner; he was an older man well experienced in general medicine. Rather than retire entirely from the arduous general practice of medicine, he took up a specialty and became an expert in a particular field; he thus became a member of a small select group. He supplemented but did not displace the general practitioner. His work was limited to consultations.

Today, owing to the greed for money, for shorter hours, and for prestige characteristic of this period, the graduate in medicine serves one or two years residency in a specialty, and come out a full-fledged specialist. Says he, in effect, "For me no general practice, no night work, no long office hours, and no credit business. I prefer general surgery. I would rather perform an appendectomy for $200 which would take less time than it takes to perform a thorough physical examination for two or three dollars."

And as the number of specialists multiplied more patients were required to support them, and the established method of limiting their work to consultation vanished. They are fast displacing the general family doctor, who has become almost extinct. So true is this that it has become difficult to get a general practitioner on Sunday, while one may die at night before getting a doctor.

To secure more patients it became the vogue on the part of certain specialists to discredit the general practitioner whose patients they wanted, and this they did sometimes subtly and sometimes brazenly.

Only recently a woman consulted me for severe intractable headache and projectile vomiting of many years' standing, for which condition she had submitted to four different abdominal operations without benefit. She had had her ovaries and appendix removed, her gall bladder drained, and a short-circuiting operation on her stomach and intestines.

She proved to have a brain tumor which was not even suspected by those who mutilated her. Another woman at about the same time came in for consultation who had had a comparable number of operations for epileptic convulsions, without benefit. She was in an emaciated condition and was having six or more convulsions every day. Blood examination showed that her epilepsy was due to hereditary syphilis, which was not even suspected by the would-be surgeons who had promised to cure her by a mutilating operation. The treatment of her hereditary condition restored her to good health and she made an uneventful recovery.

Said Dr. Paul Hawley, "Half of the surgery done in this country is done by people who are not qualified surgeons. They are general practitioners."

We have so-called national boards for the various specialists, who examine a candidate and certify him as a specialist; and we have a fellowship of surgeons, which no one can join in membership unless he receive a certain rating. But these boards and their certifications are without authority and without effect. Legislation is here indicated to give them needed authority and control. The profession must take control. If a physician wants to pursue a specialty he should be licensed by the profession when he has passed the proper requirements. In this way only can the profession and the laity know that Dr. So-and-So is competent to practice dermatology or psychiatry or any other specialty.

The one-man era in medicine is gone. The modern practice of medicine requires team-work on the part of several people. No man alive is competent to diagnose and treat every disease at the same time. We used to make a diagnosis, now we assemble them. The result is the product of several, perhaps many, physicians and technicians. Their findings are assembled by one man who goes over the whole assemblage. Once the diagnosis is accurate the treatment is usually a relatively easy matter.

Said Doctor Cabot, formerly of the Mayo Clinic, speaking to the Group Health Association of Washington, D.C.: "I have tried out the various forms of practice thoroughly. I have been in group medicine, and I can tell you at the outset that from a purely medical point of view group medicine is one hundred times better for the patient and for the doctor than the ordinary usual practice."

To apply modern technical knowledge in diagnosis and treatment we must have group medicine. We must organize measures and institutions beyond the power of the individual private practitioner to provide. A team of medical men must become the unit of medical practice instead of the individual physician.

4. The Surgical Racket

A fourth great and constantly growing evil under competitive medicine is unnecessary surgery. In the profession there is a substantial minority who capitalize upon the ignorance of the people and betray their confidence. They look upon every patient as a source of income; and with every case of illness, they ask themselves, "where do I come in, how much can I get out of this case?"

They operate upon the principle of "get all you can, charge all the traffic will bear; get it honestly if you can, but get it." A patient with a pain in the abdomen has appendicitis if he can pay. If he cannot he is apt to have an old-fashioned stomach-ache. The well-to-do patient needs a surgical operation; the poor man needs a dose of salts.

This is an anti-social policy. Sickness and death should be to nobody's advantage. No one should look to them as the hope of his livelihood. An injury to one should be felt as an injury to all.

Certain parts of the human anatomy have seemed successively vulnerable as one surgical fashion has followed another. The appendix, "God's gift to the surgeons" as the old jokes have it, the female organs, the prostate glands, the tonsils and gall bladder—these have become salients in the all-out attack on the helpless patient.

The appendix, an inert organ usually some three inches long, three quarters of an inch in diameter, and attached to the large bowel, is, of course, an "evolutionary hang-over" with no known physical function. There is nothing in the books, however, to indicate that nature left the appendix behind to be a perennial source of income for the operation-minded surgeon. Yet under a system of surgery for profit that would too often seem to be the appendix's economic function.

Many patients come to our Community Hospital complaining of the symptoms generally considered to be due to "chronic appendicitis." And many of these patients have already had their appendixes removed. In most cases the complaints are the same as those the appendectomy was supposed to have ended. Many others have easily recognizable gall bladder disease, stomach ulcer, kidney stone, pus tubes, and other ailments.

Said Dr. Paul Hawley, director of A.C.S., "I can show you where 60 to 70 per cent of the appendices removed are normal."

Nature's way of hiding the generative organs within the body of a woman results in a vast victimization of women on the part of profit-hungry surgeons.

A shocking record of performances of unnecessary operations was reported to the American Medical Association recently by Dr. James Doyle of Beverly Hills, California. Dr. Doyle said he studied the cases of 546 Los Angeles women who underwent operations in 1948, and that in each case ovaries were removed although they were normal or nearly normal. In some cases, he reported, there were not even symptoms of illness, and in one-third of the cases the diagnoses gave "nebulous reasons" for the surgery.

Said Albert Deutsch in an article in the Woman's Home Companion: "A professor of obstetrics and gynecology at a large university recently made a study of 246 womb operations during a four months period in ten midwestern hospitals. He found that fully one-third of the excised wombs were not diseased at all."

A noted surgeon, I. S. Ravdin, recently assailed some fellow surgeons for charging too much money, doing needless operations, and splitting fees. Speaking to the American Medical Association at Atlantic City he urged house-cleaning of unnecessary calling-in of consultants and of "ghost-surgery"—where a physician hires a surgeon, never seen by the patient, to do the actual operation.

"Fees charged by some surgeons," said Dr. Ravdin, "are higher than they ought to be," and the "adage of charging all the traffic will bear is unmoral."

"Many patients are being subjected to needless operations," for chronic appendicitis, gall bladder trouble, and adhesions when actually the trouble may just be emotional and not due to ailing body organs.

"It is time we became frank regarding the 'rape of the pelvis'." Dr. Radin criticized "wholesale removal" of women's ovaries and tubes, repair of tipped wombs to cure backaches, then removal when the backache returned.

I remember a case where the family doctor suggested a caesarean operation in a case of obstetrical delivery after waiting on a woman in labor for a few hours. He recommended a certain surgeon as the best man to perform the operation. The surgeon was immediately called; he came, examined the woman, and confirmed the family doctor's opinion as to the immediate need for a caesarean operation. While preparations were being made for the operation and the surgeon was scrubbing his hands, the woman emitted sharp screams, with a real labor pain, and a bouncing ten-pound baby boy was born without any doctor's or surgeon's assistance. To say that the surgeon was abashed is to put it mildly.

Said Dr. Hawley, "the normal rate (for caesarean operations) ought to be 3 to 4 per cent and there are hospitals where it runs to 15 per cent. If that many babies are born through caesarean section, that is unnecessary surgery."

5. Fee-Splitting

What increases the number of unnecessary operations is the racket of fee-splitting. Fee-splitting is what its name implies; the dividing of fees between the general practitioner who sends the patient and the surgeon or specialist who operates.

Medical societies, individual leaders of our profession, and legislators have denounced fee-splitting. Yet fee-splitting goes on secretly as a black-market enterprise. Obviously there is no way to reckon its spread. Doctors, realizing the risks they run in arousing the wrath of official bodies, do not, of course, exchange checks or conduct their splitting operations in the open, any more than did rebating monopolists in the old days. It is anybody's guess how common the practice is today. I would guess that it is much more widespread than it was in 1907, when I first began practice and was offered $100 from a surgeon to whom I had referred a patient.

Fee-splitting is illegal in many states and the offending doctor may be fined or jailed or lose his license to practice. The American College of Surgeons, organized in 1913 to restrict surgery to the honest and the able, condemned fee-splitting as "the buying and selling of patients," and required each fellow member to pledge not to practice it. But the A.C.S. (American College of Surgeons) is a surgical society and has no legal authority, and the racket continues just the same.

In 1944, the Moreland Commission of New York reported to Governor Dewey: "Kickbacks ranging from 15 to 50 per cent were paid to more than 3000 physicians in New York, Kings, Bronx, and Queens counties alone. The medical societies have seemingly closed their eyes to this widespread system." Testimony showed that referring physicians demanded kickbacks from everybody, surgeons, X-ray laboratories, surgical appliance companies, opticians, and even specimen analysis laboratories.

Some eye doctors defraud patients by taking "kickbacks" from optical houses filling prescriptions for their patients. When this racket was exposed doctors began to have the glasses delivered to them and to add 100 per cent (in addition to their fees) to the opticians' charges. This was recently revealed in Milwaukee by Willis L. Hotchkiss, Assistant United States Attorney, who commented "some doctors used to get rebates as high as $40,000 a year and they don't like to see that pile of boodle go out of the window."

Because of this racket of fee-splitting many people wear spectacles who have no need for them. A survey in the *Reader's Digest* of August and October of 1937 showed that all of its polled patients were told they needed a change of glasses just about as often as they changed optometrists.

But the most revolting type of unnecessary surgery has to do with infanticide by way of criminal abortions. If there is any doubt as to the widespread practice of unnecessary surgery, that doubt is immediately removed when we remember that it has been estimated that more than 600,000 criminal abortions are performed annually in the United States.

The performing of an abortion is so commonplace and so widespread that not a hamlet is too remote to have access to one or more physicians who are doing abortions.

Nearly every county medical society has one or more of these criminals who are doing the work for their respective communities for a handsome fee. They are known to the rest of the profession. Indeed, those physicians who refuse to perform this crime send women to other members of the society who do them regularly.

The profession has not become entirely shameless and the professional abortionist is without caste—outwardly—yet many regular practitioners and gynecologists perform criminal operations by resorting to various subterfuges.

To remove the motive for unnecessary surgical operations, it is mandatory to prevent the physician from having any pecuniary interest in his patient by putting him on a salary; and where this, for any reason, is not practicable, he may be compensated on a capitation basis.

No juror, having interest in the outcome of civil cases, is permitted to remain on the jury panel. The court removes him for cause. It is well known that every man's verdict is influenced by his own interest. It is easier to believe that a patient has appendicitis when we profit by the diagnosis.

What kind of justice could be expected from our courts if the remuneration of the judges were dependent upon their decisions, if "guilty" brought a $500 fee while "innocent" meant only $5? This position is one in which we should not place the most altruistic and high-minded of humans, and yet our doctors, in the present system of medical practice, find themselves on just that spot. Do you wonder now at my grave accusation against the medical profession? Isn't it a miracle, rather, that there are any men of goodwill left among physicians?

Under coöperative medicine, the physician on a salary has no stake in sickness, and the less sickness there is the less work he has to do and the more time he has for study and recreation. When members of the coöperative hospital association consult us, we do not try to find all manner of surgical conditions to operate upon; on the other hand, many non-member patients who come to us have had operations recommended to them, the need for which existed only in the mind of the would-be operators, and many of these have had operations that did them no good whatever.

Dr. James P. Warbasse, a distinguished surgeon, says in "The Doctor and the Public" that:

> There is abroad an idea that the physicians who enters into relations with prospective patients, on a salary basis, to serve them, is doing something unethical; any step away from the system of individualistic competitive practice is frowned upon. When we stop to think, we see that the thing called "contract" is simply an

agreement to accept a salary, and the salary basis is the way things are now being done. The President of the United States, heads of universities, the executives of great businesses, and the people who are administering most of the significant enterprises are paid with salaries. Engineers and lawyers esteem salaries. Art was at its best when the artists were subsidized with salaries. The doctors who are making the significant discoveries, the research workers to whom we look for new light on the dark places in medicine, are working for salaries— "contract doctors" all. They are not competing with one another for a living in the economic field; their livelihood is guaranteed; and they are left free to devote their talents to the finding of new facts and doing their medical work.

A cardinal principle of coöperative medicine is consumer participation.

Such participation, however, does not extend into the field of medical matters, these matters being the province of the medical staff. A doctor is an expert, and his professional work cannot be modified by a non-expert. But such control does extend into the field of business matters, and for this doctors should be grateful, for it leaves them free to devote themselves to their professional work.

Consumer coöperation has ever been fair and just and equitable. It has always treated its employees and workers fairly. Coöperative societies have ever been in favor of the organization of the employees into labor unions as a means of self-protection. The coöperative movement tends toward economic democracy.

Under coöperative medicine, the doctor is guaranteed an adequate salary and a possible bonus. He is free from economic worry. He has economic security and an assured income. He does not have to keep books, or make out bills, or look after collections. He is in the dignified position of a professor instead of that of a private tradesman. He has more time for study and for leisure.

He does not compete with fellow staff members for patients but coöperate with them. Indeed, as at our hospital, he takes a vacation for a month each year, on pay, for study and recreation, and he is not on 24-hour duty as is the solo practitioner. And when he falls ill his income does not cease; at the Community Hospital his salary is paid through 3 months of illness.

Under coöperative medicine, the young graduate finds it easy to adjust himself. Indeed he is in demand from the day he finishes his internship, as he is wanted by organized groups of physicians in every part of the country. Young graduates of medicine who came to us fared well from the day they joined the staff.

Coöperative medicine now offers these four freedoms to the doctor:

Freedom from insecurity,
Freedom for study and leisure,
Freedom for consultation with fellow practitioners,
Freedom of conscience.

And there are other freedoms as well. The freedom to tell the truth to a hypochondriac instead of coddling him in his delusions in order to keep him as a patient, the freedom to choose one's own club or fraternal organization and to refuse to join various other societies and aggregations of bores and bounders just for the sake of meeting prospective patients.

To provide a proper set of checks and balances between associations of individuals and the groups of medical men, the consumer coöperative type of government is the most effective method. Said Dr. Warbasse:

1. It is the only form of government in which no middle man is present. Hence it does not destroy the intimate and direct physician-patient relationship.
2. It is applicable to rural as well as urban areas.

3. There are existing economic forces around which it can be organized.
4. It can be put into operation now and without complicated legislation.
5. It provides an ethical means whereby the medical profession can avoid, at least partially, the oncoming of compulsory health insurance (which may yet be necessary for a certain part of the population).

"From the standpoint of organization," Dr. Warbasse continues,

> the fundamental principles of consumer coöperation apply; one member, one vote; no proxy voting; no political, racial, or religious discrimination; open membership. These principles are the basis of democracy. Through consumer coöperatives, members receive the care they themselves want. They are the ones who are insistent upon the competence of their doctors. They know that real economy is not in cheap medicine, but in better medicine.
>
> These fundamental features of organization and control are absent in many other types of health organization. With third party control, it is hard to remove the "acquisitive instinct" of the politician.
>
> When industrial concerns undertake medical care, it is often for their own good, with employees' welfare a secondary consideration. Commercial insurance companies interposing control between the patient and the physician often usurp the doctor's loyalty.
>
> No agency except an association for patients seems to be so motivated as to provide the proper relationship between the doctors and purchasers of medical services. Let it be said, however, that under the coöperative plan, lay control does not extend into the field of medical matters. Those are exclusively in the province of the doctor.

On almost every point coöperative health associations offer advantages not present in other types of organization for the provision of medical care. This is because coöperative medicine is deliberately aimed at the solution of as many economic problems of today as is possible in any one type of organization. Coöperative medicine is not a panacea. One of its faults is that in its efforts to provide the best medical care, it places its services out of reach of a great many people in the very low income groups and the unemployed. For these groups the only answer may be government subsidy.

For all these reasons, the coöperative practice of medicine seemed to me to be the best available answer to the chaotic problem, and I proceeded to devote myself to its establishment at Elk City.

Part Three

The Oklahoma Health Crusade

Chapter 10

Starting a Medical Coöperative

1929

By 1929 I had been practicing medicine for 22 years, the last 17 in Beckham County, Oklahoma. I had a large clientele and was financially easy. I said to myself, "Now is the time to put into effect the program of medical reform that I've been thinking of for the last 20 years, now or never."

To remedy the defects in the prevailing system of medical care, I decided to apply the principles of the coöperative movement to it. I determined to have a large group of people organized into an association, to build and equip their own hospital, and through a board of trustees of their own choosing to employ physicians and specialists to serve them on a salary basis.

In western Oklahoma there were more than 100 coöperative cotton gins. Each farmer who wanted to join the association had to pay $100 to build the gin, and each member of the gin had his cotton ginned on a cash basis, and received a dividend at the end of the ginning season. I figured that if the farmer could pay $100 to build a gin, he could afford $50 to build a hospital and pay $50 per year for medical and surgical care for his family.

The majority of people who cannot afford to pay for high-grade medical care and hospitalization on a fee-for-service basis can afford to pay for it if permitted to pay a given sum periodically whether ill or well. They can afford to pay so much a month or so much a year for medical care, but they can not afford to pay for every office visit, every examination, every surgical operation, and each hospitalization. As I noted in the preceding chapter, they can afford the wholesale price but not the retail price, especially when they have no voice as to what a legitimate price is to be.

The whole tragic situation was most forcibly brought to our attention when we first started the hospital. Our Board of Directors had reached an agreement whereby members of the Oklahoma State Farmers' Union could, during a period of three days, have their surgical operations free except for the payment of a minimal hospital fee. Most of the cases that came to us seeking relief were of many years' standing. Here are the histories of a few of these patients, farmers, it must be kept in mind, well above the mud-sill, who had intelligence enough to join an organization for their betterment.

Case No. 1. Piles and prolapse of the rectum of ten years' standing, ten years of suffering. This old man, 83 years of age, had contrived a sort of truss to hold his prolapsed rectum in position. He had made it himself and had attached straps to it simulating a hernia truss.

Case No. 2. A stone in the urinary bladder the size of a small orange, the victim passing blood and pus, and suffering the torment of the damned for about eight years.

Case No. 3. A woman with gangrene of the foot due to diabetes, necessitating amputation above the knee.

Case No. 4. Gall stones of several years' standing. At operation cancer was found superimposed on the gall stone, a condition which of course had been neglected.

Case No. 5. A woman with a large umbilical hernia of many years' standing. She was brought to us with strangulation of the bowel due to the hernia. The necessary operation involved a resection of the gut.

Case No. 6. Cancer of the lower bowel causing obstruction. The bowel obstruction, due to the neglect of the cancer, brought the patient to us seeking relief. Except for the ob-

STARTING A MEDICAL COÖPERATIVE 89

struction he would not have come to us, and he had been in ill health for a long time without seeking relief.

Case No. 7. A woman with incurable cancer of the womb. She had mortgaged her farm so she could pay a couple of unscrupulous "skin disease specialists" $600 for radium treatment which did her no good.

Case. No. 8. A large fibroid tumor of many years' standing, about ten pounds in weight, in a woman about 46 years of age.

Case No. 9. Another cancer of the uterus, in the later stage of the disease. This woman did not see a doctor until she had nearly bled to death. She lived on a farm and I was called out to see her at her home. I found her in a pool of blood. Her case on examination was inoperable.

Case No. 10. A cancer of the mouth. The victim of this dreadful disease had in his mouth a lower dental plate that he had made himself. He had taken a piece of wood and carved it to fit his lower jaw. He had been using it for some years. During this period he had made several dentures with nothing except a jackknife and wood. He could not afford to pay fifty to a hundred dollars for a set.

Case No. 11. A case of consumption that had developed phlebitis of one of the lower limbs, which was enlarged and swollen.

Case No. 12. A patient with cancer of the prostate gland; incurable.

With these and many comparable instances in mind, late in September 1929 I contacted the surgeon who owned the larger of the two hospitals in Elk City, and who was the president of the County Medical Society, and handed him a detailed type-written statement outlining a prepayment plan for medical care based on the principles outlined.

The plan called for 6,000 families (in my county then there were 7,000 families) who would each buy a fifty-dollar share of stock with which to build and equip a hospital, to buy the two existing hospitals in Elk City, and to build a clinic building to house the diagnostic operating staff, and who would pay $50 each year for their medical and surgical care.

Hospital care was not to be covered but was to be paid for as needed at a low daily rate. The reason for this was that the people whom we intended to reach were of the low income group and had never had any experience with paying out money as a form of insurance against sickness. The Blue Cross was not then in existence. Even today less than 4 per cent of the Blue Cross subscribers are farmers. Indeed, to insure them against hospital care in addition to medical and surgical care would increase the premium and make it prohibitive. Furthermore, except in emergency cases the farmers in southwestern Oklahoma do not go to a hospital. Prior to the building of the Community Hospital, I delivered about 3,000 babies and in no instance was the delivery in a hospital.

The prepayment plan stipulated that the medical men in the hospital territory in the county, twenty in number, were to meet and organize themselves. A given group, eight in number, representing surgery, internal medicine, and the specialties were to be assigned to the hospital where they would examine, treat, and operate on all cases referred to the diagnostic center and hospital by general practitioners, twelve in number.

Six thousand families, each paying $50 for complete medical and surgical care, would bring to the medical staff $300,000. It was proposed to pay the eight specialists $150,000 per year and the twelve general practitioners an equal amount. This sum, if it were equally divided, would pay each specialist $18,750 per year and each family doctor $12,500 per year.

How could the family doctors agree on the distribution of this amount among themselves? At any given time some doctors earn a lot more than others, and it would not be fair to make an equal division, for some doctors would be in greater demand and do a lot more work than others. The matter might be simplified by letting each member of the coöperative designate on his application the name of the physician he selects for his family doctor. At the end of each six-month period, a member might have the right, if desired, to change his family doctor for another. It would be a simple matter to pay each family doctor say $25 from the $50 accruing from each family that designated him as its family physician, the remaining $25 to go to defray the salaries of the eight specialists at the hospital and other clinic expenses. If Dr. Smith should be designated as family doctor by twice the number of families that designated Dr. Jones, then Dr. Smith would get twice the income that Dr. Jones received.

The eight specialists would have to agree among themselves as to the distribution of their total incomes.

It might be objected that all 6,000 families might not join the medical coöperative and therefore the income would not be as stated above, but considerably less. This, however, is not a valid objection, for those who did not join the coöperative would have to continue to pay for what services they received from the general practitioners or the hospital group, as they did before, which would amount to more than $50 a year per family. And it would not be long until in self-defense they fell into line as members of the association. Furthermore, under this coöperative setup, the man who is not a member of the coöperative could not employ one physician one time and another physician at some other time and evade both doctors' bills by going to still a third one the next time, for the obvious reason that the doctors in the area would for the first time be organized not on a sentimental ground but on an economic basis.

This plan I envisioned would solve the problem of the high cost of sickness, improve the quality of medical care, and enable the participants to call on the doctors for regular examinations and preventive medical services as well as medical and surgical treatment without any thought of having to pay fees; I expected too that it would remove the incentive on the part of the doctor to perform unnecessary treatment and operation.

Furthermore, I figured this reorganization of medical practice would be especially advantageous to the physicians as well as to their patients. In view of the fact that a doctor, aside from his charitable work, is fortunate if he collects 60 per cent of his bills, an adequate salary that would free him from the harassment of bookkeeping, bill collecting, and the multitude of financial end-of-the-month irritations which keep good men in a state of insecurity would be a welcome change.

Notoriously, a good doctor is a poor businessman, and notoriously too, patients think of doctors' bills in terms of crises, something to be put off until the last possible moment and then, if paid at all, paid grudgingly. To be sure, the successful Park Avenue practitioner can leave such sordid matters as collections to his highly paid secretary or lawyer, but here we are not concerned with the 5 per cent of the profession who can command fat fees and collect them. We are talking about the "run-of-the-mine" doctors in that 50 per cent of the profession which in the boom year 1929 netted an average income of $3,500 per year. We have in mind the promising younger men fighting to keep up both their chins and their appearances on an income which a skilled mechanic would scorn; youngsters starting in life with the handicap of medical school debts, running against odds in a competitive race where they are told only the fittest can survive. All that county medical societies have done for their protection is to adopt a black list against "dead beats," but this has failed of its purpose and rebounded to the hurt of the profession. A new system for medical care had, therefore, to be instituted, a system that would be as much in the interest of the doctors as in the interest of the public.

This system, I had decided, must be a cash payment in advance. It should be a prepayment for medical service, and it must eliminate all credits. Most people will pay for medical service more willingly before receiving it than after. The lawyer gets his retainer before he takes the case. At the cinema box office you pay before you see the picture. In the telephone booth you drop your nickel or quarter before you are connected.

Under present systems of competitive practice, the young man for the first five to ten years, when he is at the fullness of his ambition and strength to give conscientious service, is kept stagnating in his office, waiting, waiting, waiting. There is plenty of work but he does not have the chance to do it.

One of the most pathetic figures in life is the young medical graduate, diploma in hand, financially broke, having been to medical school four or five years and having served one or more years as a hospital interne with little or no pay whatever, and no place to go. Without any financial assistance or other direction, he is expected to fend for himself. If occasionally one is permitted to work in the outpatient department of a hospital or to occupy a minor teaching position in a medical school, not one cent does he get for his labor. Experience and opportunity to become acquainted is considered sufficient pay for his efforts.

Under a general system of coöperative medicine, the young graduate would find it easy to adjust himself. Indeed, as previously indicated, he would be in demand from the day he finished his internship, as he would be wanted by organized groups of physicians in every part of the country. He would not have to try one location after another, nor wait for patients, nor exert himself to get established and compete for a living as he would in private practice.

After a long discussion pro and con, the doctor assured me he would study the plan carefully and get in touch with me in a few days. But when two weeks went by and I did not hear from him I went to see another doctor and his son who were interested in another local hospital; they promptly rejected the plajn as being unsound and unworkable.

I consulted the doctors and sought their coöperation because I wanted the coöperative hospital to be organized without injury to any of the existing hospitals and I proposed to their surgeon owners that the coöperative association buy their hospitals and that it build a new one only when expansion would make it necessary. I proposed for every doctor to be on the hospital staff so that the people would have the widest possible choice of physicians.

But all the doctors rejected the plan. One of these surgeons wrote: "In my time I have seen many of these movements started and die out. The great difficulty lies first in trying to find 6,000 people with fifty dollars to put up for such a movement and secondly in the eternal habit humanity has of disagreeing. I am sorry but I do not think that humanity has advanced to that stage of civilization where coöperation in its broadest sense can be successfully applied."

Thus, it was by the established doctors' own decision that they were not all included from the very beginning in my contemplated plan for providing medical care on a coöperative basis to the people of western Oklahoma.

Chapter 11

The Die Is Cast

1929–1931

I was very disappointed but not particularly surprised at the negative response from the doctors. It had become evident that if a coöperative hospital were to be established in Oklahoma, it would be in spite of, and not because of, the physicians. I realized that I could count on the active opposition of the medical profession as soon as its members became aware of any real threat to their income. While these considerations gave me pause, I could not abandon the plan.

On October 20, 1929, when the country was on the brink of the most serious economic disorder in its history, I sent out a call to some of the more progressive farmers around Elk City for a meeting to be held in the basement of the Carnegie Library. Most of the men turned the evening chores over to their boys and came, wondering what I wanted. When the meeting came to order, there sat Paul E. Peeler, who was elected chairman, A. J. McKenney, S. C. Thompson, C. A. Gassner, J. W. Cain, Jesse M. Barber, W. A. Hostetler, Harry Luthy, Arthur A. Hill, E. F. Luthy, and Earl Green.

"What was it you had in mind, Doc?" Paul Peeler asked.

I began by talking about the high cost of medical care, but I stopped very quickly, because I could see after a few sentences that no one wanted to listen to that. They knew much better than I what sickness meant to the farmer. So I turned at once to the plan itself and outlined the proposed founding of the Community Health Association. We would issue memberships at fifty dollars each, which would entitle the holder to a life interest in the association and a share in its benefits and earnings. The money from the memberships would be used to build a hospital, and even if there were only 1,000 members to start with, the $50,000 would enable us to build a well-designed small hospital.

I told them that I had endeavored to secure the coöperation of the doctors in the county but without success, and that if I had their cooperation we would provide a prepayment plan giving each member of the hospital association the opportunity to pay a given sum each year for medical and surgical care for himself and family. I explained fully the plan I had offered the doctors, but added that in view of their attitude we would not be able to secure enough members at the beginning to pay salaries, but would have to start with a discount plan.

At the outset, the hospital would furnish service on a discount basis, entitling all members to a 50 per cent reduction on operations with a guaranteed maximum charge of $50. On prescriptions, members would be given a 33 1/3 per cent discount and save one-third, on dental bills, a 25 per cent discount and save one-fourth. On all general doctors' bills aside from these the members would be given a 50 per cent discount and save one-half. I saw no reason, I said, why we shouldn't attain a membership of 2,000, which would allow us to provide the finest of medical service. The Community Health Association would then be able by a prepayment plan to employ, on a strictly salary basis, a chief surgeon, a chief physician, an eye, ear, nose, and throat specialist, a urologist, a resident hospital physician, two general practitioners, an X-ray and laboratory technician, two dentists, and a druggist!

"You people," I continued, "are not getting the good medical care that is now available. Medical care has become complex, it has become a technical and a scientific problem. To practice medicine adequately requires a group of doctors, surgeons, specialists, dentists, and technicians organized around a hospital.

"Here in Elk City, a town of 6,000 (in 1929, now 18,000) people, we are without a single specialist. Indeed, in all western Oklahoma there is not a single specialist except two men who devote themselves to eye, ear, nose, and throat work. And even these two men refer many of their cases to Oklahoma City specialists. Specialists do not locate in small towns. They locate in the cities, as they cannot make a decent living in small communities; they must follow the dollar. But if you organize and pay a given sum each year, you will be able to secure these specialists because out of your annual payment you can guarantee them definite salaries.

"There are many advantages to this coöperative scheme. First of all, you get better medical care. Secondly, you get this better medical care on a cost basis. In our own town of Elk City, we have three hospitals where we should have one without their overlapping overhead expenses. These hospitals have three superintendents instead of one; three bookkeepers, three kitchens, three surgeons, three laboratories, three X-ray departments, in fact three bills for everything instead of one.

"Then again under this plan of paying when well instead of when sick, you can ward off much sickness, you get the benefit of preventive medicine as well as curative medicine.

"The doctors should like the set-up unless they are medical Midases and expect to get wealthy out of sick people. They should like group medicine and limit their work within their capabilities. They would also be free from overhead expenses, from bookkeeping, collecting, making out bills, and so on. They would be in a more dignified position, in the position of professors and men of science instead of tradesmen. And they would be more independent; they would not need to cater to morons and magnify their worst delusions. They could afford to be honest. They would not have to look upon each case as a source of their livelihood."

"This is a most wonderful idea," commented the chairman. "Of course, we laymen know nothing about running a hospital. I suppose though that a coöperative hospital would be much like a coöperative gin or creamery or grain elevator. We do not know how to run any of these coöps, but we hire a manager who does know how to run each of them. And we can do the same with the hospital; we could hire you to manage it for us—I mean the board of directors could hire you—whoever they might be, as chosen by the members of the Hospital Association."

"Yes, that's it," I said, "but I want it understood, right now, where the duties of the board of directors would begin and end. They would be responsible to the members for the business administration of the hospital and the manager would be responsible to the board. The manager would represent the board of directors between their monthly or tri-monthly meetings, just as the board would represent the members between their semi-annual or annual meetings.

"In addition to a business manager, you would need a medical director who would be entrusted with the professional, that is medical and hospital, administration. The business manager would look after bookkeeping, collecting, purchasing, and so on, and would have charge of all personnel that have to do with these duties. The medical director would have charge of all professional personnel, physicians, dentists, nurses, technicians, druggists, and so forth, and would have the privilege of hiring and firing these subject to confirmation by the board of directors. To begin with, and until such time as the business might require it, I would have to fill the place of both business manager and medical director, but the board could hire a business manager at any time they desired or the business justified it.

"At any rate as medical director I would want a contract with the Board of Directors for a period of five years. This, I admit, is unusual and in contravention of coöperative principles and practice but you can understand that this is a new venture, in fact, an adventure on my part and it will require more than the usual one-year contract as in other coöps to

THE DIE IS CAST

put the project over. I would not want to go into this unless I had five years to put it over.

"With this exception all other features of the plan would be strictly on Rochdale principle of coöperation, one member one vote, dividend based on patronage, and so on."

When I finished talking, the men remained silent for a few minutes, thinking the plan over. Then Paul Peeler spoke, "I'm with you, Doc." "Count me in," said Earl Green, and the others all agreed. They formed an organizing committee, and named me secretary-treasurer for the project. The next morning I went to the Farmers' National Bank and arranged that its president, W. E. Hocker, act as a trustee for the funds to be collected by the committee. As I left, he said: "I hope you make a go of this Hospital. I've seen too many farmers wiped out by a doctor's bill for four or five hundred dollars."

The members of the committee got to work and there were soon enough people interested to warrant taking over a charter for a coöperative hospital, capitalized at a $100,000, with shares at $50 each. Since the year was nearing its end and the farmers had little ready money, we decided to sell shares for $10 cash, the balance to be paid in a year's time. The members of the committee sold some shares among their friends, but to hasten the sale we decided to employ agents, giving them a 10 per cent commission on each sale. A good many shares were taken by my own patients, and I bought ten shares myself. To those of my patients who became members I allowed the discount for any operation performed in my little eight-bed hospital, applying the amount of the discount against their $40 note and allowing them to retain the discount when the note had been paid. Actually, discounts should have been delayed until the coöperative hospital had been established, but I wanted to make evident the advantages of joining the association, for many members who cared nothing for coöperative principles had joined only because they could save a hundred dollars or more by becoming members.

By February 1930 we had sold 125 memberships, and by May the figure had risen to 700. I found myself unable to cope with the work, so Dr. Eckrich, an excellent physician, was engaged to assist me. Both the committee and I felt so encouraged that a meeting was called for the purpose of forming a permanent organization. A board of directors was selected, a constitution was adopted, and it was decided to purchase the hospital site and start construction immediately. We would continue our sale of memberships, and by November, when the $40 notes from the members were to be collected, we would have enough money to pay for the building and equipment.

The first shovelful of earth had not been lifted before the local doctors, a round dozen of them, got together. It was one thing to have the plan on paper, but quite another actually to start construction of a building. In a manifesto published in the *Elk City News*, these doctors stated at considerable length that they would never take any of their patients to the hospital and they gave voice to that most damning of words in the medical vocabulary: "unethical."

I had felt all along that such an attack was to be expected sooner or later, so the statement did not surprise me. We now had seven hundred members behind us, enough to enable us to build a hospital, which, once established, would speak for itself. The foundation of the building was started in October, and in November we began the collection of the $40 notes. It was not until we attempted this, however, that the success of the doctors' propaganda against us became apparent. They had spread the rumor that we had no intention of really building a hospital and that the money paid in would be lost. For weeks, I traveled every day far into the night, stopping at the farms of our members and asking for the $40. Time and again I would be told, uneasily, "Sorry, Doc, we haven't got the money." In some cases, this was true, but in many the answer was inspired by the opposition from the doctors.

By the end of the month we had collected so little money

THE DIE IS CAST

that we were forced to stop work on the hospital. Inevitably, the sale of memberships dropped off, and soon the whisper grew louder: "They never meant to build that hospital." That winter was a bitter one for me. Not only did it look as though our plans would fail, but many of my patients, to whom I had sold shares of hospital stock, turned from me, and my practice, which had averaged $15,000 a year for over ten years, dwindled to a point where I wasn't even making expenses.

For a time I thought of giving up the whole project, but I could not reconcile myself to that. I had to fight the thing through. I had lived in Beckham county for eighteen years and I wasn't going to give up the most important thing I had ever undertaken without a long, hard fight.

It was most essential to get enough money to build the hospital, for that would convince the people that we were not cheating them. I went to John Simpson, leader of the Oklahoma Farmers' Union, to ask him if he could arrange a loan of $15,000 which, with the $11,000 we had in the bank, would enable us to go ahead. He persuaded the Great American Insurance Company to make us the loan, payable on completion of the building and secured by a $15,000 term insurance policy on my life. To their loan I added $10,000 of my own, receiving a note from the board of directors.

In the spring of 1931 we resumed building operations, and by the middle of August the Community Hospital, a two-story modern brick building, stood ready for occupancy. But all the money we had raised had been used to pay for the land and the building, and not enough was left with which to buy equipment. So I moved all of my own—about $10,000 worth—into the hospital, and we were ready for the formal opening.

The sight of the hospital reassured our members, and things looked so propitious that we decided to have as elaborate an opening as we could manage. We asked John Simpson, O. E. Enfield, and Oscar Ameringer to be our speakers. We built an arbor on the grounds and we barbecued seven

Community Hospital, Elk City, Oklahoma.

beeves to feed our three thousand hungry well-wishers. Everyone cheered when it was announced that Doctors Shadid and Eckrich would, for the next four days, perform free operations, subject only to the payment of fees for anesthesia, room, board, and nursing. (In those four days, the hospital took in $800 in fees.)

The time for speeches came; John Simpson made a stirring one. Oscar Ameringer a funny one, and in an effort to counteract the propaganda spread by our opponents I made a sworn statement:

> I will never own or appropriate for my own private purpose the Community Hospital at Elk City, legally or illegally.
>
> I will do my best to insure its success.
>
> I will defend it against the machinations of its enemies.
>
> I will never desert it while it is in its swaddling clothes—not until it has become a stripling and able to stand on its own feet—and then only because I am convinced that it will succeed better without me at its helm.
>
> I built and sponsored this hospital not only as a token of appreciation for what the people did for me in Beckham County, but also because I am convinced that private ownership of hospitals is wrong and detrimental to the best interests of the masses of mankind, physically, morally, and financially, in this and every other country of the world.

Chapter 12

The Termites Attack

1931

The successful opening of the hospital spiked the guns of the opposition only momentarily. Although they carried on their whispering campaign, they could no longer intimate that the hospital plans would never materialize. They had to concentrate on the accusation that I was planning to misappropriate the hospital for my own private use and profit.

They turned their main efforts, however, to another—and more drastic—form of attack; an effort to have my license revoked. The driving force of the opposition came chiefly from the surgeon owners of the hospitals who, of course, saw in the Community Hospital a direct threat to their earnings. Many of the other doctors were behind them in the fight, but some were sympathetic to our coöperative medical plan. The pressure was so strong, however, that these few ventured to express their beliefs only in private, though they did help by furnishing me with information on the activities of my opponents.

One night a doctor friend came to my home, and handed me a copy of a notice for a special meeting of the Beckham County Medical Society. Apparently the county president had sent copies to all its other members, but I had not received one despite the fact that I had been a member in good standing for twenty years. The reason for the omission was clear enough, as will be seen from the proceedings of the county medical society meeting as reported to me by my friend substantially as follows:

"The meeting will come to order," announced the president of the Beckham County Medical Society. "This is a special meeting called for purpose of deciding what to do about the Community Hospital."

Ordinarily meetings of the medical society are poorly attended and sometimes the meeting would be adjourned for want of a quorum. On this occasion, however, every member was present, for it was not only a meeting of minds but a meeting of economic interests as well. The doctors of the society felt that their livelihood was threatened and they were fearful.

"In the letter I sent you calling this meeting," continued the president, "I told you we had a communication from the president of the State Board of Medical Examiners which I will now read:

> The State Board of Medical Examiners has just sat as a court to try one Dr. R. L. Browning of Hartshorne to cancel said Browning's license, for unprofessional conduct, in that Browning has been guilty of employing steerage to procure additional practice. Browning's method was to have coal mine superintendents circulate lists of employees for their signatures authorizing the mine officials to deduct $1.75 per month from their respective wages, this $1.75 premium entitling the miner and his family to full professional services at the hands of Browning, and hospitalization in the Hartshorne Hospital which was owned by Browning. The case was vigorously prosecuted by the Attorney-General's department, and Browning was found guilty, but given a suspended sentence of two years upon his promise to desist from such practice in the future. The law is very plain along these lines and the board has absolute authority to cancel licenses where it is shown that any method of steerage is employed.

It occurs to me that you could very easily have one of your colleagues' licenses revoked for this same reprehensible practice. It is up to your society to file the charges and present them to the Attorney-General who will collect the evidence and prosecute before the board.

"You have heard this communication from the State Board of Medical Examiners," said the chairman. "What is your pleasure?"

For a moment there was complete stillness. This communication took them by complete surprise. They had on many occasions talked things over with one another, two or three of them at a time, but they had no idea what to do about this Community Hospital.

"Mr. President," boomed my friend, a short middle-aged physician, "before we can intelligently discuss this communication from Doctor McGregor and act on his suggestion it seems to me we should know what this so-called coöperative Community Hospital is about, what its purposes are, and how it proposes to achieve them. Before you fight your enemy, it is wise to know all you can about his strength and his weaknesses.

"I have in my hand a folder titled 'The Community Hospital Service Plan'. This folder states that the family membership fee is fifty dollars and that this fee is to go into 'land, building, and equipment.' " Reading from the Community Hospital folder, he continued:

" 'That this membership entitles the member and his family to discount on his medical and dental bills, and later on to a prepayment plan giving examinations, treatments, surgical operations, and laboratory work upon the payment of fifty dollars per year.'

"The folder further states, quote:

> The purpose of the Community Hospital is to make medical care available to people of low income, to improve the quality of medical care, and to make it possible

for people to see the doctor early and get the benefit of preventive medicine.

" 'A dues-paying system is very much cheaper. It is cheaper to pay so much a year to a staff of doctors and specialists than it is to pay them every time you have an examination or a treatment or a surgical operation. One case of serious illness in ten years will save enough money to pay the dues for ten years, to say nothing about needed examinations and treatments and surgical operations.

A member not on free service comes to the doctors when he must. He puts off coming because of the cost. A member on free service comes as often as he needs to without waiting until it is too late. He has a lot of work done that the other member neglects. A dues-paying system is preventive of ill health.

A doctor hired by the year, and not by the visit or by the job, is disposed to deal fairly and honestly by the member. A doctor who does not profit by giving a treatment or by doing a surgical operation is not going to recommend a needless treatment or a useless operation.

"This folder, from these statements I have read," continued the doctor, "reveals Dr. Shadid's strength but it does not reveal all of his weaknesses. His strength consists of an effort to make medical care available to people of low incomes and to improve the quality of medical care and to make preventive medical services available. No one can object to these laudable purposes. Certainly we cannot attack him or disbar him for trying to advance these ends.

"Now what are his weaknesses? The folder does not reveal them. But we do know that he is sending agents out to solicit members; can this be construed as 'steerage' within the meaning of the medical practice act? If it can be so construed his license can be revoked or suspended. If he makes the plea that he has nothing to do with these agents, that these are the agents of the corporation, then it will be up to the State

Board of Medical Examiners to determine. We do know this, however, that he is secretary-treasurer of the corporation and as such we may be able to hold him guilty of steerage in that he has employed steerers or cappers within the meaning of the law. Of course, he could make this defense. He could claim that the law when enacted was aimed at venereal disease quacks who employed agents to corral patients to their offices, and was never meant to prohibit corporations from securing members through agents, and of course he would be correct in his contention. But then, again, it would be up to the state licensing board to pass on this. As I see it, the state licensing board is the key figure in the fight if we choose to make it. Then again he is making speeches all over western Oklahoma in an effort to corral members for his hospital. Can this be considered advertising and steerage? Making speeches is a form of publicity and it may or may not be advertising from the professional standpoint. Even though it is construed as advertising, there is no law against advertising, for the law does not take cognizance of ethics, medical or otherwise.

"One more observation and I am through. Just recently the committee on the cost of medical care published its report covering a five-year period of research. The majority report, signed by its chairman, Dr. Ray Lyman Wilbur, formerly president of the American Medical Association, makes the following recommendations, quote:

> The committee recommends that medical service, both preventive and therapeutic, should be furnished largely by organized groups of physicians, dentists, nurses, pharmacists, and other associated personnel. Such groups should be organized preferably around a hospital, for rendering complete home, office, and hospital care. The form of organization should encourage the maintenance of high standards and the development or preservation of a personal relation between patient and physician.

> The committee recommends that the costs of medical care be placed on a group payment basis through the use of insurance, through the use of taxation, or through the use of both of these methods. This is not meant to preclude the continuation of medical service provided on an individual fee basis for those who prefer the present method.

"This committee," he continued, "was organized in 1927 and consisted of forty-eight persons, twenty-five of whom were physicians and surgeons of national and international reputation. The chairman of this committee is Doctor Wilbur, formerly secretary of the Department of the Interior under Hoover, and at one time president of Leland Stanford University, and also at one time president of the American Medical Association. Other members of this committee represented the great foundations, the social sciences, the professions, and the general public. This committee was given nearly $1,000,000 by nine foundations with which to prosecute an inquiry into the cost of medical care and other matters pertaining thereto.

"This report is just off the press. It is quite possible that this is the next step in the evolution of medical practice. Other countries have adopted more radical steps. Some countries have adopted state medicine, others compulsory health insurance, both under government auspices. Do we want this in this country? I know I don't and I do not believe there is a doctor here that does.

"My own feeling in the matter is this," he continued, "we should stop and consider. If we act in haste we may grieve at leisure. Perhaps we should invite Dr. Shadid for a conference and ask him to explain. The House of Delegates of the American Medical Association has not yet taken any position on this recommendation. A majority of them might be in favor in which case we would be out on a limb. For, after all, Dr. Shadid's scheme or plan seems to dovetail with the recommendation of the majority on the committee. Only he has anticipated the committee's recommendations by several years. He has organized doctors, dentists, pharmacists, nurses, technicians, and other needful personnel to give group medical care and has organized an association of patients and prospective patients to make a group payment, all of which conforms to the recommendations of the majority committee. I hold no brief for Dr. Shadid; I am with you in any action you decide upon."

The speaker was the physician who had given me the notice he had received about the secret meeting. I was, therefore, fully aware of the object of the meeting and had given considerable thought to presenting my own defense through this doctor, who was a good friend of mine. He was sold on this coöperative plan and was willing to make the foregoing speech which I had written for him.

"Mr. President," said another doctor, "I have known Dr. Shadid for many years, and I know he is a money grabber. He does not give a damn about better medical care any more than he gives a damn about poor people. This coöperative hospital association is a smoke screen behind which he does his dirty work. He wants to build a hospital for himself without using his own money. I prophesy that in two years or less the hospital will be so deep in the red that he will buy it for a song. And he will not pay any money for it either. He will pay the people fifty cents on the dollar, not in cold cash, but in examinations and operations at his own price.

"Doctor Shadid is a schemer. He is fooling these poor farmers and radicals. He is a spell-binder and has hypnotized these poor people into building a hospital for him.

"I am in favor of kicking him out of this society now. I have a notion that the previous speaker is in on the scheme. I prophesy that if we do not kick Dr. Shadid out now but let him succeed in his schemes, that he will join him. Two birds of one feather flock together.

"If this society does not kick Dr. Shadid out, please accept my resignation effective now. I do not want to associate myself with crooks—at least not foreign crooks. I am not going to tolerate foreigners coming over here and telling us how to practice medicine. This country belongs to the people who inhabit it and not to immigrants. If I had my way about it, I would expel them all and send them back to where they came from. Those are my sentiments."

This doctor was envious of my success and was a member of the Ku Klux Klan. In a K.K.K. parade through the city streets, he had been seen with his face uncovered. And he was bitter toward my friend because he had treated a case of blood poisoning (sepsis) following an obstetrical delivery. He accused my friend of having told the patient that her sepsis was due to his own lack of asepsis, although my friend was absolutely innocent of the charge.

My friend rose to reply but the president would not recognize him, saying each doctor would be heard once before any one doctor spoke a second time.

"I confess," said the president, "the first address is a complete surprise to me. I have never heard of the Committee on the Cost of Medical Care until now. I did not even know of a Dr. Wilbur who had been president of the American Medical Association."

A third doctor, a tall and kindly old fellow with a goatee and shaking palsy, stood up. This doctor was formerly a preacher.

"I am like our first speaker; I am not for taking action against Dr. Shadid. I hold no brief for his experiment. I think it is visionary, impractical. In my time, I have seen similar movements and clinics started and die out. This coöperative hospital is no exception. In two years or less, it will fold up. This is a free country. We learn by trial and error. I favor letting this hospital wash itself out."

Several men sought the floor, and were recognized in turn.

"In view of what has been said already," said one, "I am undecided what is best for us as a medical society to do. I feel we should consult our state officers."

"Mr. Chairman and gentlemen," boomed another, "I am

entirely in disagreement with the first speaker. If we ignore this socialist experiment no telling how long it will be before it folds up. It is true, you can't fool all the people all the time, but you can fool enough of them long enough to do a lot of harm and considerable damage. You and I know that people want something for nothing. And it seems to me that these dues as he calls them are but a little more than nothing. Good God Almighty! I get fifty dollars for a tonsillectomy and the hospital gets fifteen dollars for anesthetic and operating room; I get one hundred and fifty dollars for an abdominal operation like appendicitis or cholecystectomy or hernia; three to five hundred dollars for gastro-enterostomy or gastric resection.

"It has been prophesied that in two years at the most this communistic experiment will fold up and its sponsor be discredited. I am not so sure of that and even if it is true, are we going to sit here idly and let this damned foreigner corrupt our citizens and lower the standard of our noble profession? Are we going to allow a shrewd guy like that to bamboozle our friends and neighbors? You and I know that he is making promises he cannot fulfill, are we going to allow him to humbug our people?

"Look as the people he has already taken into membership, J. C. Nunley, Howard Gibson, Fannie Steinhardt, Owen Mitchell; good substantial farmers. I do not know of any poor farmers who have bought stock in the outfit. The cream of our patrons is being skimmed and I suppose we will still have to doctor those people who stay out of his experiment. Fine business!

"Listen to this" (reading from the Community Hospital Service Plan):

" 'A doctor hired by the year, and not by the visit or by the job, is disposed to deal fairly and honestly by the member. A doctor who does not profit by giving treatment or by doing a surgical operation is not going to recommend a needless treatment or a useless operation.'

" 'MORE HONEST ADVICE'! Aren't the people getting honest

service now? Are we cheating and deceiving our patients? Is a damned foreigner more honest than a native American doctor? Are you going to stand for this? Are you going to swallow your self-respect and surrender your pride? I, for one, refuse to do it. If this society fails to take action against this unethical, unprofessional conduct on the part of an alien slanderer, I shall proceed to do so. They say this is a free country; well, so it is, but this is not American freedom as we know it; it is socialism, communism, inciting to revolution as Dr. Fishbein has correctly stated. It is a foreign ideology, it is destructive of the American system of free enterprise."

Immediately several men asked for the floor.

"The first speaker," said the one recognized, "hesitates to take action till a pronouncement is received from our national officers in Chicago. I disagree. A county medical society is autonomous. We do not have to follow any policy laid down in Chicago with respect to how we want to practice medicine.

"I spent two years in college, four years in medical school, and two years in a hospital at a total cost of $18,000 and I do not want to practice medicine for a measly salary and be pushed around, take orders from superiors, follow rules and regulations, and fill out blanks interminably. I studied medicine to make a living—a good living—acquire prestige, enjoy the good will of my patients, build a home, educate my children, and lay away a competency for my old age. Every one that can is doing it. See the business men in your own community and mine, grocers, dry-goods men, real estate men, movie men. Have they invested more money than you and I? Have they studied harder? Have they denied themselves and married late as some of us have done? Do they have to wait for years to establish themselves as we do? Are they at the beck and call of every Tom, Dick, and Harry day and night? Do they ever leave a warm bed to face a blizzard? Yet compare their income with our own; their homes, their automobiles, their clothes with ours! No, I am not working for the good of humanity but for the good of myself, my wife, and my children. Take care of your own interest and humanity will take care of itself.

"I am for action now. I am for kicking Doctor Shadid out of this society. He is beyond the pale of organized medicine.

"Then I am for disbarring him and revoking his license. If we do not do that other renegades will emulate his example till in self defense we will be obliged to lower our standard and work for pittance.

"I make a motion that we drop Dr. Shadid's name from the roll, cancel his membership, and bring charges against him for steerage and unprofessional conduct."

"I second that motion," boomed a voice in the rear of the room.

"You have heard the motion," said the chairman, "what is your pleasure?"

"I rise to a point of order," said my friend, "if you expel the doctor without trial, he will appeal to the proper state authority and he will win. You cannot expel a member without trial. Why not call the doctor in on the charges we have against him, give him a hearing, and then vote to expel him?"

"If we do that," rejoined the maker of the motion, "we would build him up. He would make capital out of it and create popular sympathy. He would tell it to the world. He would use that as an excuse to broadcast his program. He would make out of himself a victim of persecution, a hero, a martyr, and put us in the villain's role; no, that would never do."

The meeting continued until each doctor had had his say. There was no unanimity in their thinking. Some were in favor of letting the experiment "wash itself out" but these were in the minority, the majority being in favor of some action. Finally, one doctor arose, obtained the floor, and addressed the chairman as follows:

"Mr. Chairman," said he, "before we take any action against Dr. Shadid it will be advisable to disband the Beckham County Medical Society or else we would be liable for libel in the event that we do not substantiate any charges that we might hereafter make. I know Dr. Shadid well enough to know that he is a fighter from way back. Should he win out, he would be sure to sue this county society for damages. If we disband the society now, we would serve a double purpose. We would be in the clear as a group, and in the meantime we would have dropped his name from the roll of membership, for when we reorganize the society, we will do so without notifying him. Be assured that action will be taken along the lines already indicated and that in the very immediate future. I move, Mr. Chairman, that we surrender our charter as a county medical society and that we disband and adjourne sine die."

The motion was duly seconded and when put to a vote was carried by a large majority.

Chapter 13

Alfalfa Bill Murray to the Rescue

1931–1932

The charge that Dr. Eckrich and I were guilty of "steerage" was ridiculous. By steerage is meant the solicitation of patients directly or indirectly through "cappers" or "steerers." This reprehensible practice was first indulged in by quack itinerant specialists in sex diseases and the medical practice act provided a severe penalty for this misconduct. The penalty provided was suspension or revocation of license. The Community Hospital Association which I organized did send agents out to sell membership in the association and the president of the State Board of Medical Examiners found it convenient to interpret the law to apply to our agents as "steerers." The charge was absurd of course, but if they took my license away the fact that the complaint was groundless wouldn't matter.

Dr. Eckrich soon got word of this attempt, and was advised by "disinterested" friends to get out before it was too late. He came in one morning, slammed the door, stood still for a moment, and then slumped into a chair.

"What's happened, Eckrich?" I asked, alarmed.

"Dr. Shadid . . . ," he stammered, "it's nothing you've done . . . but I want to leave."

"Someone showed you that letter," I said.

"Yes," he admitted, "I was stopping on the street. I don't want to leave you, I'm with you all the way on this hospital, but I can't lose my license . . . I can't! There's only one way I can earn my living, and I haven't any money saved. Without my license, I'm no use to you or anybody else."

All my assurances that we had friends, too, and that if charges were brought against us we could fight and win our case could not dispel his fears. Finally I called Father Gaerhardt, the priest who had been instrumental in bringing Dr. Eckrich to the hospital. Father Gaerhardt, who was deeply interested in the welfare of the parishioners, realized that the hospital was an important step toward better medical care for his people, and was therefore anxious to see it succeed. We talked in the waiting room for a few minutes while I explained what had happened and why Eckrich was so afraid. But nothing that Father Gaerhardt or I said to Eckrich made an impression. Finally the priest said to him wearily: "The best thing to do is to get some sleep now and try to get some perspective on the matter, and when you feel better, tell Dr. Shadid your decision. I hope you will decide to stay."

The next morning Dr. Eckrich left us and I sat down to try to find some solution to the difficulties his departure would cause. I had relied on him for most of the medical work while I was away making collections on the notes and speaking to groups of our members. Many people had joined the hospital because of their personal regard for Dr. Eckrich, and I knew their membership would lapse now that he had gone.

The immediate result of his leaving was the report, industriously circulated by our opponents, that I was hard to get along with. They also used his departure as a further "proof" of the dishonesty of my intentions with regard to the hospital. I was shocked to realize that many people whom I had considered my friends believed these statements. I had been convinced that they would come to my defense and stand with me in my fight for the hospital. Of course, a good many of them did or we could never have won out. Without the support of these staunch friends I could not have carried on the fight.

Several days later the 'phone rang, and to my surprise the voice was that of the president of the county medical society.

"Hello, doctor," I said warily, "what can I do for you?"

"Well, Shadid," he answered with considerable heartiness, "you can give me ten minutes of your time. It's important that I see you this evening."

Since he had been hostile from the beginning, I couldn't imagine why he should want to see me. However, I said that I would be in my office that evening. He was most affable when he arrived.

"Lord knows, and I know, Shadid," he began, "it's all nonsense about your trying to gull the people into buying you a hospital. You have enough money to build your own hospital if you want. But they're after you, man, they're after you! They cannot stand this notion of coöperative medicine. They want to revoke your license."

"But that's a state matter, not a county," I said. "You have nothing to do with that."

"Oh, but I have," he said significantly. "The boys know I have influence higher up and they want me to use it. Now . . . I'd certainly hate to see you squeezed out."

"I won't be," I assured him.

"That's easy to say, Shadid. Talk's cheap, but actually what can you do? Once the wheels start moving, you'll find it pretty hard to keep your head above water. And you know as well as I do that you'll be held personally responsible for the failure of this hospital. If you had to pay its debts it would take almost every cent you've managed to save, wouldn't it?"

"I'm not worried about its failing, doctor," I said, "so don't you give it another thought."

He persisted. "It would be easy to make you responsible for every penny, but I don't want to see you in a spot, so . . ."

He hesitated, and I egged him on. "Just what do you mean, doctor?"

"You know how I like flying," he began. "Well I've just

ALFALFA BILL MURRAY TO THE RESCUE

seen a new plane that's a beauty. It's fast, safe, and it handles like silk; and only four thousand dollars."

"Wouldn't you like a new car, too?" I asked him.

His face grew very red. "This isn't anything for you to joke about, Shadid!" he roared. "I have influence higher up and I'm going to break you!"

He blustered out. It was obvious that I would have to act quickly and decisively to counter the attack before it struck me full force. I knew that John Simpson numbered among his friends men active in state politics, so I went to him and told him of the attempt that was being made to take my license. John Simpson spoke to Tom Cheek, the newly elected president of the Farmers' Union; Tom Cheek accepted the challenge, and with his associate, Zed Lawter, went to Governor Murray.

"Alfalfa Bill" Murray has been ridiculed by many conservatives for his homespun ways, but he was a good friend to the Community Hospital in its hour of need. He had established the custom of addressing a weekly message to the people in the pages of the *Blue Valley Farmer* and I was delighted when the following week I saw this message from the governor:

> With reference to the foregoing statement for the *Union Farmer*, it must be remembered there is an "inner circle" of the medical association, as there is of the various class organizations in the state. These "inner circles" of doctors, lawyers, and dentists, and other class organizations, undertake to regulate and control those who are not obedient to their wishes.
>
> I want to state that there is no danger of any doctor who may be employed in that hospital losing his license. In the first place, if the medical board attempts such conspiracy, they will be dismissed by the governor and prosecuted for such conspiracy, under the laws, as will any other doctor in any such conspiracy.

As to the attorney-general, who, under the Constitution, is under the direction of the governor, he will not make any such prosecution.

So this is notice to the doctors of the state, and all concerned, that the farmers in Beckham County who sought to organize for themselves a hospital for the treatment of their families have the legal constitutional right to do so, and will be protected to the limit by the governor of Oklahoma, and any organization of more than three persons having for its purpose the destruction of the hospital, or its injury, or the taking away of the license of any physician in such hospital will, under the criminal laws, be guilty of conspiracy, and will be prosecuted by direction of the governor by appointment of a special attorney, so that any combination with anyone else, as intimidated herein, will not be available to them, as "cat's-paws," in their hands.

The farmers of Beckham County are hereby guaranteed their rights, under the law, to continue; and the same protection will be extended to any other coöperative group coöperating with the said hospital, or any other that may be organized.

This is not the first instance where the "inner circle" have attempted even to thwart the execution of the laws. When I say the "inner circle" I mean those in control of these several class organizations, not alone of the physicians, but of the lawyers, dentists, barbers, et cetera.

Signed: *Wm. H. Murray*

The governor's denunciation acted like chloroform on all the open organized activity of the medical association, but the underground sniping campaign, already in progress, was pushed with renewed zeal. The tactics once more changed from front to flank attacks.

Every method that had been discarded before as being too rough, or "unethical," was hauled out and pressed into service. As previously stated, the Beckham County Medical Society disbanded, and when it miraculously reappeared, after eighteen months, the only change apparent to the naked eye was that I was no longer a member.

Medical societies supposedly exist for the advancement of knowledge. In the twenty years that I had been a member of the Beckham County Medical Society I had never once heard anything resembling a scientific discussion. The society's chief function seemed to be to collect dues and subscriptions for the *Journal of the American Medical Association*, the periodical issued by the national parent of such county societies. Exclusion from the county society, therefore, would not have perturbed me unduly had my only loss been the learned scientific papers one should expect to hear read at its meetings.

But there was a much more serious threat in the situation. Every doctor at one time or another in the course of his medical career is threatened with a malpractice suit by some disgruntled patient. While occasionally such a suit is justified, more frequently the grounds for the charge are flimsy and sometimes they are really non-existent. Most doctors are insured against the risk of such suits, and every insurance company, when insurance is applied for, asks whether the applicant is a member of his local medical society. If not, such insurance is refused. Without such membership I was left without protection against any law suit that an unscrupulous or hysterical person might institute against me.

The insurance companies, in making this rule, are eminently practical, for they reason that a doctor who is not a member of the home society will be unable to get another doctor to appear in court ready to swear that the diagnosis or treatment of the case in question was correct. As a result of being dropped from the roll of the county medical society, I would have to pay my own way in any malpractice suit brought against me, and I suspected that I would have lawsuits aplenty once the sniping was in full swing.

It was in the midst of such troubles as these, on a cold

January day in 1932, that I received a telegram announcing the imminent arrival of a vice-president of the Great American Insurance Company to inspect the hospital and make certain that the company would be in no danger of losing its $15,000 loan. There was just one patient in the hospital when the telegram arrived, and I was afraid that unless the hospital looked reasonably busy we might not get the loan extension that had been arranged.

I phoned my wife and asked her to send down any of the children who were at home, and two of them dutifully came rushing over. That wasn't enough so I sent them back for some playmates and went out to collect a couple of friendly adults. I hurried them all into bed, and their clothes were barely whisked out of sight when the vice-president was announced. I showed him through the modestly busy hospital while my children and friends lay in bed, fairly splitting with suppressed laughter.

To my great relief, the loan went through. It is true that I resorted to deception, but I did it only because I was convinced that the hospital would ultimately succeed, and I was right; the hospital paid off its debt to the insurance company, and its debt to me; it has repaid everyone from whom it has ever borrowed. Later, people said that in addition to filling the beds with healthy ringers, I had parked two old cars in front of the building to add to the effect, but I hadn't. I hadn't thought of it.

Chapter 14

Running the Medical Blockade

The governor's forthright proclamation spiked the guns of the opposition only as to revocation of my license, for they turned their efforts to another and more sinister attack, an effort to blockade the hospital and prevent us from securing physicians, nurses, and other technicians. This mode of attack had a telling effect. It was impossible to find in Oklahoma a doctor willing to run the risk of joining the Community Hospital, so I was forced to look outside the state for medical men. This was the signal for the opposition to lay siege. They established an invisible but very effective blockade around the Community Hospital and dared any doctor to run it. With the Beckham County Medical Society as a front, the opposition by pulling all the strings it could, had assured itself of the coöperation of the State Board of Medical Examiners as well as of the State Board of Dental Examiners. As a result, any doctor from outside the state who took the state medical examination or applied for reciprocity with the announced intention of joining the Community Hospital was either flunked or refused reciprocity. And the same was true for dentists.

Dr. Abodeeley, who was a graduate from a reputable medical school and had served one year of internship in a recognized hospital in Chicago, came to join our hospital staff. He wrote Dr. Osborne for a permit pending his examination. The secretary wrote to say that since the Basic Science Act was passed by the last legislature he had no knowledge whether or not he was permitted to issue permits to practice medicine pending the examination, but that he would inquire of the attorney-general and then write him accordingly. An excerpt from Dr. Osborne's letter follows:

> As to a temporary permit to practice medicine pending the examination, I am now asking for an opinion from the attorney-general. It has been a practice of the board to grant temporary permits, but since the enactment of Senate Bill #108 known as the Basic Science Act, I am of the opinion that no temporary permit can be granted and comply with this law.

More than a month passed and the secretary did not write and thereupon Dr. Abodeeley wrote the secretary another letter asking if he had decided on the matter of the issuing of the permit. Dr. Osborne wrote to say that the attorney-general had not yet sent his opinion and that he would write as soon as he heard. His second letter to Dr. Abodeeley follows:

> In reply to your letter of January 13, 1938, will say that as yet we have not received the opinion requested on December 14, 1937 regarding the issuing of temporary permits from the attorney-general; but upon receipt of same shall be glad to give you the desired information.

Two more months passed by after the last letter and the secretary never had written as he had promised. I then went up to Oklahoma City, and requested Ira M. Finley, president of the V.I.A., to ask the attorney-general if Dr. Osborne had written him for an opinion on the issuing of a permit to practice medicine under the Basic Science Act as passed by the 16th Legislature. The attorney-general said no request for an opinion had been made by Dr. Osborne, and looked up his records to make sure that no such request had been made. According to law the secretary of the board was under legal obligation to issue the permit to the doctor, as he was plainly entitled to it.

Dr. Emerson Blake, who came and was with us for many months, was a graduate of a class A medical school and was entitled to receive his license at the December meeting of the State Board of Medical Examiners in 1936. He and I went to Oklahoma City the day he was to appear before the State Board of Medical Examiners. Dr. Blake told me that Dr. Osborne refused him a license because he was connected with the Community Hospital, but agreed to give him a temporary permit to practice, provided he severed his connections with the Community Hospital. Dr. Blake told me that he had complied with every requirement and had previously deposited $100 with the board for said license and that there was no other question involved in Dr. Osborne's refusal to issue the license. Dr. Blake is now practicing medicine at Lubbock, Texas.

Every year I wrote to the members of the graduating classes of medical schools, north, east, south, and west, and asked them to consider joining us. The first thing these doctors did, naturally enough, was to write to the local branch of the American Medical Association and ask about my standing and the rating of the hospital. The reply was such as to keep away even the most job-hungry doctor. Here is a sample:

> Your letter to the president of the Beckham Medical Association was handed to me as president of the county society, for although my address is Sayre, Elk City is in my county. The Community Hospital is in disrepute with the medical profession of the state, the head of the institution being ineligible for membership in the county society for various reasons, several of which I would not care to put in writing. I believe that if you are a conscientious, honorable gentlemen, you would

be very unhappy with him in such connections as you would have there.

I might say as a matter of justice that the head of the institution is a fair doctor, but it is the unfair and shady practices that we all object to.

H. K. Speed
President, Beckham County Medical Society

These hints about reasons that couldn't be "put in writing" and "unfair and shady practices" were as infuriating as they were untrue. There was just one "shady practice" I had been guilty of in my twenty years in Beckham County, and that was the founding of a coöperative hospital. No charge had ever been brought against me until I committed this "unethical" act. But the inquiring doctor, knowing nothing of the circumstances of the case and receiving such misinformation, had no choice but to think I was running some kind of medical racket. Certainly my eagerness to have him, a mere novice, whom no one else particularly wanted, seemed to indicate that something was wrong. Fortunately for us, there were some doctors willing to run the blockade, and I felt justified in using a subterfuge or two to get them in. Since any doctor admitting his intention of joining the Community Hospital staff automatically failed to pass his examination, I advised doctors to state on the examination form that they intended to practice in Sayre, Oklahoma City, or anywhere but Elk City. After obtaining his license he could come to Elk City.

The opposing doctors endeavored to persuade physicians' exchanges and nurses' registries to boycott us in our efforts to secure such personnel, but after my explaining matters in person at great length they were persuaded to the contrary, and refused to join in the blockade.

The secretary of the Oklahoma State Board of Nurses made a point of warning all nurses taking state board examinations to shy away from us. She made the nurses believe that they would endanger their reputation by working at the

Community Hospital. This nefarious practice did not cease until after the election of Governor Turner, for while he was campaigning for election, we donated to his campaign $250, and he agreed to put a stop to this boycott insofar as it involved the secretary of the State Board of Nurses.

The secretary of the State Board of Dental Examiners was even more venomous in conducting his part of the boycott. He even went so far as to write to Dr. Ralph Shadid, a distant cousin of mine who had joined our staff, to remind him that he had reneged on his promise not to join the Community Hospital when he took the dental State Board examination. Dr. Ralph wrote him a letter in reply saying that his father had died unexpectedly since his taking the examination, and that he had no money to buy equipment and begin private practice, and further that he found nothing wrong with the doctors at the Community Hospital as they were practicing good and ethical medicine.

During the war Dr. Ralph was the first one to be drafted with every available man on the staff (more of this draft business later) and remained in the army for some years. When released he opened an office at Bethany, a suburb of Oklahoma City. He then applied for the renewal of his license as provided by law and wrote to Dr. Longwell, secretary of the dental board. Here follows Dr. Longwell's reply:

Dr. Ralph J. Shadid
2121 N. W. 26th St.
Oklahoma City, Okla.

Dear Doctor:

Please fill out the enclosed card and return it to this office.

It seems that I can remember the statement you made to the members of the board prior to your receiving your license, and also, the letter I received from you at a later date and at the time of your connection with the hospital at Elk City, in regard to your intention, and in the latter case, in regard to the practice of dentistry in general.

It may take some time to re-instate your license, but in the meantime, please fill out the card and return it to me.

Very truly yours,
W. T. Longwell,
Secretary."

As may be seen later, in future chapters, organized medicine's persecution of those they cannot control is relentless, for when Dr. Ralph applied for membership in the Oklahoma County Dental Society, he received the following reply:

Oklahoma County Dental Society
May 13, 1947

Dr. Ralph Shadid
108½ S. E. Main St.
Bethany, Okla.

Dear Mr. Shadid:

In behalf of the Oklahoma Dental Society I am prompted to inform you that due to unfavorable evidence, your application for membership was rejected. This action does not mean, however, that you cannot re-apply for membership. Your application can again be re-submitted in six months. It would be my council to you to live such an ideal and ethical existence that sooner or later your application will meet with approval.

Might I also suggest that at times when you are in town, to make efforts to know the men in the society. I personally would like to know you much better.

Very sincerely,
Wm. E. Cole, President.

Postscript: Dean Rinehart of the Kansas City Western Dental College told them that you promised not to go to the Community Hospital. Rinehart did not allow Geo. Shadid to go back to the Kansas City Western Dental College for fear he would join the Community Hospital.

The George Shadid, above mentioned, was another dental pupil who was not permitted to finish his dental education because Dr. Ralph Shadid, to whom he was not related, had reneged on his promise not to join the Community Hospital staff.

Every dental applicant for a license who was suspected of intending to join the Community Hospital was flunked in his examination. Of course, every dentist of Syrian descent was suspect in the eyes of the secretary and Board of Dental Examiners, and therefore every such dentist failed to pass on taking the examination. One year three dentists of Syrian origin were flunked, and flunked twice each on taking the examination. Finally an appeal was taken to a member of the state legislature, William Shibley, who is himself of Syrian descent. He introduced a bill in the state legislature providing for an appeal board from the decision of the dental board, whereupon an agreement was reached whereby each of the Syrians who were flunked was licensed after taking a third examination. One of the flunked men told me that the secretary had told him that the board had sometime previously agreed on a policy of failing one-third of all graduates; that the state boards of dental examiners in Arkansas and Texas had adopted the same policy; and that the dental board in New Mexico was much more extreme, for its members had an understanding that six out of seven men should flunk their dental examinations.

I presume that the theory of the State Board of Dental Examiners (apart from its effect upon the Community Hospital) is that it would be well for the dentists already in practice to have fewer dental competitors and thus preserve the "scarcity economy" and keep down competition. In short, the practicing dentists want a monopoly—a dental closed shop. This theory and practice, also, account for the fact that we have very few dental hygienists in the United States.

Is it not anomalous for a state to charter and set up dental and medical schools and then to set up a state agency to flunk graduates from these schools? Why should dental and medical graduates be given diplomas in the first place? Is not the faculty of such schools as competent or even more competent to judge the competency of their graduates than a bunch of political appointees?

If the medical and dental schools are not fit to teach and license their graduates they should be made fit by raising their standards in teaching and licensing physicians and dentists. If they are fit then state licensing boards are superfluous and should be abolished.

I must in justice say that for a few years before his death, the late Dr. Osborne, secretary of the State Board of Medical Examiners, had completely reversed his position on the Community Hospital. He had come to the conclusion that he had been wrong all along and was being used by designing local doctors to protect their vested interests. In an interview he told a reporter that he knew nothing about Dr. Shadid but what the doctors in Beckham County had told him. He said that the Community Hospital under the law of Oklahoma had a right to exist and that in the matter of giving licenses he would not discriminate against doctors wanting to joint the Community Hospital. This was quite a reversal of his position.

The secretary of the state dental board, Dr. W. T. Longwell, however, was until his death as vindictive as ever.

Under the present medical setup, most doctors upon graduation from medical school cast around until they find a likely looking town. They then settle down and move only when driven away by a loss of practice or something equally serious; consequently, many of the doctors who were willing to come to Elk City were men who were running away from something. By no means all of them were of this type; some of our most competent staff men today came to us during this period of emergency.

I remember for instance a doctor who came to us from Baltimore as a "urologist." He came to us through a Chicago physicians' exchange and had a letter of recommendation from a prominent U.S. Senator. He was tall and must have weighed 225 pounds. His features were coarse and his general appearance did not indicate a professional man.

"Do you do urologic surgery?" I asked him.

"No," said he, "I do not do any surgery: I practice medical urology."

"Do you perform cystoscopic examinations?" (looking into the bladder through a cystoscope) I inquired.

"No, I do not."

"If you do not make a cystoscopic examination and perform no urologic surgery, just what do you do?" I asked.

"Well, I treat gonorrhea and syphilis, and when a patient is in need of cystoscopic examination or urologic surgery I send him to a hospital where such work is done," he replied.

"You send him to a real urologist," I retorted. "But your credentials say that you are a urologist and a urologist should at least be able to make a urologic examination which includes cystoscopy and urethral catheterization (including fine catheters into the bladder and through the ureters to the kidneys so as to collect urine from each kidney separately, and inject dye therein for X-ray examination). Giving shots for gonorrhea and syphilis does not make one a urologist. I have been doing this for many years. I have even been making cystoscopic examinations and catheterizations but I never thought of myself as a urologist. You are not a urologist at all. You are masquerading as one and I can have no use for your services here. Here is a check for seventy-five dollars to pay your fare back to Baltimore and you are at liberty to take the next train home."

I recall another physician who came to us as a specialist

in diseases of the eye, ear, nose, and throat. He claimed to do surgery on those organs. Two months passed and yet the record showed that he had never performed any operation except to take out tonsils. His work consisted of testing eyes for glasses and giving prescriptions for eye, ear, or nose drops.

Finally, I brought him a case of badly infected sinus (Antrum of Hymore) that positively needed surgical drainage. He wanted to treat the patient by nose drops, and so on, but I insisted that he perform surgical drainage. He grudgingly agreed but while he was performing the operation it was plain for me to see that he had never done the operation before and was in danger of inflicting serious injury to the patient's eye. Indeed not long before that we had hospitalized a patient that came to us with a brain abscess following such an operation by a novice at a state hospital. I immediately put a stop to his interference.

I remember well the moral derelict, an army doctor, who loved too well wine, women, and song. He was a suave and good-looking individual, about 55 years of age and married to a handsome woman much younger than himself. He stole the alcohol from the hospital drug room, dated the patients (when he could), and kept fees that should have been turned in to the hospital. I found out, soon enough, that he had been in the army 17 years and would have retired on a pension in 3 more years. But he had raised a check from five hundred to one thousand dollars and was about to be court-martialed when he resigned.

I called him into my office, showed him the evidence of his numerous moral derelictions, and reprimanded him severely. He left town the following day and located in a small village where many of our hospital members lived. He remained there 2 or 3 years, during which time his wife left him, and then he moved to some other virgin territory.

Another "specialist," an "orthopedist," came to us who had been a medical missionary to India. He had been with us three months during which time under one pretext or other he referred his real orthopedic cases to an orthopedic specialist in Oklahoma City. When I let him go, our enemy doctors got hold of him and had him sign a statement to the effect that I had let him go so as to enable me to keep my son, a member of the hospital staff, from being drafted into the armed services.

As a result of our difficulty in getting competent physicians, when the campaign against us was at its peak, we were exposed to sharp criticism should we have any incompetent men on the staff. Needless to say any worthless ones were discharged and given enough money to get out of the state as soon as their real characters were revealed. Some of them were alcoholics, and one, when we could least afford notoriety, committed suicide in the hospital.

He was a northerner, and his letters of recommendation were from extremely reliable physicians, so I had felt no hesitation in asking him to join the staff. He ran the blockade without difficulty, and when he reported for work he seemed like a sober, serious, and competent man. He worked quietly for about ten days, and I was beginning to feel relieved in having someone I could rely on, for the burden of the work was becoming increasingly heavy. Then one night I received a phone call from the hospital saying that he was dying.

I drove there as fast as I could, and found him on the floor, gasping for his last breath. He died a few minutes after I arrived and the nurse revealed that he had swallowed bichloride of mercury and iodine. In his pockets I found two syringes which he had been using for his morphine injections. When he could get no more of the narcotic, he committed suicide. I later learned from his parents that he had tried suicide before.

Not only were we blockaded to prevent us from securing physicians, dentists, and nurses, but the quarantine also extended to medical magazines, post-graduate medical schools, and registries of technicians.

We had the only radiologist in western Oklahoma, and when he applied for membership in the radiological society of the state his application was rejected because he was a member of the Community Hospital staff.

When our X-ray technician applied for certification by the American registry of X-ray technicians, he was told: "this will mean that you will be eligible to be certified at once when you have severed your connections with your present place of employment."

The thoroughness with which organized medicine pursues those whom it has marked for destruction is illustrated by my experience in June 1941, when I went to Chicago to take a two-week post-graduate course on fractures at the Cook County Graduate School.

When I went to the Dean's office to register, I was informed by the registrar that before I could take the course, I would have to show my credentials as a member of my local medical society. Now as we have seen I was not a member of Beckham County Medical Society, having been left by the wayside, when, in the course of the fight against our hospital, that society of which I had been a member for twenty years suddenly disbanded, and as suddenly, one year later reorganized, leaving me out.

"Sorry," said the registrar, "you cannot take this course, nor any other course. These are given for 'ethical physicians' only."

"But I am an 'ethical physician,' " I protested, "I am a graduate of Washington University, the best medical school west of the Mississippi at the time I attended. Since my graduation in 1907, I have been in constant practice and I've never been expelled from any medical society, nor have I ever been guilty of any unethical behavior. I am licensed to practice in Missouri, Oklahoma, Texas, and New York."

"Just the same," said the registrar, "you can't take the course. Many men have graduated from class A medical schools and have failed to continue in ethical practice. Sorry, but those are the rules."

I was naturally outraged. I had come a long distance at

great inconvenience to get the last word on the treatment of fractures, for the benefit of our Oklahoma farmer patients. (Naturally, at my age I wanted no academic credits for the course.) Injuries to the extremities from falls or contact with unguarded farm machinery constitute the bulk of our emergency cases. We had not been able to obtain a competent orthopedist because of the pressure put by the hierarchs on anyone announcing his intention of joining our staff. So I had intended to take on some of the orthopedic work, in addition to my other work, after the refresher course at Chicago. And I was applying at a school supported by taxpayers' money, yet, as I soon discovered, dominated by a private organization of physicians and surgeons.

Present at the interview in the registrar's office were my son, Dr. Fred Shadid, and a friend of ours, a member of the Cook County Hospital staff. The latter undertook to intercede for me with the dean and the executive committee of the school. He came back to us crestfallen. He explained that the Cook County School authorities were fearful lest in allowing me to take the two-week course (at a cost, by the way, of $125) the school would incur the enmity of the A.M.A. The Chicago hierarchs, so the school authorities feared, might even go so far as to change the rating of the school.

Before I left Chicago, I hired a firm of lawyers to bring suit against the school for my traveling expenses and time consumed on this fruitless journey.

Presently, I received this letter from my attorney:

Dear Dr. Shadid:

I have been giving careful thought and study to your situation in connection with the Cook County School of Medicine. I with-held action this long for the purpose of proceeding in this matter with due caution.

On July 3rd, I had a conversation with the attorney for the Cook County Graduate School of Medicine.

The files revealed that you have corresponded with them on several occasions for the past few years in connection with registering in their course. They state that if you had forwarded your application in time, they would have been more than glad to admit you. The attorney further stated that I may quote him to the effect that membership in the American Medical Association is not a decisive factor in determining whether or not a doctor may be registered for their course. He also stated that the next time you are desirous of registering for a course, if you forward your application in time, they will undoubtedly register you in the course you desire. As a result of this the Graduate School of Medicine has now come around to our way of thinking, namely, that membership in the American Medical Association will no longer be considered in extending registration to any reputable doctor.

I confronted the attorney with your statement that registration had been denied to you only on the ground that you were not a member of the American Medical Association. He said that this was not correct, and that registration had been denied to you only for the reason that the course was full.

I do not for a moment question your statement of the facts as to what occurred. I am inclined to believe that the Cook County Graduate School of Medicine is attempting, in a graceful manner, to rectify the situation. Please let me know your reaction to this letter at your earliest convenience.

My reaction was to test the sincerity of the school authorities by presenting them with another applicant for a course—a member of our staff and of course an "ethical practitioner," though not a member of the Beckham County Medical Society. Our doctor received the following letter in answer to his application:

My Dear Doctor:

In response to your letter received today, there is enclosed a circular listing the courses offered in the Division of General Surgery.

On page No. 16 you will find an outline of a personal course in Regional and Intravenous Anesthesia. This course is available every two weeks throughout the year. In addition to this course, the Department also offers a one-month practical course in ether and nitrous oxide anesthesia. This course is available starting the first of every month and the fee for the one-month course in inhalation anesthesia is $100.

The courses referred to are offered only to licensed medical physicians who are members of their county and state medical societies.

A registration card is enclosed, and if we can assist you further, please let us know.

Very truly yours,
Cook County Graduate
School of Medicine.

The evasiveness and pettiness of the letters reversing the statement of the school authorities that membership in a medical society is not a necessary qualification for a course in the school needs no further elaboration.

It must be remembered, however, that the Cook County Hospital is a county hospital built and supported by a county tax. It is a peoples' hospital and yet organized medicine has the unashamed effrontery to monopolize its facilities and equipment and deny their use to those whom it cannot control.

As formerly stated even medical journals joined in the quarantine, as may be inferred from the following communication:

STATE DEPARTMENT OF HEALTH
State of Oklahoma
3400 North Eastern
Oklahoma City 5, Oklahoma
Dec. 9, 1948

Lloyd W. Davis
Hospital Administrator
and Clinic Manager
Elk City, Oklahoma

Dear Sir:

I have your request to place the name of Dr. Fred Shadid on a subscription list for the journal of the Oklahoma Medical Association.

This journal cannot be ordered by popular subscription and is sent only to members of the County Medical Societies and the Oklahoma Medical Association. It would be better to take the matter up with the secretary of the County Medical Society as we can do nothing about it.

By direction of the Commissioner of Health.

Very truly yours,
James O. Wails, M. D., Director
Division of Preventive Diseases.

Here again organized medicine has a monopoly on a publication published by a state health department supported by a tax on the people of the state.

The *Journal of the American Medical Association*, edited by Dr. Fishbein, carries much advertising at a high rate. Physicians and physicians' exchanges advertise in an effort to secure physicians and specialists but for many years the *Journal* refused to accept my advertisements in my efforts to obtain physicians for our clinic. Finally, I wrote a letter to the Attorney-General of the United States and complained about this discrimination, whereupon the *Journal* wrote accepting my advertisements.

Among other public and semi-public functions that the A.M.A. takes upon itself, one is to pass upon the qualifications of hospitals and list them or refuse to list them in the American Medical Association directory.

In our efforts to secure physicians and technicians, we found it a hindrance not to have our hospital listed. We therefore wrote the Council on Medical Education and Hospitals of the American Medical Association and asked them to list our hospital after we were inspected by them.

This, under one pretext or other, they refused to do, even though they had listed many hospitals in our territory that in no way were equal to our hospital in equipment, personnel, or other requirements.

After writing many letters back and forth, I went to Chicago, on my way to New York, stopped at the A.M.A. Building and told Dr. Victor Johnson, secretary of the Council on Medical Education and Hospitals, that we meant to sue the association for violating the anti-trust laws of the United States in refusing to list our hospital because of our coöp complexion.

In the meantime, I wrote a long letter to Dr. Ray Lyman Wilbur, chairman of the Council, and explained the discrimination against us. Soon, therefore, I received the following telegram:

Dr. M. Shadid
Community Hospital
Elk City, Oklahoma

It is a pleasure to state that registration was granted.

This recognition presumably ended the last phase of a blockade which had extended over a twenty-year period, during which many other efforts to destroy us had been met one at a time.

Chapter 15

The Plan in Successful Operation

1932–1935

Apart from the difficulties caused by our enemies, we were having trouble in our own ranks, for some of our most loyal members were beginning to complain about the discount system. They pointed out that our doctors charged different fees for the same service; one doctor might charge one dollar for a treatment that cost two dollars when performed by another, under the discount system.

One of our greatest dangers was the extension of credit to members. Often when a member owed us money beyond the value of his share of stock, he withdrew from membership, forfeiting the share, as he found that easier and cheaper than paying his debt. It became increasingly clear to me that we had made a serious mistake in starting the discount system, for it still brought heavy burdens of expense to families having a siege of sickness and it could be copied by private doctors and hospitals in competition with us.

Then again it was not unusual for a member to come to us saying that a local druggist, dentist, or optician had told them that he had not received a discount on his glasses, or his prescription, or his dental filling.

Indeed two of the four competing hospitals in the county reorganized and called themselves coöperative hospitals. One was at Erick and the other in Elk City. In addition other hospitals, one at Mangum and another at Clinton, put out a prepayment plan for hospital care not including medical or surgical care. The idea was simple. They were going to kill the coöperative community hospital by starting a string of seemingly coöperative hospitals.

Suddenly Beckham County was full of hospitals willing, nay eager, to discount hospital bills and surgical fees after the manner of the Community Hospital. Operations for which doctors had formerly charged from a hundred and fifty to two hundred dollars were now performed for fifty dollars. Even dentists and druggists joined the parade and matched our discounts.

I was glad to see patients paying lower fees, but I was sure that if the coöperative hospital was squeezed out of existence, the rates would go up again, just as the price of gasoline had when the big oil companies won the first round in their fight against the coöperative gas stations. Some of our members, when they saw that they could fare as cheaply in hospitals nearer home, deserted us. We drew our membership from a large area—ten counties in the southwestern part of the state—and the opposition drive, if successful, could cripple us.

The pseudo-coöperative hospital in Elk City was managed by an ex-doctor with a genius for promotion, who had persuaded its chief physician that he could get rich quickly by joining. The latter in turn induced two other doctors to join the project, and the hospital was ready for operation and operations.

Elk City had never seen such a campaign as they put on, for the promoter knew all the tricks. He ran big ads daily in the paper, and daily he went out with his entourage of doctors and nurses to the country schools where he gave "free medical examinations" to all children. Back in his office with the addresses of the children's parents, he sent out form letters for appendicitis, diseased tonsils, "fallen" kidney, and so on. His appendicitis letter was, in part, as follows:

> In checking over the examination of the school children I find your child shows tenderness in its side and

symptoms of appendicitis. The examination also shows infected tonsils, which could cause the appendicitis infection. Proper treatment could possibly save an appendicitis operation.

I would like to examine your child again in my office. There will be no expense to you, as I am willing to give you this examination free.

If your child has symptoms of appendicitis, naturally you should have it treated; if you do not, an operation will be necessary in time. Many deaths occur from ruptured appendix, and I know you do not want your child to take a chance on that.

Do not hold back bringing your child to my office on account of money, for as staff physician of the Standifer Hospital of Elk City, arrangements can be made, I assure you, for the money.

Looking forward to seeing you and your child in my office shortly, I am . . .

Many anxious parents brought their children to our hospital as a result of this letter, and with the exception of a few children with diseased tonsils, the various diagnoses were absolutely at variance with the facts. It was "business" pure and simple, and unfortunately these doctors got a lot of money from poor unsuspecting fathers and mothers. But this was enough for the promoter. He decided to run a contest, and the following sort of glowing announcement, looking like an advertisement for a soap contest, was soon appearing in the paper:

Free automobile trip to California! Choice of either new Ford or Chevrolet for sixty (60) memberships sold! (No limit to the number of cars to be given away.) $1.50 cash prize on each membership sold! Bed room furniture, living room furniture, cedar chests, sets of silver, and sets of dishes as extra prizes to be given away every three months!

THE PLAN IN SUCCESSFUL OPERATION 143

This sort of advertisement for a hospital, however, made people suspicious, and business at his hospital began to slump noticeably. It was then that the promoter decided to get the backing of the Farmers' Union. He presented his case so plausibly to Tom Cheek that Cheek turned him over to the Beckham County Union. When the Beckham County group promptly rejected his idea, he went to an adjoining county and proceeded to sell the idea of sponsorship of his hospital to the officers of the union.

They decided to call a special meeting of the officers of the Farmers' Union locals in the county to discuss the sponsorship plan, and they asked the promoter to speak to them. I sat in the audience taking notes while he talked. He was painting a very attractive picture of his hospital, working up, I could see, to something far more binding on the Farmers' Union than mere sponsorship. When he saw me sitting there, writing down everything he was saying, he suddenly began swallowing his words, and he ended rather abruptly without mentioning his plan, asking only that the Farmers' Union sponsor his hospital. I don't know whether the men were uninformed, or had been "persuaded," but someone promptly moved that the hospital be endorsed and another man seconded the motion.

I couldn't sit still any longer. I jumped up and asked permission to address the group, but the chairman denied me the floor on technical grounds. I appealed directly to the audience, asking for a chance to speak, and they voted unanimously to hear me. I told them in the most forceful words I could find what people in Elk City thought about the hospital in question, and why, and I asked them not to sponsor it. Some of them were impressed, but enough were still attracted by the promoter's proposal to vote that three men meet with him and me at the Community Hospital in two weeks to attempt some sort of joint plan.

I went at once to Oklahoma City to look up the incorporation papers of the group. I felt sure that his hospital was not a true coöperative with control in the hands of the members. I was right. The promoter had merely filed a typewritten declaration of trust. Capital stock with a value of $160,020 was to be issued at $30 a share, and the three trustees, a nurse, the chief physician, and the promoter, were to have complete and undivided control of the organization and all its funds. Now a coöperative either is a coöperative or it isn't, and as long as a promoter, stockholder, trustee—call him what you will—is to make a profit out of an enterprise it is no coöperative, no matter how many times it uses the name coöperative in its prospectus or other publicity. A true coöperative is owned by its members and no one else.

In the proposed promotion, the stockholders, or shareholders, had no right to ask for any kind of accounting. The hospital itself had been a private home, and in its palmiest day it could not have been valued at any more than $25,000. Now it was being capitalized at $160,000, half the money to go to the nurse who was the nominal owner, and the other half to the promoter and the chief physician.

This was all the information I needed, and when I presented these facts about the "coöperative" to the members of the Farmers' Union they had to be restrained from throwing its organizer out bodily. It was the beginning of the end for that scheme.

But, as I saw it, there was one thing we had to do. We had to become a dues-paying or a prepayment group. This was the only cure for our difficulties. The discount system was a failure. It had been adopted merely as a stop-gap, until such time as the membership was large enough so that a prepayment plan would enable us at least to pay the doctors' salaries.

So I worked out a prepayment plan, and a scale of prices which I knew would preclude cut-throat competition from the doctors and dentists, and would give the hospital sufficient income, if and as our membership increased.

The prepayment plan was as follows:

For one person $12.00 per year
For two persons 18.00 per year
For three persons 22.00 per year
For four or more persons in the family 25.00 per year

For these dues the family was entitled to medical examinations, treatments, surgical operations, and laboratory work at the hospital.

Home visits in town $1.00, plus ten cents a mile each way in the country. Hospital bills, medicines, anesthetics, etc.:

X-ray of teeth	50 cents per film
Extraction of teeth	50 cents per tooth
Full dental plates (vulconite)	$25.00
(lucitone)	35.00
Cleaning teeth	1.00
Filling	1.00
Crowns	7.00
Bridges, per tooth	5.00
Gold fillings	5.00

In 1937, the prepayment was increased as follows:

One person	$16.00
Two persons	24.00
Three persons	30.00
Four or more	34.00

For dental care:

X-ray of teeth	75 cents
Extraction	75 cents
Filling	$1.50 cents
Cleaning	1.00
Treatments	50 cents
Dental surgery	50% discount

Impacted teeth	$5.00
Gold work, crowns	7.00
inlays	6.50
reset inlays	50 cents
Dentures, upper and lower (lucitone)	65.00

At the present time, since inflation hit us hard, the prepayment plan for medical and dental care is as follows:

One person	$18.00
Two persons	30.00
Three persons	36.00
Four or more	40.00

Heretofore, all physiotherapy treatments and laboratory work were free, but now are given at a discount of 50 per cent, and diathermy treatments at 50 per cent discount.

Superficial X-ray therapy	$2.65 non-members	$4.00
Deep X-ray therapy	3.35 non-members	5.00
X-ray fluoroscopic	3.00 non-members	4.50
X-ray pictures	33⅓ discount	
Free refraction, moderate charge for glasses		
Metabolism test	2.50 non-members	5.00
Electrocardiogram	6.00 non-members	9.00
X-ray of teeth, per film	.75 non-members	1.50
Extraction	1.00 non-members	2.00
One filling	2.00 non-members	4.00
Cleaning teeth	1.50 non-members	3.00
Treatment	1.00 non-members	2.00
Dental surgery	50% discount	
Impacted teeth	5.00 non-members	10.00
Gold work,		
crowns, per tooth	10.00 non-members	20.00
inlays, per tooth	8.00 non-members	16.00
reset inlays	1.00 non-members	2.00
Dentures, upper and lower	70.00 non-members	100.00

THE PLAN IN SUCCESSFUL OPERATION

The initial prepayment plan seems ridiculously cheap to those who are not familiar with economic conditions as they existed in 1931 and up to 1936. Our members, nearly all farmers, had no money; farm products were never cheaper in the history of the United States. And there was complete drought. Many nurses were willing to work for room and board, although I never paid less than $60 to a graduate and never less than $30 to a nurse's-aid, plus room and board. When we dedicated the hospital in 1931, we were able to purchase seven cows for a barbecue for ten dollars each.

To keep doctors at the hospital I had to sacrifice my own income. In 1931 and 1932 I had an income of about $125 to $150 per month; in 1923 it had been $200 to $250 per month. I did not make enough to live on from my actual practice, but prior to the building of the hospital I had acquired a backlog of about $100,000 from private practice. I owned two business buildings in Elk City and one in Mangum that netted me several hundred dollars a month from rents, and so could well afford to take the loss on income from practice. In private practice I had earned $15,000 or more per year. My income since the hospital was built never at any time equaled my previous income from private practice. Even when I retired from the staff of the Community Hospital in 1946 my salary was $900 per month. Figuring my income since the hospital was built, and comparing it with my income prior to that date, with due regard to the depression, the experiment had cost me a minimum of $60,000. But to me the experiment has been worth much more than it has cost.

The initial prepayment plan was adopted in early 1932, and during that year only 100 members subscribed to the plan.

In those hard days of drought and depression they were bound to be particularly skeptical of any new plan that cost money at the outset. Since it was impossible for me to leave the hospital, I had to find a way to bring the people to me. I had learned, long before, that people came to meetings and listened to speeches if refreshments were served. So for two months, five evenings a week, I invited twenty members for dinner, and after the table had been cleared I spoke to them, somewhat as follows:

> Medicine is a progressive science which daily becomes more complex. It is no longer possible for one or two doctors to know all there is to know about medicine. The family doctor has now become a signpost pointing the way to different specialists, and today adequate medical and surgical care is possible only through the attention of a group of medical men.
>
> The examination of a patient is a job requiring the coöperative skills of four or five people. Under present systems of medical practice one doctor is expected to do the work of these five people by himself. Perhaps his patient has blood in his urine; the doctor needs to have the special knowledge of a urologist, who specializes in kidney, bladder, and venereal diseases, to find out where the blood is coming from. It may be from a bladder tumor, or a kidney stone, or an obstructive prostate gland, or a more general disease.
>
> A large percentage of the old men operated on in western Oklahoma for prostatic obstruction die from the operation. Yet the Mayo Clinic reports that their mortality following this operation is less than two per cent. We cannot all go to the Mayo Clinic, and even if we had a Mayo Clinic in western Oklahoma, it would be prohibitive in cost to you and your neighbors.
>
> In western Oklahoma we do not have a single specialist in urology. We do not have a brain specialist, a child specialist, an orthopedic specialist, or any other except one or two eye, ear, nose, and throat specialists. You cannot afford these men individually, but you can afford them collectively—coöperatively. That is one of the reasons for this coöperative hospital. Two thousand of you can pay twenty-five dollars a year for your fami-

lies and with the fifty thousand dollars you will collectively have, you can hire eight or more doctors and specialists who will provide you with free examinations, free treatments, and free surgical operations for a year without any additional charge.

Collectively and coöperatively you can have the expensive equipment necessary for thorough examination and treatment: X-ray machines, metabolism machines, electrocardiographs, laboratories, radium, physiotherapy equipment, and the like. In all of western Oklahoma we haven't a single blood bank, an X-ray treatment machine, or any radium. They're too expensive for private doctors, and therefore you do without the best that medical science can offer.

Many of you have paid from three hundred to a thousand dollars for one case of illness. Under a prepayment plan, three hundred dollars will pay your doctor's bill for twelve years, and a thousand dollars would pay for a lifetime of protection.

In addition to examinations and treatments when you are sick, under the prepayment plan you can receive the benefits of preventive medicine. At the present time, doctors are occupied with the two per cent of the population that is sick. The figures are reversed, though, when it comes to the amount of money spent in this country on preventive medicine—ninety-eight per cent of the medical dollar goes for treatment, two per cent for prevention.

Now the tragedy of this situation will be apparent when I tell you that a large percentage of illness can be checked in an early stage. But under the present setup, the patient doesn't go to a doctor for a slight illness—he can't afford to. As a result, he may have high blood pressure and shortness of breath that results from heart and arterial disease over a long period of time. A doctor may be consulted for an advanced condition of glaucoma which usually results in blindness, whereas the condition existed for years in a curable form. Cancer is curable before it metastasizes or is disseminated into the organism, and yet one in every ten deaths is caused by cancer.

Listen carefully to this: It is estimated that one-third of the deaths in the United States every year are preventable. And why this tragic failure? Because under our system, the doctor is a private tradesman with services to sell—and only sick people will buy them.

Coöperative medicine will improve the condition of the doctors by freeing them from the uncertainties of private practice: the charity cases, the burden of uncollectable debts, the overhead of office and equipment, the waste of time. It will give the doctor a chance for regular hours, the use of all essential facilities, freedom from economic pressures."

The result of this educational campaign was that our dues-paying membership went up to three hundred, and since these members really understood what the hospital was doing, their long-range view and their devotion to the principles behind it made them fight to keep it going. They also became proselytizers and set about bringing many new members into the fold. The tide seemed to have turned and I was heartened even more when we were able to obtain an excellent eye, ear, nose, and throat specialist, as well as a good general man for the staff. I could now get away from the hospital for short periods and I began to go up and down western Oklahoma, speaking before farmers' coöperative associations and civic groups explaining our plan.

By 1934 our prepayment membership was up to six hundred, and we were able to increase our medical staff until it numbered five men, in addition to myself: an eye, ear, nose, and throat specialist, a urologist, two internists, and a dentist.

The prepayment plan put the Community Hospital on a firm basis. The pseudo-coöperative hospital had collapsed.

THE PLAN IN SUCCESSFUL OPERATION

They copied our shadow (plans and literature) but not our spirit. They were not sincere in their efforts. They meant simply to defeat our purpose and put an end to our existence. Their insincere imitation of our plan and their complete failure redounded to our benefit so that in 1935 over 1,100 members paid their dues and we had on our staff eight salaried doctors and two dentists.

Under the discount plan our members came to see us for emergencies, as they had formerly done, but under the prepayment or "dues" plan, as we call it, they came oftener and had much more work done than ever before. They would come for physical "checkups" and for preventive services. Formerly the majority of cases of appendicitis would come to us in a ruptured state. Now a ruptured case is a rarity among our members; indeed when a patron comes in with a ruptured appendix we are almost certain that he or she is not a member of the hospital association.

Formerly they would insist on the doctors delivering their babies at home and when we refused they called competing doctors. It is different now. The babies delivered at the hospital in 1950 numbered 269, in 1951, 202; in 1952, 221; and in 1953, 250.

Formerly they utilized hospital care only in emergency cases. Now they avail themselves of it much more readily and without any urging. Formerly they would come with diabetic gangrene of the foot, or diabetic coma, or in a late stage of pellagra or consumption, but now all such cases that come to us are from the non-member population in this and adjoining counties.

Since we adopted the prepayment plan competing doctors, dentists, and druggists could no longer tell our members "you got no discount," and try to wean our members away from us. They were, of course, unwilling to serve our members on a prepayment basis. In other words they could no longer meet our competition, or were unwilling to do so.

Then again the "missionary work" that I had carried on began to bear fruit. I made hundreds of speeches over southwestern Oklahoma before farmers' gin and elevator coöperative associations. A coöperative cannot be said to have succeeded when it has merely obtained a large volume of business, unless its members have also developed a feeling of responsibility and ownership and take pride in its achievement. There are really two stages in the organization of a coöperative association. The first stage is devoted to enlisting a membership which represents adequate volume for the support of the association. The second stage is that of mobilizing the membership for participation in the affairs of the association and for mutual contact between the individual member and the management. Loyalty based on understanding of the policies and problems, and a feeling of ownership resulting from participation in the affairs of the association, assist it in meeting its problems or in facing any crisis that may develop.

The large majority of our members are farmers and many of them are of the low income group. They have a practical and conservative bent of mind. They are not easily sold but once sold they stay sold. They fully appreciate their prepayment plan and many of them say they would not accept $500 for their $50 interest in the association.

When we adopted the prepayment plan in lieu of the discount plan we reorganized the association as a non-profit, non-dividend-paying association. The shares of stock were replaced with lifetime memberships. These $100 memberships are not now transferable unless the member dies or moves away a distance of one hundred or more miles.

Our experience in the organization and administration of the Community Hospital brought home to us the need of a permanent monthly periodical, The Community Hospital Bulletin, which would not only keep the membership informed on the problems and doings of the coöperative hospital, but at the same time serve as an instructor in matters of health and hygiene.

For a while after the failure of the pseudo-coöperative hospitals the opposition was quiescent. It seemed wise during this breathing spell to consolidate our forces. We had lost two staunch supporters; Governor Murray was out of office and John Simpson, who had been a loyal and devoted friend of the hospital, had died. I hoped that the Farmers' Union could be persuaded to assume sponsorship of the hospital, which would make it possible to fend off further attacks without the bitter warfare of the past. At the annual meeting of hospital membership in 1934, I urged that a resolution be passed asking the Farmers' Union to sponsor the hospital. Convinced that it was a sound move, the membership voted it through, and Tom Cheek was asked to present the resolution to the state convention of the Farmers' Union.

This time the Farmers' Union readily saw the advantages of such a move and at the state convention voted for the resolution. Our charter name was changed from the "Community Health Association" to the "Farmers' Union Co-operative Hospital Association". This action put the Union on record as being willing to fight for us, and since it was a politically powerful group, we would have a strong ally in any future struggle.

It should be mentioned here that since we adopted the salary system in 1935 we have paid the doctors a bonus from the medical fees received from non-members of the hospital association, with the stipulation that such a bonus may be paid only after all hospital expenses have been paid and with the additional stipulation that such bonus may not exceed the net surplus to the hospital each year.

This brief breath-space, and the additional strength secured by improving our financial system and obtaining Farmers' Union sponsorship, were to serve us well in the increasingly dangerous and bitter struggle ahead of us.

Chapter 16

Success Arouses Greater Hostility

1935–1936

The Community Hospital continued to move ahead steadily and securely. We had gained many more members; we had increased both the size and the quality of our medical staff and our equipment; we were giving our members better and better medical care. But despite our success the fight against us was far from ended.

In 1935 the federal government, alarmed over the situation among those whom Thomas Jefferson called "our most valuable citizens, the cultivators of the soil," took a hand at tackling the tough problem of ensuring medical care for farmers.

In 1935 I received a letter from an official of the Resettlement Administration, a letter which seemed to indicate that the coöperative idea might be adopted widely. The communication, which was signed by Dr. Robert Olesen, read:

> The Resettlement Administration, with which I am associated as Medical Director, appears to be confronted with the same perplexing problems of medical care that must have prevailed in Beckham County prior to the establishment of the Farmers' Union Co-operative Hospital Association in Elk City.
>
> Because the Association seems to offer very many organization suggestions which will prove useful not only to the Resettlement Adminstration, but also to

SUCCESS AROUSES GREATER HOSTILITY

other agencies of the Federal Government, I am anxious to learn at first hand of the various features of your medical care plan.

Knowing that you are beset and probably disturbed by very many visitors, I hesitate to insert myself in the same category. I trust, therefore, that you will be quite frank in telling me if my proposed visit would be an inconvenience. At the same time, I can assure you that what information I can acquire and transmit to the Resettlement Administration, and other agencies, will go far in solving a problem that is acute and pressing.

I wrote to Dr. Olesen at once, inviting him to visit us and assuring him that any representative he might send would be welcomed. Shortly thereafter two Resettlement men, one from Oklahoma City and the other from Dallas, appeared at the hospital. When we had finished showing our visitors around and they had inspected our records, the Dallas man asked how many of our memberships still remained unsold.

"About five hundred," I said.

"Would you like to sell them to the Resettlement Administration for our families?" he asked.

"I'm sure the board of directors would agree," I said, very pleased. "They've been planning to borrow money to build a new wing for the hospital, but if the remaining shares are sold no loan will be necessary."

The Resettlement men explained their plan to us. They would instruct their agents to make loans to Resettlement clients for membership in the Community Hospital and we were to send the applications to the Washington Office for approval. The five hundred shares were quickly subscribed, and we filed our request in Washington.

The Beckham County Medical Society immediately called a meeting and passed a resolution condemning the project, and a little later the American Medical Association adopted a resolution submitted by an Oklahoma doctor, one of our principal enemies, who moved that:

WHEREAS, It has been reported to the House of Delegates that plans are about to be consummated for the loan of federal money to individuals to enable them to subscribe for stock in an existing coöperative hospital at Elk City, Oklahoma and

WHEREAS, The hospital referred to is not operated in accordance with the Principles of Medical Ethics of the American Medical Association or in conformity with the special rules of the association governing hospitals and is managed by a physician who has been expelled from his county medical association, and

WHEREAS, The reported plan for federal aid for this or any other hospital similarly situated, whether given directly or indirectly, under guise of gifts or loans to individual stock-holders or prospective stock-holders, is contrary to public policy and to the interests of the medical profession; be it

RESOLVED, That the Board of Trustees be requested to investigate the existing situation immediately, not only with respect to the reported situation in Elk City, Oklahoma, but also with respect to the general policies of the federal government, and to take such action as it deems proper to protect the interests of the public and of the medical profession, and be it further

RESOLVED, That if the Trustees think it wise, a copy of these resolutions be transmitted to the President, the President of the Senate, the Speaker of the House of Representatives, the Director of the Budget, and the Undersecretary of Agriculture in charge of the Rural Resettlement Administration.

The American Medical Association always indignantly denies any assertion that it plays politics, much less than it plays politics well, but certainly the action that followed this declaration would make one think that they were adepts. The next thing we know Dr. Olesen had been replaced by Dr. R. C. Williams, who promptly announced that he was

SUCCESS AROUSES GREATER HOSTILITY

coming to visit the hospital himself. Until he had made his inspection, the money, naturally, could not be paid.

When, some months later, Dr. Williams and Harvey P. Vaughn, coöperative specialist for Resettlement, appeared, we showed them the hospital and the records, and introduced them to the members of the staff. By that time we had a staff of eight men, seven of whom were graduates of grade "A" medical schools. We mentioned, with considerable pride, that we had on our staff the only urologist in the whole of western Oklahoma, and that we were, indeed, the only genuine clinic functioning in the region. Despite the very interesting and enthusiastic report of the coöperative specialist who accompanied him, Dr. Williams cancelled the applications that the five hundred Resettlement families had made for membership in our hospital.

In view of the American Medical Association's stand against us, I did not find Dr. Williams' action particularly surprising. Apparently he thought it essential to devise a plan that would meet the approval of the A.M.A., for in a report issued by the Farm Security Administration, dated November 1, 1938, Dr. Williams stated: "The Farm Security Administration has developed plans under which more than 78,000 low income farm families of 20 states are being helped to obtain medical care at a cost which they can afford."

Under this plan each Resettlement family pays twenty-five dollars a year to a common fund, and chooses its own doctor, who renders a monthly bill which is paid out of this common fund. By this means the A.M.A.'s principle of "free choice" is upheld.

As was to be expected, only members of the American Medical Association were eligible for payments from this fund, thus automatically excluding all the doctors on the staff of the Community Hospital. But that such a ruling very definitely limited the "free choice" of Resettlement families did not seem to trouble the leaders of the American Medical Association in the least.

Some months after the plan had been put into operation, a Resettlement client came to us for a confinement. We had to tell her that the Community Hospital didn't participate in the fund and gave her the name of a hospital which did. She replied that she had already been there, but that the hospital had refused her admission because the fund already owed it three hundred dollars and it would take no more Resettlement clients until the debt was paid. She was certainly in a more unfortunate position than a charity patient, and all because the doctors in the fund were raiding it as though it were a private gold mine.

The service plan of the F.S.A. medical coöperative was established by Dr. Williams after he came to our hospital and studied our plan. In order to appease the medical profession he had to modify more than one important feature of our plan to suit the producers of medical services, the physicians. He had to discard group practice in favor of private individualistic practice of medicine; he had to abandon consumer control; he had to retain the fee system. As a result, the character of the service not being group practice, it is less than satisfactory or adequate. Lack of consumer control does not stimulate enthusiasm on the part of the lay members. And the retention of the fee system instead of the capitation or salary system brought about chiseling on the part of the doctors. The fee system has no part in any coöperative set-up. The motive of profit is destructive to any coöperative endeavor. Under the fee system there remains the temptation to give unnecessary treatments, to perform unnecessary surgery, and to make useless examinations. The prepayment fund is never sufficient to meet the bills of the doctors and necessitates their revision downward. This makes for dissatisfaction among the honest physicians whose bills are fair and just. On the other hand, the unscrupulous physicians are amply rewarded.

The fees for professional services are set by the local professional groups themselves and not by the F.S.A. or the clients of the F.S.A. Not only that, but fees are, with few exceptions, identical with those ordinarily charged in local practice. In other words, except where there is consumer participation under a set of by-laws and a board of directors, chosen by the consumers, the local health association is reduced to a collection agency for physicians.

The poorer farmers need more medical care than the average farmers, for it is well known that sickness exists in inverse ratio to the economic level. Furthermore, in many of these health associations, membership is often limited to a hundred families or even less. It is axiomatic in the insurance business that larger groups would obtain a better spread of risks and larger pools of funds. In this case, larger pools of funds would mean better medical care, wider scope of service, and better pay for those rendering the service. The F.S.A. group of borrowers, with a relatively high incidence of illness from disease or accident, constitute a bad risk from the standpoint of actuarial soundness.

Can anyone say honestly that these associations, handicapped as they are from the standpoint of organization, management, service, and actuarial soundness, have failed? Some counties contained but one or two hundred clients and therefore the money coming from such a limited clientele to individual physicians is necessarily small in amount. Is it any wonder doctors looked upon this service as a "glorified relief service," and that they actually treated these patients like charity patients—an attitude not calculated to engender loyalty and to promote a successful association.

What if these associations were to be recognized as bona fide consumer coöperatives so that their members might discover the significance of self-help and mutual aid? Would that not arouse their enthusiasm? What if the remuneration of the family doctor, to be chosen by the member, was based on a capitation system (so much per year per family) instead of the fee system?

Indeed, one physician in Ohio told of 36 families now members of the unit who, prior to the establishment of the F.S.A. plan, had received service from him. Of the total charges of $900 only $150 could be collected. If these families had had a group plan at that time he would have received about $700 at the present rate of payment.

The year after the Resettlement project episode, early in 1936, I received a letter postmarked Lawton, Oklahoma. I knew no one there, so I opened the envelope with curiosity and looked for the signature, but there wasn't any. I guessed the letter was one of those threats that had been so common since the hospital had been started, but I saw quickly that I was wrong, for it said:

> Enclosed you will find a copy of a bill to be presented to the legislature in January. These were distributed to the doctors on the east side of the state in Tulsa; and were given to me by one present but not in sympathy with their scheme. I understand that the following night the doctors from the west side of the state met in Oklahoma City.
>
> Now their scheme is this. They have raised a slush fund by assessing each member of their organization ten dollars per capita and have employed a former Speaker of the House to spend this fund putting the scheme through. These proposed amendments to the Medical Practice Act have been drawn to look innocent, but they openly state it is to put your institution and others out of business. If they succeed in buying enough representatives to vote the proposed amendments, they will then have a string on them, and will use it to slip through the so-called Basic Science Law, which will eliminate both osteopaths and chiropractors. [The Community Hospital has no interest in osteopathy or chiropractic.]
>
> I am reliably informed charges are to be brought before the medical board at the next meeting to revoke your license. This is to be done in order to hurt your influence with the legislature, the governor, and the people. These amendments would take this law out of

SUCCESS AROUSES GREATER HOSTILITY

> the hands of the governor and the state, where it rightfully belongs, and puts it under that political bunch, the Oklahoma State Medical Association. Of course, you can see why they want this.
>
> You should immediately get up a petition and have all your friends and stockholders sign it. Then take as many as you can in person and call on the governor; inform him of their scheme to discredit you before the legislature meets, bringing these charges before the medical board; and if he has the guts that Governor Murray had, you can stop it.

Once again I was indebted to a doctor who didn't dare openly to ally himself with our forces. If the doctors were finally resorting to such schemes as this, any sympathizers we had would have to be very cautious unless they wanted to be crushed along with us by this juggernaut. The situation was a serious one, for either of the opposition's measures was sufficient to cripple, perhaps to kill, the Community Hospital. I don't want to seem to overemphasize my own importance, but I had been with the hospital since its birth and I had worked hard for it, and the loss of my license might endanger it seriously. As for the attempt that would be made to legislate us out of existence, its success would mean the end.

A week later, a friendly doctor brought me the following notice which was addressed to him:

> Dear Doctor:
>
> The Physicians, Dentists, Druggists, and Nurses Association meeting has been changed from the 29th of June to the 22nd, at 8:00 p.m., at the Bon Ton, Hobart, Oklahoma. There will be fireworks.
>
> This is a free-for-all, so come in and get it off your chest. This is your meeting. Bring your druggist.

This note was only one of a number announcing a series of meetings that summer, fall, and following winter.

I thought it would be nice to see the fireworks and participate in the free-for-all, so I decided to go to this meeting at the Bon Ton along with one of our staff doctors. When we arrived we found a good-sized gathering of doctors, with a scattering of nurses and druggists, the latter dragged in because we employed a druggist at the Community Hospital.

We sat down and after a short time the meeting started with an informal roll call; everyone was asked to rise and give his name and address. When I arose and said "Dr. Michael Shadid, Community Hospital, Elk City, Oklahoma," there was a sudden hush and everybody turned to look at the demon. The secretary of the meeting was confused by this unexpected development so he turned for a hurried consultation with his companion on the platform. When they finished, the secretary straightened up and said, "Will all those who are not members of the Oklahoma State Medical Association please leave the meeting?"

Then I did something I have never been able to explain to my own satisfaction. I got up and left. I have asked myself many times since why I did this, but I don't know. I should have stayed and dared them to throw me out. But I left with the staff doctor, who looked a little puzzled by my actions.

But more meetings were held from time to time. Doctors, nurses, druggists, and dentists were urged to pin down the candidates for the legislature from their districts until they had commitments from them to support an amendment to the Medical Practice Act that would put the Community Hospital out of business. At the same time the doctors collected levies for the fight; individual doctors were assessed from ten to twenty dollars, and hospitals were required to contribute anywhere from twenty-five to a hundred dollars. In August this little paragraph signed by the "Legislative Committee" of the Oklahoma State Medical Association, a group of three doctors, appeared in the *Oklahoma State Medical Association Journal:*

> So that you might be able to go to your candidates for the Legislature and the Senate with something definite, you may advise them that we propose to change the Medical Practice Act, so that it will do away with corporation practice, just as the lawyers have seen fit to do with their good local practice act, as well as the dentists in their practice act that was passed last year.

The lawyers, it is true, had advocated and obtained the passage of such a statute, but the dentists, in the "Registered Dentists of Oklahoma Act" had incorporated a special amendment for the coöperatives which stated: "Providing that nothing contained in this Act shall prohibit a coöperative corporation, school, college, or university from employing dentists or dental hygienists to render dental services to their employees." Obviously, the doctors were wrong when they said the dentists had barred the Community Hospital, but it made a good talking point: "If the dentists protect themselves, why shouldn't we?"

The following affidavit speaks for itself:

> October 3, 1936
> Recently I was sitting in a doctor's office in Waurika, Okla., Dr. J. I. Hollingsworth, waiting on him to finish some business with me. Dr. J. M. Thompson of Walters, Okla., was in the office and the two were discussing the recent state medical meetings. Dr. Hollingsworth asked Dr. Thompson if he had sent in his $10 that had been assessed to each member of the association. Thompson told him no and asked what the assessment was for, as he had not attended this association meeting. Dr. Hollingsworth told him that Dr. Speed of Sayre, Oklahoma, who was head of the legislative

committee, had stated that it was to buy the legislature just like the Chiros and others did. Dr. Hollingsworth also stated in the conversation that it might take more than the first $10 assessment.

Signed: *Byrne Ross*

The above subscribed and sworn to before me this 3rd day of October, 1936.

Ethel Pearson
Notary Public

My commission expires June 9, 1938.

It was soon to become apparent that these friendly warnings had a substantial basis in fact.

Chapter 17

The Courts Rescue My License

1936–1940

On November 6, 1936, I, along with two other key doctors on the staff, received a summons citing me to appear before the State Board of Medical Examiners on December 9 to show cause why my license should not be revoked for unprofessional conduct. The charges against me were for advertising, fleecing the public, and "steerage," or soliciting patients. And the complaint was signed, not by a doctor or any prominent citizen, but by a janitor almost unknown even in his own community. The document requested me to file my answer to the charges with the secretary of the board within twenty days and to deposit with him my license allowing me to practice medicine in the state of Oklahoma. The situation was a dangerous one, for not a single doctor had ever successfully defended himself against the State Board of Medical Examiners. There had never been an appeal in the courts from a State Board decision; usually there were not grounds for such an appeal, as the State Board customarily exercised with discretion its powers in regard to revocation.

Well, I wasn't going to give up without a court fight. I was going to take that summons to court, and have the status of the State Board determined. My feelings about the whole set of ridiculous charges, and the answer I would make in court, were pretty well summed up in an article "It All Depends on Whose Ox Is Gored," which was printed in the

Community Hospital News, our little monthly bulletin for our members:

> Now it is a fact that our doctors are absolutely innocent of every one of these charges. Dr. Shadid has lived in Beckham County for over twenty-five years, and has a host of friends and followers, else he could never have put over the Community Hospital and persuaded more than two thousand families to build a hospital for themselves. If he had not been an honored and respected physician, do you imagine he could have done this?
> As to advertising, Dr. Shadid never advertised, but, for the sake of argument, is it a crime to advertise? Is there a law against advertising? If so, has any doctor's license ever been revoked in this state for advertising? And would not a law against advertising be unconstitutional and an infringement of personal liberty?
> Who ever heard of Dr. Shadid or any staff member soliciting business? It is an unmitigated falsehood, like the advertising and fleecing charges.
> Again, are there doctors in the state guilty of advertising? Are there some who are guilty of fleecing the public? Are there doctors guilty of soliciting patients? We know of many such physicians, and we know of other guilty of heinous crimes. But have they been prosecuted and brought to justice? Not that we have noticed. Why?
> We know of one doctor who capitalized his hospital and sold shares through agents for fifty dollars each, and copied the Community Hospital plans almost word for word, and yet that doctor is a member of the same county medical society of which Dr. Shadid was a member for twenty years. Why was he not accused of steerage and the solicitation of patients?
> We know of other physicians who founded a corporation and went out and sold membership and solicited business by multigraphed letters. They are members of

THE COURTS RESCUE MY LICENSE

the same Beckham County Medical Society of which Dr. Shadid was a member. Were they sued and made to appear before the State Board of Medical Examiners to show cause why their license should not be revoked? They were not. Why?

Dr. Shadid organized a coöperative hospital for the people. It is their hospital. They have a deed for it. These other doctors organized corporations, not on coöperative lines but on a profit basis for themselves. Does that justify the persecution of Dr. Shadid and the winking at the acts of these other doctors?

Why then single out the Community Hospital and its staff for vicious attack?

Merely because it has succeeded where the others have failed. Professional jealousy, extreme selfishness, a chip on the shoulders of a few competitive doctors who own hospitals in the immediate vicinity of the Community Hospital and who feel that their business has been injured through the success of the Community Hospital—that is the answer. We can name those doctors. Everybody living in Beckham County and surrounding counties knows them. Their names already are anathema to people who believe in honor and justice and fair play, to everyone who frowns on skullduggery and crookedness in all places, high and low.

When this article appeared, our members were thoroughly aroused over this new attempt to destroy their hospital, and many of them came to me asking if there was anything they could do. Two members even wanted to kidnap our chief opponent and tar and feather him, and I had great difficulty in persuading them that this would hurt our cause rather than aid it. The most effective action was taken by Tom Cheek, who circulated a questionnaire among five hundred members of the Farmers' Union, asking them if the hospital had saved them money, and if so, how much. They all answered that it had been a great saving to them—a saving running anywhere from fifty dollars to two thousand dollars. The questionnaire asked also what they thought of the hospital, and many of the farmers replied that they wouldn't take a thousand dollars for their memberships.

Typical comments on the questionnaire ranged about as follows:

". . . We think more of the few dollars invested in the Community Hospital than of any investment we have ever made, and of Dr. Shadid as a doctor and surgeon, and I think this bunch fighting him should be sat down on so hard that it would jar their ancestors for four generations past and all their future followers so inclined."

". . . If the lowdown undermining doctors can succeed in destroying our hospital, I think we would be done a great injury and injustice . . . All these slugs care for is their own selfish greed."

". . . I feel that my sixty-seven days last year in any other hospital would have taken our home and as it was the doctors saved my leg, and my home, too. This is just part of our visits, there wasn't room to name all our savings."

The editor asserted categorically that not one of the several hundreds who filled out the questionnaires showed any indication of dissatisfaction with the service or with charges or with the treatments given. The tone of the leading newspapers in Oklahoma was especially significant. Elsewhere when organized medicine attempted to overthrow a liberal group of doctors for making medicine available to more people, as in Los Angeles, the newspapers were lukewarm editorially, but it was different in Oklahoma. R. M. McClintock, political writer for the *Daily Oklahoman*, made the following pertinent comment:

Public medicine seems destined to become one of the issues in the regular session of the legislature. The Oklahoma State Medical Association, which has raised the issue in its effort to revoke Dr. Shadid's license, . . . seems determined to push it to a conclusion.

The State Board of Medical Examiners may revoke Dr. Shadid's license. But that would only throw the matter into the legislature. The State Board is a creature of the legislature. Nothing is more certain, from present indications, than that if the medical association pushes the issue against Dr. Shadid, it will run into a tremendous storm in the legislature, with results that may prove most harmful in the end to the medical profession itself . . .

The Elk City doctor . . . is no quack. For years he was an honored and successful practitioner in Elk City. . . . So far as this observer has been able to discover, no charge of malpractice has been lodged against Dr. Shadid or any member of his staff. Dissatisfied patients may be found, as of any hospital and of any doctor. But the fact that the hospital has had to be enlarged three times would seem to indicate that, on the whole, it is filling a real need. . . .

These are times in which the coöperative ideal is spreading widely. From the political standpoint, it would seem to be the worst of all times for the doctors to seek to punish one of their number, unless they have more serious charges against him than that he has been relatively successful in putting into operation a plan of coöperative hospitalization.

I gave very little thought to the whole matter because I was so busy with the hospital and the legislative fight, and as a result I looked at my calendar one morning and got quite a shock. Eighteen of the twenty days I had in which to file my answer to the State Board's charges had passed, and I had done nothing about it. I hurried to Gomer Smith, and asked him to help me. Gomer Smith was a well-known liberal lawyer, greatly feared by the public utilities because of his skill in extracting judgments against them in favor of poor individuals. I had barely started the outline of the problem when he interrupted:

"Have you surrendered your license yet?"

"No," I said, "I thought—"

"Who's your district judge?"

"Judge Keen."

"Friendly? Has he backbone?"

"Yes, he's friendly," I said. "He was elected by the farmers and working people. As for backbone, I don't know. I've never made a physical examination of him."

But Gomer Smith was already on his way to the outer office where, while I sat by, he dictated a brief restraining the State Board of Medical Examiners from revoking my license. When the brief had been typed, we jumped into my car and drove a hundred and twenty miles to Sayre, the county seat.

"No, he isn't in now," said the court clerk. "I expect he's holding court in Cheyenne by this time."

We climbed back into the car and went through more miles of dust until we came to Cheyenne, a little town near the state border. The court was in session as Gomer Smith strode to the bench and started to put the brief before Judge Keen. The judge didn't look up from the text he was reading, but he said:

"You'll have to wait until Court has adjourned."

"But, your honor," said Gomer Smith, "this is about the Community Hospital—"

"I won't sign anything against it," Judge Keen said firmly, "you're wasting your time."

"Your honor," pleaded Gomer, "this is for the hospital, and it's urgent."

Judge Keen slammed shut his lawbook and without any hesitation he signed the injunction against the State Board. Gomer Smith was so happy he was walking on air, and all

THE COURTS RESCUE MY LICENSE

during the long drive home he was figuring out the lawsuits for libel and malicious prosecution to bring against the doctors. When we arrived at Sayre, we stopped to have the district court clerk make out copies of the injunction to be sent to each member of the State Board. And right here I should say that it would be unjust to make it appear that this scheme had been evolved by the entire board. When I visited the individual members of the board later they told me they had been greatly surprised when they received copies of the injunction; as they knew nothing about the entire action. To the best of my knowledge, the secretary of the board was the only member active in the vicious fight against me.

The injunction caused him, and his fellow plotters, great concern. In a council of war, they decided to take the matter to the Oklahoma State Supreme Court and they selected an expensive, high-powered attorney to present their case. The attorney went before the Supreme Court asking for a writ to nullify Judge Keen's injunction, on the grounds that a district judge had no jurisdiction over the State Board under the terms of the Medical Practice Act. The Supreme Court was on the spot, for the Medical Practice Act said nothing that empowered the State Board of Medical Examiners to revoke a license on such grounds as "fleecing the people," and Gomer Smith, at the drop of a hat, was ready to disprove the steerage charge. The case was clearly an attempt on the part of the board's secretary to revoke a license on flimsy charges.

After considering the problem, the Supreme Court asked for briefs, and both Gomer Smith and the opposition attorney submitted long documents. Then the Supreme Court fixed June 22, 1937, for the oral argument. All our members had been told of the coming hearing, so when the dignified justices in their black robes filed in, they saw before them a courtroom brimful of poor farmers in blue overalls. The farmers listened attentively to their own lawyer and then to the opposing attorney, who felt so desperate that he dragged in the old "red" herring with the charge that a bunch of radicals were behind the Community Hospital. Our farmers hardly looked the part of dangerous reds.

When the oral arguments had been presented, the Supreme Court adjourned for further consideration, and some months passed before it made a ruling.

Finally, to our great satisfaction, it refused to issue a writ of prohibition as the doctors had asked. The wind was out of the opposition's sails, and they did not present the matter for further hearing in the courts. To emphasize their deflated state, I let it be known that if ever I was brought into court to defend the injunction I would sue the opposing physician for libel.

The denial of the writ of prohibition by the Supreme Court of Oklahoma did not end the legal battle, but it made the temporary injunction of the judge of the district court permanent, preventing the State Board of Medical Examiners from trying me. The conspiring doctors could still come into the district court, if they wished, and try me on the charges of unprofessional conduct, steerage, and fleecing the people, and argue the case before the district judge, and contend that I should be turned over to the State Board of Medical Examiners for trial. Knowing full well, however, that they had no case, they steadfastly refused to do that. Furthermore, they knew that so long as the charges hung over us and were never adjudicated one way or another there would be a cloud on our reputation that would effectively prevent physicians and other personnel from working for and with us.

When it finally dawned on me that these were the reasons that the legal battle against me had not been pushed by the conspiring doctors and the issues brought to a conclusion, I went to see my attorney, and he promised to force the opposition to come into court or else clear me of all their charges. This he proceeded to do, and on the 10th day of February 1940, I had my last tilt in court with the doctors'

THE COURTS RESCUE MY LICENSE

conspiracy. Gomer Smith continued to represent me and the assistant state attorney pleaded the case of the doctors.

In the meantime, it should be stated, there had been a gerrymandering of the judicial district and Judge Keen, who had issued the original injunction, had been removed to an adjoining county seat. The judge who took his place disqualified himself so the Chief Justice of the state sent in another judge, an able jurist named Lucius Babcock. Judge Babcock came from central Oklahoma. The case was "too hot" for any judge in western Oklahoma to handle. The wide-spread membership of the Community Hospital had political influence throughout western Oklahoma. Furthermore, about one-third of the members of the Oklahoma Farmers' Union resided in the Seventh Congressional District, in which nearly all the members of our Community Hospital lived. A local judge would prejudice his chances for re-election by ruling against the interests of Community Hospital. A judge coming from a distant part of the state would be immune from so much political pressure.

We decided, nonetheless, to bring what pressure we could. We interviewed a great many members of the Farmers' Union in the county in which Judge Babcock lived and had them come over to our trial and sit in the front seats where Judge Babcock could not help seeing them. We also spread news of the trial in the *Oklahoma Union Farmer* and sent a letter to each member of the hospital association apprising him of the date and place of the trial and urging him to be present. All our members were, to be sure, fully aware of the importance of the issues to be settled.

It was a nice clear, cool winter day, that 10th day of February. Only five hundred of the farmers who drove into Sayre could crowd into the courtroom, which was supposed to seat only two hundred. The conspiring doctors were conspicuous by their absence. They were more than content to let their attorneys face the judge alone. The story of what happened can best be told, perhaps, by quoting the account of the trial as printed in the *Daily Oklahoman* of Oklahoma City. It should be said here that the Oklahoma City dailies, both owned by the same corporation, had always been impartial and fair in their treatment of news of the Community Hospital. Charles Saulsberry of the staff of the *Daily Oklahoman* was present and wrote the following front-page account of what happened:

MEDICAL BOARD IS BARRED FROM TRYING SHADID

Babcock Grants Writ of Prohibition
Against Examiners

Sayre, February 10th. Coöperative medicine in Oklahoma won a court victory Monday when Lucius Babcock, district judge assigned here from Oklahoma City, granted a writ of prohibition barring prosecution by the State Medical Board of a four-year-old charge of unprofessional conduct against Dr. M. Shadid, Elk City Community Hospital head.

In house frocks, overalls, and Sunday clothes, a crosssection of western Oklahoma took the day off to attend the most significant hearing the Beckham Country district courtroom has entertained in years. More than 500 spectators were crowded into accommodations for only 200, even against the judge's bench, as Judge Babcock announced his decision.

At noon, the throng broke its suppressed excitement to cheer and whistle at a statement by Gomer Smith, Oklahoma City attorney for Doctor Shadid. Among the crowd, obviously, were many of the 2,000 heads of families who make up the membership of the Farmers' Union Co-operative Hospital Association, incorporated as a non-profit institution.

THE COURTS RESCUE MY LICENSE

Conspiracy Is Charged

Smith charged a conspiracy on the part of two western Oklahoma hospitals' heads "to destroy the Community Hospital of Elk City" in persuading an employee of one of them to file the original charges against Doctor Shadid. The demonstration came when Smith said: "it looks to me like, of all these 2,000 heads of families, these doctors could have found someone to say they'd been fleeced, besides one of their own janitors."

Judge Babcock held that the complaint signed by B. F. Oliver, Sayre, Nov. 2, 1936, did not specify sufficiently the nature of the charges against Doctor Shadid.

Appeal is Undecided

Fred Hansen, assistant attorney general who headed the opposing side, said he did not know whether an appeal would be taken until his office conferred with the medical board.

Courtroom attendants thronged about Dr. Shadid when he left the court.

Smith built his case on the doctor's right, before a quasi-judicial tribunal, to know the exact nature of the charges brought against him.

"Doctor Shadid's hospital is charged with operating a 'bunco game,' with hiring fellows to persuade the people to come in and be fleeced, but the complaint does not say who these 'cappers' and 'steerers' are, who hired them, and who was fleeced," Smith said.

"Their complaint must be specific not only of the complaint alleged but in the particulars of the act, if Doctor Shadid is accused of violating the law. Instead, the complaint draws only a set of legal conclusions. The real question is whether the medical society can run the Elk City Community Hospital out of business so it won't take business away from the hospitals of Clinton and Sayre.

"Doctor Shadid would not be prosecuted in due process of law, but on a breach of ethics which the board thought it was empowered to legislate and tell the doctors to follow it or it would revoke their licenses. They have already kicked him out of the county and state medical society and the American Medical Association and that is all they can do."

References to the "cappers" and "steerers" provision of the state Medical Practices Act were frequent after Smith challenged its constitutionality for the lack of specific definitions of the words. "Cappers" he said, were decoys for gamblers. "Steerers" were come-on men for confidence men.

Use of Salesmen Charged

The complaint charged Doctor Shadid with authorizing the use of "cappers" and "steerers" as stock salesmen to solicit membership in the hospital association and offering prizes for salesmen. It also alleged that the hospital advertised "free" services and misled the public, which by reading further in the advertisement discovered that such services were free only to members. Use of the radio, pamphlets, and platform talks to advertise the hospital also were charged.

"Doctor Shadid and other professional men at the hospital are on fixed salaries and have no interest in its income," Smith said. Originally charged before the medical board with Doctor Shadid were Dr. B. O. McDaniel, Dr. J. K. Nealon, and one other physician. Smith said disposition of their cases probably would be reached by stipulation with the medical board on the outcome of the Shadid case.

"None of the types of advertising prohibited by laws was published by the hospitals," Smith said.

THE COURTS RESCUE MY LICENSE

Judge Lucius Babcock's decision granting a writ of prohibition barring prosecution of me by the Oklahoma State Medical Board on the flimsy and foolish charges made against me in 1936 seems to have permanently cooled the ardor of the conspiring doctors so far as any further court action is concerned.

Chapter 18

The Fight in the Legislature and on the Ballot

1937–1940

In 1937, while my case was before the State Supreme Court, we also faced a legislative battle in a state legislature which Governor Murray had dubbed "the best legislature that money can buy." The doctors, having failed to destroy the hospital by revoking the licenses of the medical staff, doubled their efforts to put us out of business by a legislative enactment. And for a year previously they campaigned to elect to the legislature the kind of men who would do their bidding.

I was glad that the Community Hospital had been put under the sponsorship of the Farmers' Union two years previously, for we were going to need its help as never before. I went to Tom Cheek with the anonymous letter mentioned in a previous chapter and he was sufficiently impressed by its warning to take me to Pat Murphy, the State Commissioner of Labor. Commissioner Murphy felt that the letter should go at once to Governor Marland, and both Tom Cheek and I were pleased when he offered to accompany us. I was reassured by the prospect of this interview with Governor Marland, for I believed from what people said of him that he would be as ready to help us as Governor Murray had been.

But when I watched the governor's expression as I unfolded the story of the letter and the conspiracy I began to have doubts. When I had finished he asked:

"What is this Community Hospital of yours?" I was visibly taken aback, and Tom Cheek tried to explain: "You remember the hospital, the one Governor Murray made the proclamation for in 1931."

The governor said he had no recollection of it.

"Governor Marland," I said, "there are two thousand families dependent on the Community Hospital for medical attention, and this note contains a serious threat to their well-being. Won't you please act at once?"

The governor toyed with the letter. "There is nothing I can do," he said. "Certainly you can't expect that I will act on an anonymous letter. I will ask the State Health Commissioner to investigate the situation and report to me. That's all I can do."

As we left, both Tom Cheek and I realized that the situation was more serious than it had been before, because we had lost our one means of stopping the doctors without a knockdown and dragout struggle. The State Health Commissioner was no hero, and the last thing he wanted to do was to offend the Oklahoma State Medical Association. We knew the kind of consideration he would give our complaint.

Since the governor wouldn't help us, we had to fight it out alone. So I wrote a pamphlet called "The Doctors' Seven Years of Conspiracy," and issued fifteen thousand copies of it. Copies were sent to our members, to members of the legislature and of the State Supreme Court, and to all executives at the State House. I tried to arouse support and sympathy among the people of western Oklahoma by writing articles in the *Oklahoma Union Farmer* and various labor journals. In my pamphlet I said:

> This fight is not a fight of the medical profession of the state—it is a fight waged by a few doctors, living in the immediate vicinity of the Community Hospital, who think they have suffered some financial loss on account of our success.
>
> These selfsame local doctors lately called their county

medical society members together and passed resolutions against the Federal Resettlement Administration for attempting to extend aid to their low-income farmer clients to enable them to purchase membership and service in the Community Hospital. They went so far as to extend a two-dollar-per-day rate for room, board, and nursing to Resettlement clients and to agree to charge them only twenty-five dollars for a major operation. They agreed to do this provided the Resettlement Administration would withdraw aid to its clients in the form of buying membership in the Community Hospital, which it agreed to do.

Even now, at this writing they have henchmen going around soliciting citizens in Roger Mills County to sign a petition requesting the authorities in said county to have the County Commissioners violate their contract with the Community Hospital in caring for their poor. Every imaginable obstacle they have placed in our path to "Stop the Community Hospital!" Like a drowning man, they grasp at every straw.

They have pressed into their service and conspiracy a few unthinking doctors in key positions. In order to overthrow us, they have gone before doctors and county societies over the state, and misrepresented us, and played on their prejudices; and gotten a lot of money to lobby through the legislature a nefarious bill to put us out of business so as to protect themselves from any possible financial loss.

They would have you believe that the legislature passed a dental act last year, aimed at us. This is untrue, for the committee of the legislature that had the dental act under consideration interviewed us and were glad to put in an exemption in favor of coöperative corporations, as they had no idea of forbidding us from practicing dentistry. The act was aimed at itinerant dentists who travel about the country and make extravagant claims in their advertising, thus deceiving the general

THE FIGHT IN THE LEGISLATURE

public. This statement may be easily substantiated by reading the dental act.

To enact the legislation the doctors are asking for would put the hospital out of business and would cause loss to the twenty-four hundred farm families of over $150,000 invested in the hospital, and would deny to twenty thousand families who are members of the Farmers' Union in this state the opportunity to receive a similar protection by organizing similar hospitals.

You can pass such legislation and receive the plaudits of a few self-seeking surgeons, but you will have to answer to the common people of the state, and to your consciences.

Beware of what you may read or hear. Come to Elk City and western Oklahoma. Visit the people in the town and on the farms, and ask them what they think of the Community Hospital, and the doctors and specialists in it!

For six years, now, the self-seeking medical politicians have been trying to get my license. If they had had any justification, they would have succeeded in so doing. They are interested in me because, as they have said many times, if they could frame me and get my license, they would get rid of that "damned Community Hospital."

I make no brief for myself, for I shall soon retire from the active practice of medicine and surgery by death or by my own volition. Ninety-nine doctors out of every hundred in the state hold no grudge against me. I can visit them individually and receive the usual courtesies of the profession.

I plead for the Community Hospital, which is the first coöperative hospital in the nation. I plead for the fifteen thousand men, women, and children who put a hundred and fifty thousand dollars into the hospital, from their pittances, and for the hundred thousand men, women, and children in the Farmers' Union in this state who are going to have access to this, and similar, hospitals on a basis they can afford. I plead for the underprivileged, the disinherited, and the poor. . . .

As we had feared, the State Health Commissioner was not going to help us. He made a report to the governor, after talking at length with our arch-enemies, but never once consulting us, urging that the governor do nothing about the Community Hospital situation, for it was much too hot for gubernational hands. This was just about what the governor wanted to hear. Formerly a rich man, who had been stripped clean on Wall Street, Marland was trying desperately to rebuild his prestige. He had the choice of a try for the United States Senate or political oblivion after his term of office was up in 1938, because the governor of Oklahoma cannot succeed himself. Naturally, he decided on the Senate, and when a group as seemingly powerful as the Oklahoma State Medical Association said "No," the governor was glad to repeat it.

At the same time I addressed an open letter to a member of the Beckham County Medical Society—a man who had been most active in the attacks on me and on the hospital. It read, in part, as follows:

> You object to farmers owning a hospital coöperatively in order to save for themselves, but at the same time you do not object to owning stock in a gin to save yourself from profit-making gins, owned by private corporations. Consistency, thou art a jewel! Or does it depend on whose ox is gored?
>
> You have accumulated lands, houses, and riches. Why object to my helping a lot of people to help themselves? Some of the doctors in your town told me that you objected to the Community Hospital on the grounds that it has taken some of your patients away from you.
>
> From the inception of the Community Hospital, you

fought me on every occasion. You would have the people believe that I advertise to cure anything. You would have people believe that the Community Hospital promises to do things it does not do, when we have five thousand dollars as security with the state government to ensure that we carry out our word to the people.

Those who know me best know that all my life I have been devoted to the coöperative movement, that I organized the Community Hospital not only at great personal sacrifice of my professional income but even at my own expense, because of my lifelong ambition to do something as a contribution to human uplift.

You conspired to destroy the Community Hospital. You have met in the dead of night with other conspirators trying to think out schemes to eliminate the Community Hospital as a competitor, and but for Governor Murray you would probably have succeeded. I will tell you how to compete with the Community Hospital. Do it on economic and legitimate grounds, not by playing politics and calling me names, but by serving your fellow men better and cheaper, and more honestly and more faithfully.

The fight you are making for Mammon is a losing fight. The coöperative movement is bigger than any man or any set of men. The cause of the people is the cause of righteousness, and must prevail. Every coöperative enterprise had to contend with selfish interests and had to fight its way to success, and this hospital had to do the same. You, and those like you, will soon pass away. But the cause of the people will prevail!

The profession of medicine is an honorable calling. The people in their collective capacity are going to redeem it from its low estate and restore its ancient precepts—the precepts of the Golden Rule and of Jesus of Nazareth.

Social medicine is on the way. The people have a knack for meeting their own needs, and solving their problems. The success of the Community Hospital—phenomenal as it is—cannot be explained by saying it is unethical. It cannot be brushed aside so easily as that. The Community Hospital is a social phenomenon of deep and lasting significance. It must be studied with an open mind and sympathetic understanding. Facts are stubborn things, and must be approached from the scientific standpoint. The Community Hospital has succeeded because it has met a long felt need. It is in tune with the times.

The day of individualism in medicine, as in many other fields, is past. We are living in a period of transition from a system of "laissez faire" to a system of order in human relations. Those who would survive must accommodate themselves to changing conditions in human affairs or else they will be flattened by a steam roller, impersonal and ruthless.

Despite all our efforts the Community Hospital was in a difficult spot. The doctors had picked their candidates where they could, during the campaign, and relied on their slush fund of forty-four thousand dollars to do the rest, once the legislature convened. We were going to have a stiff fight all along the line. Tom Cheek offered to direct our legislative campaign, and when the legislature convened in January 1937, our legislative committee included representatives of the Farmers' Union, the various labor unions, and the Veterans of Industry of America, and beat the opposition to the draw by seeing that our bill was introduced first. This bill, offered as a substitute to the doctors' bill, enabled a civic body, such as a church, or a nonprofit organization like the Farmers' Union, or a labor union, to organize a coöperative hospital. Its second provision was that a doctor's license could not be revoked by the State Board of Medical Examiners without giving the doctor an opportunity to defend himself in his district court.

The doctors' bill, on the other hand, made it illegal for a corporation to practice medicine, and forbade anyone "to provide medical care under any name other than his own" under penalty of revocation of license. It further stipulated that all members of the State Board of Medical Examiners (seven in number) must be chosen by the Governor from a list of twenty-five names chosen by the Oklahoma State Medical Association.

There they were, again trying to concentrate power in the hands of the Oklahoma State Medical Association. But we beat them to the gun, and the House of Representatives voted in favor of our bill seventy-three to sixteen, as the doctors fell back in consternation. They went into a huddle, and within twenty-four hours the slush fund was pouring its oil on the troubled waters. When our bill came up for consideration in the Senate, it was referred with amazing promptness to a committee, where it was buried till adjournment, but we had fought the doctors to a standstill.

Despite the eagerness of the Senate to render service for money received, our chief opponent did not introduce the doctors' bill. He decided it would be useless. But since the Community Hospital was not to be overthrown by legislation, he decided to sell his hospital rather than compete with us. Upon the theory that a state hospital, where people of low income could secure free care, would put the Community Hospital out of business, he offered his hospital for sale to the state.

The whole handling of the legislation, the entire situation, was typical of corrupt politics. The Clinton Hospital was nominally owned by the Baptist Church, so that the real owning doctor might be free to praise it without blushing. I don't see how he could help blushing anyway, for the hospital, which had about thirty-five beds, had a first mortgage of $45,000, a second mortgage of $22,000, and tax indebtedness amounting to $10,000. It would be possible at that time to build a new hospital at a standard cost of $1,000 per bed, but for this rickety Clinton Hospital, limping along with $77,000 worth of debt, the real owner set an asking price of $175,000.

And, to quote R. M. McClintock, columnist in the *Daily Oklahoman:* "What argument does the taxpayer think was used to convert a House vote of 50 to 47 (59 is required to carry) against purchase Thursday, into a vote of 63 to 47 for the purchase Friday?" The bill for the purchase of the hospital for $175,000 was passed by the Senate as well, and ultimately came up to Governor Marland for signature. With one eye on the United States Senate, he signed the bill, but he had the amount reduced to $115,000.

When the Oklahoma State Medical Association met that summer for its annual convention, the meeting had hardly been opened when a member of the legislative committee rose to say that the session of the sixteenth legislature had been an expensive one for the association, but that the matter was not to be discussed at the meeting. So the doctors kept their mouths shut.

But despite the cost to the doctors, and the corruptness of the Clinton Hospital deal, they had done one excellent thing during the sixteenth legislature. They had pressed for passage of the Basic Science Act, which required that any person seeking a license to practice healing in Oklahoma be required to take an examination in the basic sciences of anatomy, physiology, pathology, chemistry, and bacteriology. The bill was passed, and the chiropractors were effectively prevented from coming into the state, for they have about as much use for a knowledge of chemistry or bacteriology as a hog has for astronomy.

Like every honest doctor, I was in favor of the Basic Science Act, for the chiropractors had been allowed to practice their quackery too long. Then, very unexpectedly, something happened. Since according to Oklahoma law a bill that has failed in the legislature can be brought directly before the people for a vote, we decided to circulate the necessary petitions among our members to insure an unbi-

THE FIGHT IN THE LEGISLATURE

ased presentation of our cause to the people. Tom Cheek offered to take charge of the drive and draw up the petition. He brought it to me for inspection, and I read it. Yes, that was our bill all right, but when I came to the end of it, it had been amended.

Tacked to the end of our bill was a paragraph reading: "No applicant for a license to practice the healing arts in the state of Oklahoma shall be required to take an examination for such license before a board of examiners whose membership does not wholly consist of examiners who are active practitioners of the school of the particular healing art of which such applicant is a member."

Surprised and angered, I asked Tom Cheek why that amendment, which would kill the purpose of the bill, had been added.

"Well," said Tom Cheek, "during the fight in the legislature, when I was lining up support, the chiropractors said they'd help us, and they did. When they found out we were going to circulate a petition they asked if they could get in on it, and I said I didn't see why not. They got a raw deal on that Basic Science Act...."

"They got what they deserved!" I said. "That amendment has to be taken out at once!"

"Now, Doc," said Cheek, "that's not fair. They've got a right to live just the way we have. There's got to be medical freedom just like any other kind."

"Look, Tom," I said, as earnestly as I could, "these Chiros have fooled you. They're not real healers of the sick—not sincere. There may be some things they can do to help certain conditions in the sick. But they claim they can cure everything. What would you think of me as a doctor if I claimed I could cure all cancers, for instance? You'd call me a quack. And that's what they are. We can't do anything that will encourage them. I've been fighting for the people now for nine years, so they can have better medical care, but that doesn't mean for one minute that I'm not a doctor, and willing to fight for the profession, too. No self-respecting doctor can align himself with quacks, and that's what you're asking me to do. I'll quit first even if I have to sell popcorn for a living."

But Tom Cheek wasn't convinced. Like many another fair-minded but uninformed layman, he believed in "medical freedom"—actually the freedom of anyone who so desired to prey on the sick. While I was away from town Cheek called a meeting of the board of directors of the Community Hospital, and they agreed with him on the matter. They were all sincere men, and if a meeting of the entire membership had been called, I have no doubt that the vote would have been in favor of the chiropractic amendment. I felt I had to reverse this decision, so I asked for a board meeting the following week, and there explained the situation and made an impassioned speech against the amendment. I stated that I couldn't associate myself with the hospital if the amendment were allowed to stand on our petition. It was one thing, I said, to face professional persecution for attempting to improve medical practice, and quite another to face it for encouraging quackery. I wasn't in sympathy with this amendment, and I couldn't stay with the hospital if it were allowed to go through.

My speech wasn't enough to convince them I was in earnest and they voted me down. There was only one thing I could do, and I did it with great reluctance—I turned in to the board of directors my resignation and the resignations of my staff, to take effect as soon as the initiated measure with the chiropractic amendment was printed and circulated. Then I told Tom Cheek that if those resignations were accepted I would go before the next state convention of the Farmers' Union and tell the farmers why. He withdrew the amendment, and in two months' time we secured sixty-six thousand signatures to our petition, six thousand more than was required by law to submit it to a vote of the people. The conspiring doctors immediately contested the sufficiency of the signatures, but the Secretary of the State, after giving them an open hearing on the matter, dismissed their objec-

THE FIGHT IN THE LEGISLATURE

tions as invalid. Whereupon they appealed to the State Supreme Court, and there the petition rested from 1937 to 1940, and was released by the Supreme Court about sixty days prior to the November election of 1940, and declared to be a ballot petition. At this general election, the coöperative hospital bill and a graduated land tax measure were submitted to the voters.

Following is the official vote on these two measures in the election of November 5, 1940.

The graduated land tax, state question 215, initiative petition 166, carried in all but seven counties, received:

Yes votes	408,559
No votes	196,711
A plurality of	211,848

The coöperative hospital bill, state question 241, received:

Yes votes	294,346
No votes	212,701
A plurality of	81,645

You would think that both of these measures would have become law and under a just government they would have. But not under Oklahoma justice. Under Oklahoma law a voter not voting for or against a given initiated measure is counted as having voted against that measure.

At the same election the budget-balancing amendment, a state administration measure (really fathered by the state Chamber of Commerce) submitted through the legislature, state question 298, received:

Yes votes	149,412
No votes	75,830

And a Board of Regents amendment submitted through the legislature, state question 300, received:

Yes votes 137,205
No votes 82,268

Both of these measures, although they received fewer total votes and a small plurality vote, have become the law of the land. The *Oklahoma Union Farmer* had the following to say editorially:

> The farmers and laborers carried the Graduated Land Tax in Oklahoma by more than two to one. Under the rules of justice this is a law now. Our Coöperative Hospital also carried by an overwhelming majority. The silent vote in any land where it is allowed to be counted, either for or against legislation, is unjust before God and man.
>
> Representative government can not long endure and tolerate this undemocratic rule. It has no place in a democracy. The people who go to the polls and vote for a measure and the opposition who vote against a measure should be recorded and those votes alone should determine that measure.
>
> The majority always rule in a democracy. A totalitarian rule no doubt would count the silent vote as it suited the dictator, either for or against a measure.
>
> The citizens of Oklahoma will rid this state of that danger and that evil. We will ask the legislature for relief and if it is not given we will have our forces so organized that we will put it over by the initiative and referendum in the face of this silent vote proposition.

Which was fine, but too late to help us, so our political efforts were simultaneously, and thereafter, directed in another channel entirely.

Chapter 19

Candidate for Congress

1940

After the court battle ended favorably in 1940, I was quite convinced that the hospital was secure against further attacks, but I was equally convinced that voluntary coöperation without government support could not solve the health problem of the low-income people. Many of our members who had paid $10 on their $50 stock dropped out and did not finish the payment. Many others quit paying their dues. At one meeting of the board of directors, I recall, 600 members who had made a $10 payment, years before, or had merely signed a note for $50 for a share, were cancelled out.

It is true that our membership grew larger from year to year, but that was due to the fact that as we succeeded more and more business men and prosperous farmers joined the association. Indeed at this writing, both bankers and most of the leading business men of Elk City are members of the Community Hospital. While I was glad to see these people, who had formerly turned up their noses, join the hospital, I was not happy at the thought of seeing the poor people, for whom I had planned over the years, drop out or fail to join.

Then too, the voluntary coöperative health movement, inspired by what we had done at Community Hospital, seemed to be catching and holding the interest of groups here and there over the country. A coöperative health association was organized and functioning at Washington, D.C., another at Amherst, Texas, but in most places we found it difficult to get people to pay the initial membership fee with which to build and equip a hospital or health center. The people who needed it the most could least afford to pay for it.

I felt that the government should make loans to such coöperative health associations to enable them to build and equip their physical facilities, just as they have done to Rural Electrification associations. Further, I felt that the government—local, state, and federal—should pay coöperatives for the medical care of people with little or no income.

In every civilized country in the world, government made some provision for the medical care of the indigent—why not in the United States? I approached the late Congressman Massingale in an effort to get him to sponsor such a health bill. His reaction was negative.

"If I should sponsor such a bill," said he, "the doctors in my district would decapitate me at the next election."

I approached other congressmen in other districts and all reacted alike. "The medical association is too powerful," said one of them, "for any congressman to buck."

I began to think in terms of running for Congress myself to sponsor the legislation.

I knew, to be sure, that I was well known over the district. I had practiced medicine in it for over thirty years. My fights to establish and protect coöperative medicine had kept my name before the people of the region constantly.

But as a practical politician, there were other factors one had to consider. It was generally known that I was foreign born. Would my enemies be able to use that fact to defeat me? Where there enough hospital members and progressives in the district to put my candidacy across? Many of my friends thought that there were. So I told them to sound out the sentiment in the district in some way to be sure. Shortly, they brought me a petition signed by over 1,200 voters asking me to make the race.

In my political innocence, I thought, with such a block of

CANDIDATE FOR CONGRESS

voters asking me to run, that all I needed to do to be nominated would be to broadcast a few speeches over the local station KASA, without putting in a personal appearance in every town in every county in the district. But I was soon disillusioned for the organized doctors, who in 1936 had gotten together a slush fund of $44,000 with which to buy the legislators and outlaw our hospital, and who had gotten a poor unknown janitor to swear out a complaint of unprofessional conduct against me in order to try to take away my license to practice, soon joined with the politicians and ransacked the district for dishonorable men who would go out and abuse, vilify, and lie about me for pay. So in self-defense, I went over the district to let the voters look at me and find out for themselves that I did not have horns, cloven hoofs, and tail, as they were being told. And I presented my platform everywhere in speeches so that the voters would become as familiar with my ideas and voice as they were with my appearance.

But before things got that far along, the members of the Farmers' Union and the Community Hospital who had circulated the petition and secured signers gave a testimonial dinner in my behalf at Casa Grande Hotel in Elk City and invited me to address the four hundred representative citizens assembled from all over the district.

Once my candidacy was announced and my campaign launched, it did not take my professional enemies, the doctors, long to begin their dirty work. In Elk City, my campaign workers had made a huge sign reading "Shadid for Congress" and had had it stretched across the main street with the enthusiastic consent of the owners of the buildings to which the sign was anchored. It disappeared one night shortly after it was put up. Investigation showed that the doctor who had tried to compete with Community Hospital by converting his little private hospital into a spurious coöperative had hired a man to take the sign down.

The mayor of Elk City that year happened to be a doctor. He was asked to locate the sign. In a few hours the sign was returned but the hoodlums who took it down were never apprehended. Another doctor of the town loudly offered to pay the fine of the guilty party if ever brought to trial. All over the district Shadid posters and "Shadid for Congress" signs were torn down by organized gangs while the advertisements of the other candidates were left unmolested.

At Sayre, county seat town, where the leader of the doctors conspiring against the Community Hospital lived, the city fire sirens were set going during my speech although there was no fire. I accused the doctor publicly of being responsible for this wanton interruption and called upon the sheriff, who was present at the meeting, to put a stop to the annoyance or I would make a speech in every school house in the county to defeat him for re-election. The sirens stopped shortly thereafter. The doctor never denied the accusation.

At Cheyenne, while I was making a campaign speech, a group of boys, hired by the opposition, were setting off firecrackers up the block from where I was speaking. This was done deliberately, of course, to try to break up my meeting. My opponents were, evidently, very much afraid of letting the people hear me undisturbed so that they might make up their own minds on the issues and personalities of the campaign.

During the last weeks of the campaign the conspiring doctors and the opposing politicians joined to open the floodgates of falsehood and slander. I tried to keep track of these libels during the campaign and especially during the closing weeks. At Cordell, it was reported that Dr. Shadid was a Communist. At Hollis, it was whispered that Dr. Shadid had been an enemy spy during the last war. At Cheyenne, it was told that Dr. Shadid had a German Nazi from New York running his campaign. In Carmargo, it was rumored that even Dr. Shadid's wife was fighting his nomination for Congress. In Altus, it was asserted that New York Communists had contributed $8,000 to his campaign. In Eldorado, it was claimed that if Dr. Shadid were nominated he would recommend only Syrians for appointment to offices. At Reed, it was said that Dr. Shadid was a fifth columnist, although it is doubtful whether any one could then have told what that was. In Mangum, it was alleged that Dr. Shadid was a Turk. In Lone Wolf, it was spread about that Dr. Shadid was cheating the Farmers' Union out of the Community Hospital. In Hobart, it was claimed that Dr. Shadid was a millionaire. Down at Carter, a preacher, of all people, asserted that Dr. Shadid was an atheist. Over at Roosevelt, the campaign manager of another candidate showed a photograph of a check, a pure forgery, for $500 made out to Dr. Shadid from the Communist Party. Down in Tillman County, a Methodist preacher went around claiming that Dr. Shadid was a chronic drunkard unable to attend to his regular duties. And at Gage, it was rumored that Dr. Shadid had drowned one of his daughters because she had married an American. I submit that I do not believe that any other candidate for nomination for Congress in all American history ever had quite the variety of lies told about him as I had told about me.

It seemed that there were any number of preachers and editors for sale in this campaign of falsehoods. Several preachers circulated around the district advertising the fact that they were preachers and then spending their time spreading all manner of falsehoods against me.

The following, from the *Vici Beacon*, is a sample of what some of the anti-Shadid papers were saying editorially:

THE PEDDLER OF RUGS

Down the street he comes, a man apart, knowing no friend; his queer dress, his hooked nose, his broken speech and queer mannerisms set him aside from the rest—the peddler of rugs.

On his arm a gaudy display of rugs and scarfs, gleaming like jewels in the sunlight. Sparkling tinsel and glistening silk, yet alas, they bear no blessing of a known manufacturer, a thing made only to sell thru picturing of the faults of others. Bearing a guarantee of a foreigner whom you will perhaps never see again.

Nor are the political rugs as exemplified by the candidacy of Dr. M. Shadid of any better quality. These rugs, too, glisten in the light of hard times, they are smooth; but what lies under the surface?—Will they, like the peddler's rug, fade, will they become a thing forsaken, dirty, unfit to have around?

After the first washing what will we have?

They carry not the blessing of a Washington, Jefferson, Lincoln, Wilson, or Coolidge. They do carry the blessing, however, of every socialist, or ex-socialist I know. You count them over—every one you know—no preamble of the Constitution teaches class hatred and the "down with the rich" doctrine that Shadid does—but the old socialist newspaper, "Appeal to Reason" did.

No American parentage glorifies this person, and no American philosophy blesses his doctrine. We need no off-color Jews as congressmen, nor do we need off-color capital-baiting lines of thought in our national make-up.

A young woman, Sari Scott from Los Angeles, who was writing a play, later produced by Margo Jones at Dallas as "Oracle Junction," about the hospital, spent two weeks at Elk City getting information about the Community Hospital. On finding this editorial in my files she was enraged and wrote the editor of the *Vici Beacon* the following letter:

To the Editor
The Vici Beacon,
Vici, Okla.

Sir:
Yesterday going through the files in Dr. Shadid's office to obtain material for the forthcoming motion

picture production of "A Doctor for the People," I read an article from your publication dated July 4, 1940, entitled "The Peddler of Rugs." A more disgraceful commentary on ignorance and bigotry I have never read. It is inconceivable that a paper, purportedly democratic, could print those rabble-rousing words of superstition. They make a travesty of Independence Day.

A peddler of rugs you call Dr. Shadid. Did you know that when he carried a satchel of cheap jewelry to sell across the continent, when he sold these ornaments to housewives to save money to go to college—that in another satchel he carried books, text books on American history, English, algebra? That after tramping the road each day, at night he studied these books—with no teacher to guide him—but so well that he was able after only a semester of regular college curriculum, to enroll in the Washington University school of medicine at St. Louis? Did you work so hard for your education? Did you obtain an education? From the pitiful ridicule to which you stoop in the aforementioned article—I wonder.

To the thinking minds of our nation, Dr. Shadid has made history. He has won an honorable niche of pioneer integrity in America's hall of fame. Were I in your position, I would publish an editorial—on the 4th of July this year—and to the best of my ability make amends for my folly.

Sincerely yours,
Sari Scott,
Los Angeles, Calif.

May 29th, 1945.

Since the campaign against me did not at any time mention coöperative medicine or health insurance, but was devoted to socialism, communism, and my foreign birth, I resorted to the use of sarcasm and humor, about as follows:

Ladies and Gentlemen: Before getting to the kernel of this talk let me blow away some of the chaff my extinguished opponents have stirred up in this campaign against me. I say extinguished opponent because from what I can make out, all nine of them have already agreed there is only one man in the race and that's me.

Well then, the first charge my united opponents make is that I am a Socialist. I deny the allegation. I used to be one but when the New Deal adopted my platform I had no other choice than either to go with it or to desert my convictions; so now I am a New Deal Democrat, or to be precise I was one long before the New Deal was known.

The second charge is that I am a Communist and in proof thereof they declare that sometime ago I was cited before a legislative committee to prove that I was not a Communist. Well I appeared before the honorable body in company with some twenty college professors and ministers of the gospel, and from what I read in the Oklahoma City papers it seems that the committee decided that while it might be all right to investigate a red-hot horse-shoe it would be plumb foolish to pick it up and put it in the pocket for further reference.

The third charge is that I wasn't born in this country. And here my extinguished opponents "really got the goods on me." However, there are some mitigating circumstances that should be mentioned. In the first place when I was born, some 120 miles from where Christ was born, I was too young and inexperienced to know enough about geography to instruct my parents where I wanted to be born. However, in the event of my election I solemnly promise to do better next time.

Perhaps I also may add that when I came to this country at the age of 16 I was already able to read, write, and speak fluent English, all of which the bulk of my distinguished opponents still have to learn if judged by their vocal and literary utterances. Furthermore, when I came to this country I had clothes on my back whereas they arrived stark naked.

The last and most serious charge the confederation of Congressional near-candidates hurled at me is that I am only a doctor and what business has a doctor to dabble in politics. And all I can say to that is, I believe the first duty of government is the greater good for the greatest number. I am in politics for the single purpose of bringing the art of healing to more people than enjoy it now. Otherwise I confess there is a vast difference between a good doctor and a successful politician.

To prove my statement, it required four years of high school, four years of medical school, two years as an interne, a number of post-graduate courses, and thirty years of intensive and extensive practice to make me the doctor I am. But whoever heard of a politician requiring any other qualifications for his job other than being a good handshaker, back slapper, and baby kisser on top of possessing an oily tongue, an elastic conscience that permits him to be all things to all men, coupled with a memory short enough to forget the morning after election what he had promised the night before.

Don't tell me that it takes any other qualifications than above mentioned to make a successful politician. Why you and I know of County Clerks that never kept books; County and State Treasurers that never had enough money of their own to get used to the rustle of the greenbacks; lawmakers that never wrote a law; highway commissioners that never turned a shovel of dirt. You even may know of congressmen that, for all we heard of them after they left home, might have gotten lost, strayed, or stolen on their way to Washington. And last but not least you may even have heard of governors who know so little about their own state that every time Uncle Sam got ready to build a dam wide enough to churn electric generators they had to call up the lawyers of their Wall Street campaign contributors for advice on how to join Uncle Sam.

Well, I am sorry I lack the qualifications for a successful politician but doctors are that way. For instance, what good would it do a man with a mangled hand if the doctor gave it a hearty shake? How would you feel if you came to a doctor bent over with lumbago and he slapped your back? What would mothers think if you brought your baby, suffering from colic, to the doctor and he kissed it instead of taking the wind off its little tummy? Sure we doctors are handicapped when it comes to politics. We even don't dare to promise our patients to treat them in the good old-fashioned way of Jefferson and Jackson's time. Think of starting an operation by hitting the patient on the head with a wooden mallet, instead of giving him an anesthetic. Or to come closer to home, think of curing high blood pressure by bleeding the patient, or inflammation of the bladder by going to the nearest creek for a can full of leeches and let the undertaker do the rest, as was done in Abe Lincoln's day.

It's no use to deny it. We doctors either have to keep up with the march of science or join the grand army of has-beens, while all the successful politician has to do, to stay in the swim, is not be caught with a new cure for an up-to-date evil.

Then when it comes to promising, we doctors are still more handicapped. When a politician doesn't make good his promises the people take it for granted and let it go at that; but when a doctor promises to cure a patient and doesn't deliver the goods, his relatives put a stone on his grave and let the world know what kind of a liar the doctor is.

If I were a real, honest to goodness politician, I would promise every farmer a farm, every teamster a team, every bank clerk a bank, every homebody a home,

CANDIDATE FOR CONGRESS

and every housewife an electric washer with free juice thrown in for good measure. I would promise a bigger pension to the aged, free schooling to the young, and a furnished nest to every loving couple. I would come out for more government spending and lower taxes. I would promise everybody something at the cost of nobody. I might even do still better by simply orating from the stump—come on everybody, trot out your wishes and if there is anyone among you that forgot something I solemnly promise that in the event of my election I'll think it up for him.

That's the stuff out of which successful politicians are made and you know it. However, being a licensed healer and doctor and not a certified politician I will promise you folks only three things, all of them in my line.

The first is that if you elect me to Congress, and you will, I shall do my human-best to spread the message of social and coöperative medical care. I believe that the most precious possession of man on this earth is a healthy body and mind. I believe that it is our Christian and patriotic duty to give every American the best medical care his country has to offer. As things stand now only the rich can afford the best medical service. The middle class made up of farmers, wage-earners, small merchants, salaried and professional men get the second class service and to get even that, are often pauperized in the process, while the poor at the bottom get what is left—which I assure you, as a doctor of thirty years of practice, is nothing particular to write home about.

I am proud to say that the kind of new medical care you and I have stared in this 7th Congressional District has spread until by now all the larger cities of this country boast of some kind of a coöperative medical center. But why only the centers of population? Why not bring the blessing of coöperative and social medicine to every town, hamlet, and school district of the country, and the principal reason why you will send me to Congress is to give me, the father of coöperative medicine, as I am known from shore to shore, the sounding board to spread this message.

The second thing that I faithfully promise is that I will do everything within my power to keep war from these shores. And if that requires the last American dollar and drop of sweat. I shall vote that it be given.

"And lastly but foremost I promise that I would rather be carried dead out of the halls of Congress than vote to send a single American boy, be it by plane, warship, or merchant vessel, into the hell over there. For during my thirty years of practice I have seen many amputated arms and legs, enough blinded eyes and cruelly disfigured faces, enough disembowelled trunks and shattered bones to make me understand the meaning of wholesale slaughter complimentarily called "war."

Well, folks, I have told you what I am. I told you where I stand. I told you what I will do after you have elected me, as you will. Now good night and sleep tight. I leave it to you to do the rest.

But my professional and political enemies, determined to do everything in their power to defeat me, overlooked nothing in political chicanery. They set up their dummy candidates, members of the Farmers' Union to reduce my strength. And they sent William Simpson—son of the late John Simpson, national president of the Farmers' Union, who had been a staunch supporter of the Community Hospital from the first—to go out over the district contacting local Farmers' Union leaders to point out that "after all the Farmers' Union cannot afford to support a foreigner for Congress." John Simpson would have turned over in his grave had he known his son was up to such business.

The opposition to my candidacy was promoted not only

by the doctors in my county of Beckham and the 7th Congressional District and by the state adminstration, but also by the Oklahoma State Medical Association, where secretary sent out partisan letters addressed to doctors, dentists, and funeral home directors.

The dentists were appealed to, in order to defeat me, because at the Community Hospital we had two dentists who served our members on a discount basis. The funeral home directors were contacted because we were considering the organization of a coöperative funeral home to render service on a cost basis in connection with the Community Hospital.

In spite of the vicious campaign against me, I was runner-up in the primary, standing second among the ten candidates. Over ten thousand voters in the seventh district had an attitude of fair play, a feeling of tolerance, and the sense of vote on real issues.

The vote stood as follows:

Massingale	17,038
Shadid	10,422
Wickersham	9,251
Dacus	5,718
Horton	4,067
McKenzie	3,359
Hogg	1,097

Chapter 20

Running for Congress Again

1940–1941

A few months after his re-election Congressman Massingale died, and it became necessary to select a successor.

My supporters over the district began urging me to run again. They figured that my nomination would be a pushover.

As the campaign developed, it became evident that there was no doubt about my securing a plurality of the voters. The betting odds were 2 to 1 and in some places 3 to 1, but there were few takers.

The political opposition in the state, headed by the governor, Leon Phillips, was desperate, and an effort was made to enact a bill providing a run-off in *special elections*. The election laws in Oklahoma did not provide for a run-off primary between the top candidates. The candidate receiving a plurality was declared the nominee. Now an effort was made to enact a bill providing for a run-off primary between the two top candidates *but not in the general primary—only in a special primary election*. The legislature had already, on a previous occasion, voted against a run-off in the regular primary. In the lower house the vote had been 75 to 35 against a run-off in general primary elections. The members did not want to vote for a run-off in the general primary because they wanted to make sure that when they ran for office again they would not have to receive a majority of all votes cast in order to be elected. In Oklahoma, in most of the counties, winning a Democratic primary is equivalent to election, as the Republicans are greatly in the minority. Therefore the bill introduced was purposely worded to provide for a run-off *only in a special election*. This would not in any way prejudice the re-election of the incumbent law makers for a special election is a rarity. In short, the proposed law was aimed solely at my candidacy. The politicians thought that my nomination was assured, for they were certain that I was sure to receive a plurality of votes, but in the case of a run-off, between myself and the next highest candidate, if they could put the bill through, I would be sure to be defeated. Of course, they were probably right in their reasoning that I could not win a majority of votes in a run-off primary.

The efforts of the law-makers to pass this bill took a good deal of the time of the legislature but it was eventually defeated. Ex-Governor Murray, who once before had come to the rescue of myself and the Community Hospital, gave it as his considered opinion that such a law would be unconstitutional and, as he was chairman of the constitutional convention when Oklahoma was admitted to statehood, his opinion carried weight. Then, too, there were men in the legislature who believed in Americanism and fair play and fought this legislation.

Unable to head off my anticipated victory by special legislation and yet determined to deflate my candidacy, the state senate set up an investigating committee and summoned me by subpoena, along with others, before it. Among these others were a Presbyterian minister, a director of religious education at the State University, and several professors from the same institution. We were all being investigated for "subversive activities" but I was considered the prize "catch." Anything to hurt me politically was considered quite in order. Our subversive activities consisted of being members of the executive committee of the Oklahoma Federation for Constitutional Rights.

The attempt on the part of my professional and political

enemies in the legislature, my testimony before the committee of the state senate for "subversive activities," and my appearance in district court to defend the temporary injunction against the State Board of Medical Examiners on February 10, 1941, were all good campaign stuff. And I used these incidents in my speeches over the district.

In the previous campaign, in addition to the money donated by the local doctors and politicians, outside money was poured into the district from other doctors and politicians in the state. In the eleven counties in the districts, no less than a hundred men and women were engaged to speak and to circulate rumors and to print editorials against me.

But this campaign was ominously different. Nothing was said about my being a Socialist, Communist, or foreigner. I said to my wife that the opposition had decided they could not defeat me except by stealing the election.

With the special election over you may imagine the surprise and disappointment that prevailed generally among my friends when the voting was reported as follows:

Wickersham	8,062
Shadid	7,585
McClintic	7,555
Chamberlain	7,315
Wimberly	5,858
Keen	2,394
Kawks	1,094
Rogers	340
Cannon	130
McLemore	73

No reasonable explanation could possibly be put forward to explain the small vote of 7,585 cast for me except that the administration machine, having failed to defeat me by special legislation, had decided to steal the election. The total vote cast in this special primary election of 1941 was 40,408, which was about 20 per cent less than the vote cast in the regular primary election of the year before. Even if we presume that I did not win any protest votes as a result of the fight in the legislature, an absurd assumption, or as a result of my victory in the District Court, and discounting the 20 per cent of the votes cast the previous year that did not vote in the special election, I should have received about 11,500—a difference of nearly 4,000 votes unaccounted for.

It does not help to explain this loss by stating that the winner received only 8,062 votes, which was about 1,200 votes less than he received the year before. We do not say that all the votes stolen from me were given to Mr. Wickersham; they were spread among the other candidates. This much we feel certain about. In Beckham County they were given to Mr. Wickersham; in Kiowa County they were given to Mr. McClintic; in Tillman County they were given to Mr. Chamberlain; in Jackson County they were given to Mr. Wimberly—by a previous understanding among the medicos and the politicians.

Prior to the election secret meetings were held in different parts of the district between the doctors and the politicians bent on defeating me to find ways and means to steal the election. First, they tried to unite their efforts behind one candidate, but could not agree upon any one of them, so they decided to defeat me by stealing enough of my votes in different counties and giving them to various candidates according to a pre-conceived and pre-arranged plan.

There can be no other explanation in view of the fact that my supporters were on the whole more enthusiastic than the supporters of any of the opposition, and even more enthusiastic, because they thought victory certain, than they had been the year before. They turned out in the same proportionate number as the supporters of the opposition candidates.

That the election was stolen, and that the administration was well aware of that fact, is further shown by the refusal of the State Election Board to recount the ballots, in violation of the election law, which required only a deposit of $250 for each county to have the ballots recounted. I deposited $2,000 to have eight of the eleven counties of the Seventh District recounted. Further proof of the theft is the fact that although three of us had been given about the same number of votes, no other candidate except myself was interested in recounting the ballots. My vote in Beckham County, my home county, in 1940 had been 1,898 while in 1941 it dropped to 1,419. This was not the first time in Beckham County that an election had been deliberately stolen.

There is not the least doubt in my mind, or in the minds of my thousands of friends and supporters in the Seventh District and throughout the state, that the election was actually stolen. We could have shown that it was stolen, or otherwise I would not have put up $2,000 to have the votes recounted in eight of the counties. When I put up the money I said, "I know before hand that the State Election Board will not order a recount of the ballots, for its Democratic members are a part of the administration's political machine and bent on defeating me by fair means or foul." The State Election Board consisted of three members, one Republican, who voted for recounting the ballots, and two Democrats who voted against a recount. But in case this episode seems too strange to credit, or my case against my opponents too flimsy, or the whole affair too long ago to matter, I have grouped in the next chapter three extraordinary episodes of more recent vintage.

Chapter 21

Three Extraordinary Episodes

1. The Heitholt Bequest: 1938–1951

One day in 1938 an elderly man came to see me from Enid, Oklahoma. His name was Henry Heitholt. He was unable to urinate due to prostatic enlargement, and had been told he needed an operation. On examination, I discovered he had a very bad heart leak, and because of his advanced age, I advised against it and treated him for two weeks in the hospital with remarkable benefit.

On leaving the hospital he came to see me after paying his bill and said, "Doctor, I see many poor people and many poor farmers come here for treatment. I am sure they are not all able to pay for their hospitalization. If you will drive me home, I have $10,000 I do not need and will give to the hospital." Needless to say, to Enid we drove forthwith, and parked in front of the First National Bank. Mr. Heitholt led the way to the cashier's window and said, "Mr. Duerkson, give Dr. Shadid a check for $10,000." Mr. Duerkson turned pale and nervously wrote the check and handled it over.

Henry Duerkson was an employee of the bank who had gained the confidence of Mr. Heitholt to the extent of keeping his books and managing much of the estate. In fact, Mr. Heitholt roomed and boarded with the Duerksons during part of his time. Mr. Heitholt told me that Mr. Duerkson did not approve of his giving the ten thousand dollars to the hospital. Duerkson furthermore was to be the executor of the Heitholt estate.

Once, before the hospital was built, I had met Mr. Heitholt. I was looking for a loan and Oscar Ameringer, editor of *The American Guardian*, told me that a Socialist by the name of Henry Heitholt of Enid had struck it rich in oil and might lend me the money with which to build the coöperative hospital. I went to Enid and met Mr. Heitholt at the Lions Club. I told him what my mission was but he flatly refused. Later I learned that he was peeved at Mr. Ameringer, who had made some demands on him for donations.

Two years after his hospitalization, Mr. Heitholt again came to me with bladder obstruction as before and asked me to operate on him. I told him he might die on the table because of his heart condition, but he insisted that I operate regardless of risk. After a week or ten days of preoperative care, we operated with a successful result and an uneventful recovery. He was then 87 years of age.

Again, on leaving the hospital, he gave us ten thousand dollars and in appreciation of his benefactions the Board of Directors gave him a written statement agreeing that he could, as long as he lived, come to the hospital for examinations, treatment, and hospitalization, and when well, for room and board without compensation. This pleased Mr. Heitholt immensely, and thereafter until his death he came to us frequently for check-ups and other medical care.

Henry Heitholt was born in Germany in 1853, and landed in New York in 1873. He went west following his trade of woodworking, ironworking, and blacksmithing until he reached Millard, Nebraska, where he settled in 1876. In Millard, he became acquainted with Lavinia Mangold, whom he married at Omaha in 1882 when he was 29 years of age. She died in 1917 from tetanus, which resulted from a thorn injury received while tending her rose bushes. Their only surviving offspring, Harry, committed suicide in April 1925, by shooting himself after a quarrel with his father over the building of a fence.

The father of Lavinia Heitholt was Michael Mangold,

THREE EXTRAORDINARY EPISODES

who was the town banker and wealthiest citizen of Millard, Nebraska. Funds inherited as a bequest from Mr. Mangold had enabled Henry Heitholt to purchase 800 acres of land for $4.00 per acre around Pampa, Texas. This acreage was leased for minerals twice, for ten years each time, for thirty-five thousand dollars to the Cabot Company.

Mr. Heitholt was a frequent visitor at my home, and we became close friends. One day he had me drive him to his acreage around Pampa and showed me seven oil-producing wells on his property of 800 acres. I asked him why he did not have more oil wells drilled, to which he replied, "I don't know what to do with the money I have, so I decided to leave the oil in the ground for you to develop, for I have willed my estate to the hospital."

In 1941 Mr. Heitholt became ill on the streets of Enid and was rushed to a local hospital in Enid. He insisted on being taken to the Community Hospital at Elk City, but this was refused. When I learned of his illness, I went to see him. He told me that he had been requesting the hospital to move him to Elk City but without success. He told me he had been in the hospital a month and his bill was $1,500. "Now Doctor Shadid," said he, "don't leave Enid unless you take me with you."

I immediately called his doctor in an effort to put him in an ambulance and take him to Elk City. Soon thereafter Mr. Duerkson, the executor of his estate, Mr. James Howard Wilson (a member of the law firm of Wilson and Wilson, father and son, in whose custody was the will of Mr. Heitholt), and his physician, Dr. George T. Ross, came to the hospital and made every effort to hold Mr. Heitholt in Enid rather than see him go to Elk City. But I finally was able to comply with Mr. Heitholt's wish and removed him in an ambulance to Community Hospital in Elk City. A few days later he was visited by a tenant farmer of his who volunteered the information that as the ambulance drove away, Mr. Wilson remarked, "There goes our will."

This remark, coupled with the efforts made to hold Mr.

Heitholt in Enid, strengthened my suspicion of foul play with reference to Mr. Heitholt's will. Mr. Heitholt had told me on several occasions that he had willed his whole estate, less a few thousand dollars to near relatives, to the Community Hospital. Indeed, at one time, on the occasion of the annual meeting of the hospital association, he came before the meeting and publicly told the delegates that in addition to the $20,000 he had already given to the Community Hospital he had willed his estate to the hospital. I therefore told Mr. Heitholt of my suspicion and suggested that he send for a copy of his will from Wilson and Wilson, his attorneys at Enid.

"I will think it over," said Mr. Heitholt, "although I think everything will be all right as I have three witnesses to the will." Two days later Mr. Heitholt developed a severe chill and died August 5, 1941.

You can imagine my consternation when a will was read in court in Garfield County, Oklahoma, on October 4, 1941, which bequeathed the estate to the "Northern Oklahoma Co-operative Hospital Association," and provided that if, after two years, a coöperative hospital had not been built in Enid, then the estate should go to the coöperative Community Hospital Association at Elk City. I had never heard of the proposed coöperative hospital at Enid, and do not believe Mr. Heitholt had either, or he would naturally have mentioned it to me during our close friendship, and would probably have discussed any such idea with me frequently and thoroughly.

It developed that on January 5, 1939, two years prior to the death of Mr. Heitholt, Wilson and Wilson, his attorneys, had secured a charter from the State Capital for a "dummy" corporation, which they named "The Northern Oklahoma Co-operative Hospital Association." This corporation was formed by twelve men, and at the time of the opening of the will in court six of these men had moved away or died. The chairman of the twelve sponsors, Harve Topley, was a man hardly known in the community, and he later testified in

THREE EXTRAORDINARY EPISODES

court that he had never met Mr. Heitholt or knew him. I say a "dummy" corporation because Mr. Heitholt had never mentioned such a corporation, and no effort was ever made to publicize it or sell stock or membership in it. No office was named for the corporation and no place of meeting.

I went to see Mr. Henry Glasser, an attorney of Enid, to find out if there was something I could do about it. I assured Mr. Glasser that the will, except the signed last page, had been re-written to keep the funds and the estate with Mr. Duerkson and Wilson and Wilson.

"I am very sorry," said Mr. Glasser. "I can't take the case, for yesterday I wrote Governor Phillips and advised him that Mr. Heitholt lacked testamentary capacity at the time of making the will, and as he had no heirs, the estate should escheat to the State of Oklahoma." At Mr. Glasser's suggestion, we called Mr. W. J. Otjen, an attorney of Enid, who came to Mr. Glasser's office and was employed by me.

On August 2, 1943, I received a letter from Mr. Otjen telling me that Wilson and Wilson would assist me in getting a bequest of ten thousand dollars provided I withdrew from the case and assisted them in their efforts to get the state to dismiss its claim. In reply I wrote Mr. Otjen and told him that I had no personal claim on Mr. Heitholt's estate, and that I could not accept $10,000 as a settlement for the hospital, whereupon Mr. Otjen withdrew from representing the Community Hospital.

Subsequently, I hired Gomer Smith, the attorney in Oklahoma City who had previously defended me when an effort was made by the State Board of Medical Examiners to take away my license to practice medicine. After a period of time Mr. Smith came to Elk City to see me, and made me a proposition similar to that of Mr. Otjen, but I turned it down. Later on I employed Dudley, Duval, and Dudley, a law firm of Oklahoma City, without result other than the payment by us of fees and expense accounts.

This last will and testament touched off a legal battle in the courts of Garfield County which lasted ten years. As I have mentioned, the will was admitted to probate October 4, 1941, and immediately thereafter an appeal was taken by the State of Oklahoma seeking reversal of the will's being admitted to probate on the grounds that Henry Heitholt lacked testamentary capacity at the time of the execution of the will, and as he had died without heirs, claiming that the estate should escheat to the State of Oklahoma.

Upon trial in district court under Judge J. W. Bird, the state was overruled, but an appeal was taken to the State Supreme Court for failure to allow the state a reasonable time for the continuance of the trial. The decision by the district court was reversed January 5, 1943, by the Supreme Court for abuse of discretion by the trial court, in the failure to grant the state a reasonable time to prepare for trial.

The trial of the State vs. will of Henry Heitholt was then tried under Judge O. C. Wybrant, district judge, and judgment rendered February 7, 1945, which affirmed the testamentary capacity of the late Henry Heitholt, as questioned by the state, and the will was ordered to probate.

The State of Oklahoma then took appeal from Judge Wybrant to the Supreme Court, which was briefed and argued, and it was not until January 17, 1950, that the decision of Judge Wybrant was affirmed by the Supreme Court.

The State of Oklahoma having lost its claim upon the estate, there remained the litigation between Community Hospital and the "Northern Oklahoma Co-operative Hospital Association," the dummy corporation promoted by Wilson and Wilson, who had written the will of Henry Heitholt and had it in their possession.

About this time Harry Glasser, who for nine years had represented the State of Oklahoma against "The Northern Oklahoma Co-operative Hospital Association," came to the Community Hospital at Elk City and stated that according to the will of Henry Heitholt the estate, or the residue thereof, should go to the Community Hospital. In his brief to the Supreme Court, while representing the State of Oklahoma, Mr. Glasser had asserted that, if the state were not

THREE EXTRAORDINARY EPISODES

entitled to the estate, the residue should go to the Community Hospital at Elk City. After extended discussion with the hospital Board of Directors, Harry Glasser and his son Joe were employed to represent the Community Hospital. A contract was signed giving the Glassers $1,000 retainer fee plus 20 per cent of whatever proceeds accrued to the hospital and an additional $500 in the event that the case went to the Supreme Court. This contract was signed February 15, 1950.

The lawyers representing the "dummy" corporation known as "The Northern Oklahoma Co-operative Hospital Association" were Mr. Blumhagen of Watonga and Mr. Coldiron of Enid. Mr. Duerkson and Wilson and Wilson were, of course, fighting to keep the estate from being settled.

During this litigation, I testified that Henry Heitholt had told me many times, and the last time two days before his death, that he had willed his estate to Community Hospital, that he had so stated publicly before the annual meeting of the Community Hospital Association, and that in my judgment the will had been corrupted inasmuch as only the last sheet of the will was signed by Mr. Heitholt.

After many preliminary skirmishes in district court under Judge Musser, the attorneys for the estate, Wilson and Wilson, presented to the court a bill for $90,000 for attorneys' fee. Our attorneys immediately filed a petition to disallow, stating they were excessive. After many months of kicking around, Wilson and Wilson, who were aligned against us with the "dummy" corporation, approached our attorneys and said if we dropped our petition to disallow the Wilson claim, they would get out of the case entirely and show no favor to either side. With great reluctance and with practically no other choice we consented. The judge then allowed the $90,000 to the Wilsons.

After many sessions in district court, Judge Musser, who had allowed the $90,000 fee to Wilson and Wilson, handed the residue of the estate to the "dummy" corporation—The

Northern Oklahoma Co-operative Hospital Association. We immediately took an appeal to the superior court under the judgeship of Judge John F. Curran. Much more briefing and court work passed and on the tenth anniversary of the probating of the will, October 4, 1951, Judge Curran handed down his decision stating that the Northern Oklahoma Co-operative Hospital Association was neither functioning nor in existence and, reversing the opinion of Judge Musser, directing that the residue of the estate go to the Elk City Hospital.

A notice of appeal was immediately made by the "dummy" corporation to the State Supreme Court; and soon after this, talk of compromise came from all attorneys representing all sides.

It should be mentioned at this time that the most valuable asset of the Heitholt estate was the 800 acres of oil-producing land upon which the Cabot Company had a million-dollar carbon-black plant. In spite of the fact that the Cabot Company's lease was running out and that it would be very expensive to remove such a plant, Howard Wilson and Herman Duerkson sold the property for a fraction of its value to the Cabot Company without the knowledge of the litigants in the case. Furthermore the expense of litigation to date in paying attorneys' fees, expensive briefs, court costs, and so on had reduced the estate to about $175,000. We were fearful that an appeal to the Supreme Court would mean another ten years during which time the attorneys and executors of the will would exhaust the estate. Therefore when talk of compromise followed this appeal, we felt that we had no choice and agreed to the following statement.

Accounting of estate as follows: (after taxes)

Cash	$36,369.42
U.S. Bonds	20,952.00
U.S. Treasury bills	89,750.40

THREE EXTRAORDINARY EPISODES

Notes	12,937.75
Total	$160,00 9.57

Payment to lawyers and other litigants:

H. A. Duerkson	$1,050.00
Northern Oklahoma Co-op	22,500.00
McKeever & McKeever (attorneys with Glasser)	7,500.00
Hugh Conway	7,500.00
Henry Johnston	3,000.00
Glasser & Glasser	28,480.34
Will Wright (auditor)	1,205.45
Wade Thomasson, Cecil Buckler, & H. E. Schwartz	315.00
Total	$71,570.79
Balance left to Elk City Hospital	$88,438,78

I should mention that in the will left by Henry Heitholt he bequeathed $3,000 to the Mangold heirs, who were distant heirs of his first wife. A provision was included in the bequest, that in the event they contested the will this bequest was null and void. The Mangold heirs contested the will in 1941 during the first probate. The heirs were a man and woman—one had died by time of settlement, and Henry Johnston (former governor of Oklahoma) appeared for the other Mangold heir throughout the last year of the trial. To prevent him from appealing to a higher court—on a nuisance basis—the $3,000 settlement was paid directly to Johnston— we question whether the Mangold heir received any of this— the heir never made an appearance in court.

Milton Worrell was a tenant living on a farm owned by Mr. Heitholt. He was allied with the Community Hospital as a witness to the fact that one of the Wilsons made the remark, "There goes the will," when I departed with Mr. Heitholt from the Enid Hospital. As part of the payoff, the farm was given to Mr. Worrell by the Wilsons, to prevent his testifying in our favor.

Thus an estate forth well over half a million dollars in 1941 was looted by attorneys and their greedy fellow-conspirators, through forgery and bribery, until we were forced to settle for one-sixth of that amount after a ten-year battle.

2. The Draft as a Weapon: 1941–1945

After Pearl Harbor, a fine opportunity to close our hospital presented itself with the advent of the "Procurement and Assignment" service for physicians and dentists. The doctors, having been defeated in their ten years of conspiracy to close our hospital by fair means or foul, now decided that by drafting all doctors and personnel of military age at the Community Hospital, they could realize their purposes. The "Procurement and Assignment" committee of Beckham county, where our hospital is located, declared every man on our staff of military age to be available and reported their names to the state headquarters of selective service at Oklahoma City. Forthwith my son, Dr. Alex Shadid, volunteered his services, as did one of our two dentists, one laboratory technician, and our only druggist.

In the meantime, in order to keep my second son, the only key man of military age left us, I sat down and wrote the following letter to Dr. E. S. Kilpatrick, chairman of the Military Preparedness committee, in which I said:

> Dr. Fred is absolutely essential to the continuation of this hospital and if you persist in reporting him as available for military service you will have shown discrimination that is unjustified in the present circumstances. I, therefore, call upon you to reconsider your action and strike Dr. Fred Shadid's name from the list of availables.
>
> The office of Procurement and Assignment for Physicians in Washington, D.C., has laid down the principle

that the government does not wish to draft physicians who are essential in their present position to the delivery of medical care to the civil population. For this reason as medical director of the Coöperative Hospital, I request that Dr. Fred Shadid's name be removed from the list of those available for military service.

There is no doctor on our staff who has confined a single woman out of the one hundred who were confined last year except Dr. Alex Shadid and Dr. Fred Shadid. We see in our offices in the 'Out-Patient Clinic' from seventy to one hundred and fifty patients daily and Dr. Alexander used to see more patients than anyone else and most of these patients will now have to be seen by Dr. Fred Shadid.

My letter fell on deaf ears and the committee chairman did not condescend to reply. We appealed our case to the state committee only to be told shortly thereafter that the state committee unanimously declared Dr. Fred Shadid available. Soon thereafter the state chairman resigned his position and another doctor was appointed in his place who I thought was fair-minded. I paid this new chairman a personal visit and had a long consultation with him. He agreed to be absolutely impartial in the matter and to look into our dilemma. Instead of making the investigation himself he sent a committee of three doctors to investigate the availability of Dr. Fred Shadid. These three doctors were members of the state committee of Procurement and Assignment and had already declared Dr. Fred available. This committee made a report about us loaded with falsehoods and half truths.

We then appealed to the area chairman in Texas, who before even receiving my letter in rebuttal of the committee report declared Dr. Fred available. Finally, I went to Washington and laid the case of the Community Hospital before the national chairman of Procurement and Assignment, who promised to give the matter sympathetic consideration, only to write us later that the national committee found Dr. Fred available.

All these doctors of Procurement and Assignment are medical hierarchs. All are opposed to coöperative hospitals. Appeals from one hierarchical committee to another are useless. For one of them to stand out against their determination to close up the Community Hospital would be fatal.

We had one recourse left—to appeal to the President of the United States. The Board of Directors of the Community Hospital appealed to Mrs. Roosevelt, who directed us to General Hershey. In the meantime we circulated a petition to the President among people in southwestern Oklahoma and secured 13,000 signatures asking the President to intervene. This petition was sent to the national Farmers' Union office at Washington to be given the President as a last resort.

Meanwhile, I appealed to Senator Pepper of Florida, Senator LaFollette of Wisconsin, and Senator Elmer Thomas of Oklahoma and to the Manpower Commission headed by Paul McNutt. Soon thereafter, a Doctor Brooks, of the Public Health Service, a liaison officer between the Manpower Commission and Procurement and Assignment, came from Washington to investigate. Dr. Brooks made a careful investigation. He was fair and sympathetic and made a map of western Oklahoma showing the number of members of the hospital in each community and the number of doctors, if any, in those same communities, the number of patients, the number of obstetrical deliveries, and so forth, and took the map and report back to Washington with him. This, more than anything else, seemed to hinder the activities of Procurement and Assignment and to pour cold water on their machinations. Dr. Brooks was very fair because as an employee of the United States Public Health Service he was independent of the A.M.A. for between these two setups there has never been any love lost.

During all this time the local draft board refused to draft Dr. Fred as recommended by the local, state, and national Procurement and Assignment committees. One member of the local draft board, a crony of our chief medical enemy, was all set to draft him and used every trick to get the other two men to agree but these two were adamant despite threats, trickery, and all kinds of political pressure.

Early in 1945 an emissary from the office of the U.S. District Attorney appeared before the local draft board and told them that he was going to send me to the penitentiary for evading the draft of my son, Dr. Fred Shadid, but without avail. Still later, but before the war ended, F.B.I. men came to see me in an effort to investigate the availability of Dr. Fred Shadid; on their showing their credentials, I told them that the F.B.I. had more important business elsewhere and showed them the door.

Fortunately the two men on our local three-man draft board realized the serious consequences of closing our hospital at a time when many a community near by had no doctors at all, and stood out against the pressure of the P. and A. These two understood that the sudden withdrawal of medical care from 2,400 farm families who, together with those outside the coöperative, were sending us on the average of 500 patients a week, would be nothing short of a major catastrophe—a catastrophe to which the P. and A. was singularly oblivious.

3. Polio in Politics: 1949–1952

During February 1949 Carl Thompson of Clinton, Oklahoma, district representative for the National Foundation for Infantile Paralysis, called upon my son, Dr. Fred Shadid, who was then medical director of the Community Hospital, and asked him if he would set up a unit in the hospital for the care of poliomyelitis cases, and told him that in that event they would send him to Denver to take a course in its treatment and defray all of his expenses.

Dr. Fred agreed and went to Denver and took the course. On his return he called a meeting of the Hospital staff (physicians, nurses, and technicians) and delivered a lecture on the diagnosis and treatment of polio cases. Mr. Thompson was present at the meeting and was agreeably surprised, saying that although he had been in the work for many years he had never heard an abler or more instructive dissertation on the subject.

But it is one thing to satisfy a representative of the National Foundation for the Infantile Paralysis and quite another thing to please the county medical society, for they immediately called upon Mr. Thompson and told him that they would not send a single patient to the Community Hospital. And to make their boycott effective they got in touch with the Oklahoma State Commissioner for crippled children and objected to any recognition of the Community Hospital—which recognition was essential before the National Foundation for Infantile Paralysis would make available any money from the March of Dimes to the crippled children entering the Community Hospital with polio.

Soon thereafter Mr. Thompson and Dr. Robert J. Neville, a national representative of the foundation, called upon Dr. Fred and apologized for this complication, saying that before their funds could become available, the Community Hospital would have to be recognized by the State Commission for Crippled Children.

Now the Oklahoma commissioners had said they could not recognize the hospital unless the Beckham County Medical Society accepted our doctors' applications for membership.

But the Beckham County Medical Society had refused to accept our membership unless we adopted their prepayment plan (the Blue Shield) and discontinued our own. This we could not do, for that would do away with group practice and preventive medical services, abolish consumer control, and destroy the coöperative idea upon which the Community Hospital was founded.

So Dr. Fred bid Mr. Thompson and Dr. Neville goodbye, and the next morning called in the newspaper reporters and gave them the entire story. This was published and immediately public opinion was aroused. A group of women from various civic clubs called upon Dr. Fred, and the story was again related to them. Later, three women representing the civic council went over to Sayre to interview Dr. H. K. Speed, then president of the county medical society, and the interview which was published in the local papers was as follows:

> Mrs. Earnest Mobley, president of the civic council: What would be your attitude toward our having a polio isolation ward in Elk City?
> Doctor Speed: We would be against it and wouldn't let it happen.
> Mrs. Mobley: But why?
> Dr. Speed: It would need more supervision and trained men.
> Mrs. Mobley: Why does not the county society approve the Community Hospital?
> Dr. Speed: Because they are not recognized.
> Mrs. Mobley: By whom?
> Dr. Speed: By the county society.
> Mrs. Mobley: That is you, why don't you recognize them?
> Dr. Speed: If I were to tell you all these details I'd be sued for damages.
> Mrs. Mobley: If you tell the truth you can't be sued. You don't libel any one with the truth.
> Dr. Speed: If you were men, I would throw you out; I left the door open but you would not take the hint."

This published interview aroused the public to fever heat. At a called meeting of citizens, plans were formulated to start immediately a "March of Dollars" campaign to finance aid to polio victims at Community Hospital. At the same time a telegram to the Foundation in New York was sent by the county chairman for the polio drive, Mr. Bill Ansley, informing them of this plan, and stating that their next drive, as far as the Foundation was concerned, would be futile. A day went by, and Mr. Ansley received a telegram with apologies and sundry explanations for the misunderstanding and assurance that the Foundation would be glad to help polio victims. Again to the public belongs the victory.

Following upon the heels of this episode, the worst polio epidemic in Oklahoma history struck. The polio ward at Community Hospital was filled, as were other wards in the state. Ours being the only hospital in western Oklahoma equipped to care for polio cases, patients were brought to us from the whole southern and western part of Oklahoma. The hospital staff worked day and night caring for these patients. As I write, in 1952, the hospital has 90 polio cases.

Chapter 22

Happy Ending, for Oklahoma

1950–1952

After 20 years of bitter struggle with organized medicine our problems in obtaining needed personnel grew more difficult. Due to the growth of our membership and improvement of our facilities our business had increased tremendously. To carry our patient loads we needed to increase our clinic staff, and as we were still ostracised by "organized medicine," this needed personnel was hard to recruit.

It should be recalled that when a doctor cannot join his local county medical society he is:

1. Stigmatized as being unethical or a quack.
2. Refused malpractice insurance.
3. Refused admission to post-graduate courses in medicine and surgery.
4. Not allowed to attend clinical meetings of the Oklahoma state and district societies.
5. Not allowed to become a recognized specialist, for he is not allowed to take the necessary examination before his respective specialty board.
6. Denied consultation with fellow practitioners.

In addition to this, other personnel working at the hospital, such as X-ray and lab technicians, were equally ostracized and were not permitted to register with their respective agencies.

This situation became intolerable, and during the summer of 1950 our doctors resolved to settle this old standing problem one way or another. Legal advice told us to exhaust every means available to settle it through proper medical channels.

For years we had tried every honorable means to gain admission without avail. More than once we had submitted our applications, but they were never acted upon. The last report we had was to the effect that at a meeting of the society the president and one ex-president were in favor of admitting our doctors but that a majority were vehemently opposed, and that serious argument for and against us took place. Finally, when Dr. Fred again submitted the application for membership, the secretary of the society answered as follows:

Dr. Fred Shadid,
Elk City, Okla.

Dear Doctor:
   Herewith returned are your applications for membership in the B.C.M.S. (Beckham County Medical Society).
   Section 2 of the by-laws requires that the applications be endorsed by 2 members of the Beckham County Medical Society.
                              O. C. Standifer, M. D.
                              Secretary.

But as the majority in the county society were still opposed no doctor would endorse the petitions; Dr. Fred then wrote saying that the American Medical Association and the Cooperative Health Federation of America has agreed that any group of physicians practicing medicine in accordance with the 20 principles they set forth would be eligible for membership in the A.M.A.

To this communication he received the following reply:

Fred Shadid, M. D.
Elk City, Okla.

Dear Doctor,
This will acknowledge receipt of your letter. It will be taken up at the next meeting of the society.

Speaking frankly, but in no sense for the society, I would say that I would never vote for your admission to the society until you practice medicine like the rest of us and quit tying people up with contracts to have a certain doctor or group of doctors.

As you have found out any individual doctor can do with his vote pretty much as he pleases and any county society can admit or deny membership as it pleases and to hell with any higher authority. Is this frank enough?
O. C. Standifer, M. D.
Secretary, B.C.M.S.
but personal

To a letter from Dr. Fred, Dr. Standifer wrote as follows:

That it is the opinion of the individual members at the county society meetings: if the plan under which the doctors on the Community Hospital staff practice medicine were modified, so as to allow the subscribers to the plan to have free choice of physicians and hospital; then in that eventuality, it is the opinion of the individual doctors of the Beckham County Medical Society present at the particular meeting of the Beckham County Medical Society, that the individual doctors practicing on the Community Hospital staff would not have a great deal of trouble getting a member of the Beckham County Medical Society to endorse their individual applications for membership.

Who is Doctor O. C. Standifer? Dr. Standifer is the same doctor who, when I sought his coöperation, before organizing the coöperative hospital, said my plan was economically unsound and unworkable, and that he would be happy to meet its competition. He said nothing about the plan being contract medicine (because it is not) or being unethical. On the contrary, when he saw the Community Hospital succeeding, as told in a previous chapter, he organized the hospital with which he was connected, The Standifer Hospital, into a pseudo-coöperative hospital for personal gain, and threw all ethics to the wind.

At the same time that I was, he too was served a notice to appear before the State Board of Medical Examiners to show cause why his license to practice medicine should not be revoked. Immediately he dispatched an attorney to see the members of the State Board and beg them for mercy, promising to liquidate his pseudo-coöperative hospital.

Again, Dr. Fred had sent the following communication to the county medical society.

September 3, 1945
The Beckham County Medical Society,

Gentlemen:

When my father embarked on the project of the Coöperative Hospital, he meant to do so without injury to vested interests in hospitals existing at that time in Elk City, or to the general practitioners in the trade area of Elk City, Oklahoma.

He took the project in typewritten form to Dr. Tisdale, who promised to examine it and let him hear from him. But when two weeks passed with no word from the doctor, he took the matter up with Dr. O. C. Standifer and his father. The doctors rejected the plan as visionary, and Dr. O. C. Standifer said that they could meet the competition. The plan is outlined in one of the books he has written entitled "Principles of Coöperative Medicine." It is called the "ideal set-up," and you can read it on pages 84 to 89 of said book.

We are now willing to set up this plan and publish it and send it to our members as well as to all people living in the trade territory of Elk City, allowing all family doctors and hospitals in the area to participate on that basis if they so desire.

It is my sincere belief that, if the doctors and the hospitals would undertake the execution of this plan wholeheartedly, we could demonstrate to the profession throughout the United States that a program has been found which will bring medical and hospital care within the reach of the people, making obsolete the need for compulsory health insurance and state medicine. Under this program, we would be in a position to ask for state or local subsidy to cover people without means.

Of course, under this plan, there are some difficulties that must be ironed out and some adjustments to be made, but where there is a will there is a way.

I have given this matter considerable thought and this proposition is the best that I can think of. If it is not agreeable, then it is up to you to counter-proposition. We are willing to do any reasonable thing short of destroying the idea of coöperative medicine.

Our work at the Community Hospital is ethical in the highest degree and we feel that we are fully entitled to membership in the Beckham County Medical Society. The American Medical Association has receded from its former stand against pre-payment, and the Oklahoma State Medical Association has indorsed the system at a previous convention. The physicians in the Milwaukee Medical Center, Milwaukee, Wisconsin; in Group Health Association, Washington, D.C.; and other places like Los Angeles, California, have been admitted to their respective county medical societies, so your attitude toward us is no longer tenable and we hope that you will reconsider your action.

> Yours truly,
> *Fred V. Shadid*, M. D.

The reply to the foregoing communication was the same as before. Nothing would satisfy the county society doctors except "fee for service," and, so far as prepayment was concerned, it had to be the Blue Shield or no prepayment plan at all. In other words, we would have to destroy the coöperative idea in medicine, and sell the hospital to private enterprise.

What is the Blue Shield? Well, it is a prepayment plan sponsored by the A.M.A. (American Medical Association) for the purpose of thwarting Truman's Health Insurance Bill. It provides only *partial* protection against the cost of surgical operations and obstetrical cases. I say partial, because it reimburses the patient for only part of his surgical fee. For example, a Blue Shield subscriber is allowed $100 for an appendectomy although he may have to pay $150 to $250 for his operation. The Blue Shield allows $100 for a brain operation, yet the patient may be charged two to five hundred dollars for the operation. For a hysterectomy or a caesarean operation he is allowed $100 but may have to pay $250 or more to the surgeon.

Furthermore, though few surgical operations can be performed without previous examinations, laboratory services, or X-ray, under the Blue Shield nothing is allowed for diagnostic services. Nor is anything allowed for blood transfusion, plasma, or tissue examination, all standard procedures in surgical treatment.

The Blue Shield, as I said, was born out of the need to mollify Congress, and thus ward off National Health Insurance. It does not provide for preventive medical service, or group medical care by a group of physicians and specialists. And, because it is based on fee-for-service, the cost is constantly rising because too many physicians are continually chiseling and performing unnecessary examinations and surgical operations. Also, there is no consumer participation, although the plan is called a non-profit plan, and the "best that money can buy."

Failing to arrive at an amicable understanding with the

Beckham County Medical Society, appeal was made to the Oklahoma State Medical Association. A committee representing the association consisting of the secretary, legal counsel, and six physicians met with a committee representing the Community Hospital and made an effort at settlement, but without success. Nothing would satisfy the A.M.A. physicians except that which would destroy the coöperative idea in medicine.

As a last resort, it was decided to take our case to court, as the petition stipulates, "that upon the conclusion of the trial the plaintiff, the Farmers' Union Hospital Association, and the eleven individual plaintiffs in behalf of the total membership, have and receive from the defendants, jointly and severally, and that the defendants pay to the plaintiffs, as compensation for the damage sustained as a direct result of the acts and things done by the defendants in violation of the anti-trust laws of the State of Oklahoma, and of the common law of the State of Oklahoma against conspiracy in restraint of trade a minimum sum of $100,000 and that said damage, according to law, be trebled, and as trebled the damage be assessed in the sum of three hundred thousand dollars."

The petition, the most brilliant in medico-legal history, was written by William H. Hamilton, a member of the firm of Arnold, Fortas, and Porter. Thurman Arnold is a fight-loving westerner who has one of the best legal minds in the country. Within five years, as assistant attorney-general in charge of the Anti-Trust Division of the Justice Department, he filed 230 suits against alleged conspiracies in restraint of trade—more suits than had been filed in the entire previous history of the Sherman Act.

William Hamilton, who took charge of our litigation, was for 25 years a Yale law professor. I had had lunch with Mr. Hamilton in New York some ten years previously, at which time he told me that we could successfully sue the Beckham County Medical Society for damages, and compel them to accept our doctors as members of that organization. Mr.

Hamilton was a member of the committee on the cost of medical care and in his dissenting opinion showed a very profound knowledge of the medical situation. An abler counsel to take charge of our case can hardly be imagined. We were indeed fortunate to secure his services. His brief is a historic document.

Our suit was filed in August of 1950. The first move of the defendants was a motion to "Quash," which meant that we did not legally serve the defendants with summonses as the law requires, Later they asked for additional time to file pleadings in the case. Afterwards they filed a "motion to make more definite and certain to strike." Still later they filed an application to disqualify W. P. Keen, the district judge, on the pretext that he was biased and prejudiced in favor of Community Hospital, and friendly towards Dr. Michael Shadid—all these and other delaying tactics.

The Oklahoma State Medical Association was backing the Beckham County Medical Society in its defense. A member of the House of Delegates of the state association said that "because the county society is in difficulty and fighting for principles we believe in, the state association will give its moral and financial support to the Beckham County Medical Society." And, at a meeting of the Council of the Oklahoma State Medical Association, Doctor McHenry, president of the state association, made a motion as follows:

> Moved that the house of delegates approve the employment of the law firm of Keaton, Wells, Johnston, and Lytle to defend the law suit of the Beckham County Society with the instructions that the Oklahoma State Medical Association pay the legal fees and expenses of this firm, and with the understanding that the members of the county society pay the fees and expenses of their local attorneys and the court costs incident to the defense of the suit. IT IS UNDERSTOOD THAT THE OKLAHOMA STATE MEDICAL ASSOCIATION ASSUMES NO RESPONSIBILITY FOR PAYMENT OF ANY JUDGMENT WHICH MIGHT BE REN-

DERED. Motion seconded by Forest Etter, M. D., Bartlesville. Motion Carried.

While our litigation was pending, two other consumer coöperative plans carried their fight to the courts. These court cases raised the same basic legal question that our law suit raised:

1. Do lay people have the right (a) to organize plans for prepaying their physicians' services, and (b) to make financial arrangements with physicians of their choice to furnish these services?
2. Do medical societies have the right to block such plans in the name of "medical ethics"?

The first case was that of a coöperative hospital association I had helped to organize some years back—Group Health Coöperative of Puget Sound at Seattle, Washington. The medical society had been charged with excluding Group Health staff physicians from the use of local hospitals. The Supreme Court of the State of Washington, in November 1951, reversed an order of the lower court, and found "reason to believe that the purpose of the society in restraining competition extends to the ultimate extermination of all contract practice by the coöperative."

The society had declared that the conduct of the physicians of the staff of the coöperative was "unethical"; they could therefore not be admitted to membership in the medical society. Non-membership in the society meant exclusion from the staffs of all local hospitals. Moreover, physicians currently members of the society who consulted with any Group Health staff doctor regarding a patient of the coöperative would be deemed guilty of "unethical" conduct.

The court's decision held that the medical society used the word "unethical" in a special and abnormal sense: to indicate, not lack of professional morality, but mere nonconformity with the Society's economic policy of opposing the coöperative's health insurance plan. In the words of the court: "the exclusion of appellant physicians from the staff of hospital upon the sole ground that they are practicing contract medicine, is unreasonable, arbitrary, capricious, and discriminatory."

In the course of the testimony physicians on the staff of the Group Health coöperative explained some of the advantages they had found in group practice under contract with the coöperatives:

> Physicians are "enabled to give better service under the coöperative's group prepayment plan than is usually possible where doctors carry on separate practice: increased opportunities for, and convenience in, effectuating referral of patients to other doctors to take advantage of various specialties." Staff members have "access to more and better equipment and laboratory facilities; improved quality of service because of constant surveillance of other members of the staff; opportunities for consultation, staff conferences, refresher courses, and post-graduate studies."
>
> Staff doctors have the advantage of "better organization of time as, for example, the rotation of emergency night calls service; greater incentive to give patients proper treatment; security of professional income regardless of daily patient load; and disassociation of the business aspects of the service, so that the doctors may devote themselves entirely to professional matters."

In the second case, in March, 1952, a Superior Court of the State of California upheld charges made by the Complete Service Bureau (a group-practice prepayment plan) that the San Diego Medical Society had conspired to coerce the doctors on the Bureau's staff to desist from continuing to serve the Bureau. The medical society had claimed that the thriving Bureau was a corporation illegally engaged in the practice of medicine. In refutation of this accusation, the judge said that the object of group health plans is:

> to provide a low-cost medical care to their membership without profit to any agency. The fact that the California Physicians' Service (an insurance plan wholly owned and controlled by the medical society) is subject to control by doctor members, and that Complete Service Bureau is subject to control by patient members, does not operate to make the one a lawfully conducted organization and the other unlawful.

Concerning the medical society's accusation that it was "unethical" for the Bureau to solicit members, the judge ruled: "There is nothing illegal or unethical in soliciting members to join an organization which will provide them with a medical service plan. This has been the practice for years, and has had the tacit approval of the public, including public officials and the medical profession."

Other significant statements by the court in this case were:

> "The fact that Complete Service Bureau and other non-profit corporations offering a medical service plan have drawn and are sustaining members numbering in the thousands is an indication of the favorable reaction toward them."

> "The reality of the whole thing is that these voluntary organizations are here; they are part of our times, and it may be, as some witnesses think, that they are the answer to socialized medicine."

> "Group practice may siphon off some of the fees which otherwise would go to the individual practitioner, but there are many who have a contrary opinion of this. They hold that group practice will be beneficial to the profession as a whole as well as to the public. The increased interest in health and medical service would have the natural reaction of bringing many to the

individual practitioner who otherwise might be prone to defer their visits to a doctor's office."

Both the Puget Sound and the San Diego cases covered similar issues. The San Diego decision explicitly affirms the right of consumers of medical services to form an organization for prepayment purposes and to make contracts with doctors of their choice. The Puget Sound case denies the right of the medical society to discipline doctors on grounds which while called "ethical" by the society are actually economic—such as objection to competition.

These two current cases convinced the defending lawyers that their defense was hopeless, and the best they could do was to settle out of court with a face-saving device in the form of a contract in which the Community Hospital agreed to certain propositions.

This was done and settlement out of court was effected; our entire medical staff was admitted to membership, and this was heralded as a "great red-letter day for western Oklahoma."

Did this contract touch upon any of the issues involved in the law suit? Not at all. We still publish our monthly bulletin; our doctors are still on a salary, not on a fee basis; we still have our own prepayment plan; we are still a coöperative association; our Board of Directors is elected by the members and both the medical director and the business manager are responsible to them. Our constitution and by-laws are still as they were, a coöperative constitution and standard coöp by-laws. The society doctors were given the privilege of using our hospital, which they previously had had. Our hospital had always been an open-staff hospital; that is all non-staff doctors had the privilege of caring for their patients in the Community Hospital without any distinction, and, in fact, a few such doctors had been taking advantage of that privilege for years.

As previously stated the "contract" was a device to save face. There were many physicians in the Oklahoma State

HAPPY ENDING, FOR OKLAHOMA

Medical Association who were opposed to supporting the Beckham Medical Society. They had to be mollified. The State Medical Journal said the suit cost the state association $12,575.49 and "that it is the feeling of the Council that this matter should be a closed chapter in the history of medicine in Oklahoma and that no further comment should be made."

At a recent meeting of the Beckham County Medical Society, December 12, 1952, Dr. M. J. Sugarman, medical director of the Community Hospital, was elected vice-president of the society and Dr. Fred Shadid was elected a member of the Board of Censors.

When the news of the settlement was announced in the press, many forward-looking leaders in the Oklahoma State Medical Association wrote or telephoned their congratulations. In addition, many leaders in the coöperative movement in the United States wrote or wired congratulations.

With this complete vindication, we felt that the Oklahoma phase of our crusade for coöperative medicine could be considered won, and I decided to concentrate on wider horizons, where I had long been engaged in spreading my views across the nation.

Part Four

Horizons in Coöperative Medicine

Chapter 23

Coöperative Medicine Across America

During the years I was battling the medical hierarchy for the right to provide medical care in Oklahoma on a coöperative basis, I naturally kept constant watch on the progress of similar plans elsewhere, and their struggles against the A.M.A. octopus and its political stooges, while the public was duped by its pervasive propaganda, calling every truly coöperative medical plan "unethical," with a totalitarian-style corruption of the true meaning of the word, and a totalitarian disregard for facts and for honorable methods of controversy.

Unfortunately my own experience with organized medicine is not unique. Other individuals and groups trying to meet the medical needs of our time met the same sort of unscrupulous opposition from the would-be medical monopolies. The doctors of the Ross-Loos Clinic in Los Angeles, the medical group of the Milwaukee Medical Center, the medical group of Trinity Hospital in Little Rock, Arkansas, and the medical staff of Group Health Association in Washington, D.C., all felt the heavy hand of organized medicine and were expelled from their local medical societies for offering medical care on a prepayment basis. The medical oligarchs were determined to nip in the bud any form of medical practice, no matter how good and how effective, that had the possibilities of reducing their income, or changing the system they found so remunerative and power-yielding.

Michael A. Shadid, M.D.

In 1936, I spoke at the annual meeting of the Co-op League of the United States at Columbus, Ohio. In my address I suggested the establishing of a bureau of coöperative medicine. Subsequently, in 1937, the Bureau of Coöperative Medicine was organized with Dr. James Peter Warbasse, dean of American coöperators, as chairman and Dr. Kingsley Roberts as medical director.

From the beginning the Bureau adopted a conciliatory attitude toward the American Medical Association, of which, incidentally, Dr. Warbasse and Dr. Roberts are both members in good standing. The first plank in the Bureau's platform reads as follows:

> We believe that, to justify itself, any departure from the existing medical economic system must do two things at the same time. It must demonstrate a system whereby those who wish can budget their complete medical costs, and at the same time provide a method whereby the doctors concerned can practice better medicine.

Despite their conciliatory approach and despite repeated conferences with leading representatives of the A.M.A., the 1937 report of the Bureau of Medical Economics of the American Medical Association had this to say about the most comprehensive of the six plans projected by the Bureau of Coöperative Medicine:

> This proposal would introduce a type of medical practice only slightly different from club practice and voluntary insurance. There is nothing essentially "coöperative" about it. It seems safe to assume that the introduction of such a scheme would tend to encourage the spread of other schemes strikingly similar to the "club practice" which filled England prior to 1911.

In his authoritative volume, "Voluntary Medical Care Insurance in the United States," Dr. Franz Goldman, associate professor of medical care at Harvard School of Public Health, wrote:

> Actually all of the physicians who in the thirties assumed the leadership in organizing group practice plans were punished for their action. They were expelled from their medical society and consequently lost the hospital privilege, teaching appointments, opportunity for consultation, the right to accreditation by specialty boards, and the possibility of taking out malpractice insurance policies or obtaining malpractice defense without great cost. Their hospitals were removed from the list of hospitals registered by the American Medical Association.

How true this indictment was may be proved by citing a few prominent examples of such persecution.

Early in 1929, the employees of the Los Angeles Department of Water and Power approached Doctors Ross and Loos, who were running a private and highly successful clinic, and asked them to work out a group medical plan for the department employees. Doctors Ross and Loos arranged a two-dollar-a-month-per-person plan of medical care to cover medical and surgical work, medicines, and drugs, and up to ninety days of hospitalization. The plan worked out well, and by the end of the first year, the group had a staff of eight doctors and a membership of almost four thousand subscribers.

In its early stages the Ross-Loos medical group went unnoticed by the Los Angeles County Medical Society, but once its success was apparent, Doctors Ross and Loos were summarily expelled from the county society for "unethical conduct." They appealed to the California Medical Association, which upheld the county group. Then Doctors Ross and Loos went directly to the Council of the American Medical

Association and obtained their reinstatement on the grounds that they had not had a fair trial. It must be remembered, of course, that this clinic is privately owned by the physicians who operate it. Since that time the group has been allowed to continue, but it has been hampered by the A.M.A. whenever it has tried to obtain doctors who lived in other states. No doctor entering California to join the Ross-Loos group is eligible to join the A.M.A. and as a result, he cannot hospitalize patients in Los Angeles hospitals, which are closed-staff organizations.

Two years later, however, the A.M.A.'s action was harsher when seven doctors in Little Rock, Arkansas, worked out a group medical plan to give low-cost care. The doctors incorporated their Trinity Hospital as a proprietary hospital under the laws of Arkansas and set in operation a plan to give almost complete medical care, and up to six weeks hospitalization, at a basic rate of two dollars per person per month. Starting in 1931, when the depression was at is worst, the Trinity Hospital in four years built up its membership to 1,550 subscribers, with an additional 1,878 patients in the families of the subscribers. But in the process, all the doctors were forced to resign their membership in the A.M.A. because of the protest of the local medical society.

One of the bitterest fights between the A.M.A. and a privately owned group occurred in 1936 when the Milwaukee Medical Center was asked to work out a low-cost medical plan for the employees of the International Harvester Company. Soon there was a staff of seven doctors, a membership of twenty-five hundred, which with dependents meant a total of seven thousand five hundred patients. Medical care was furnished to members—and is today—at a cost of three dollars a month per family, with hospitalization extra. The initial attack by the county medical society was an elaborate charge that the Milwaukee Medical Center was trying to circumvent recently passed legislation stipulating that only county medical societies could practice contract medicine. In addition, it accused the Medical Center of "conduct tending to defeat the purpose of the county society," "solicitation and advertising," and "contract practice contrary to sound public policy." The case was taken to the council of the A.M.A. and after ten months the council upheld the local society. Meanwhile, other tactics had been adopted forcing one Milwaukee hospital after another to withdraw the use of its facilities from the Medical Center. When there remained only two hospitals to which the Center's members could be admitted, the Milwaukee Trades Council stepped in, raising the issue of "free choice of hospitals by union members of the Center." It also announced that the union would boycott the Community Chest, which subsidizes the hospitals from publicly subscribed funds, unless the Medical Center doctors were allowed staff privileges.

I have saved for the last a group that has been one of the most successful and has certainly become the most widely known of medical coöperatives because of the federal government's action in its behalf against the American Medical Association. The Group Health Association of Washington, D.C., was organized for employees of the Home Owners' Loan Corporation and for other government employees.

The Washington group has had a lively history. It had scarcely filed its incorporation papers when the American Medical Association instituted the most vigorous drive of its career. Its representatives poured into the national capital with advice for the Medical Society of the District of Columbia, and in short time doctors who were contemplating joining the group were given dire warning and the directors of local hospitals were advised not to coöperate with the Group Health Association.

As a result, the struggling group encountered infinite difficulty in hospitalizing its cases; one patient, according to a Group Health Association official, had just been given a morphine injection preparatory to an appendectomy when the hospital suddenly refused the use of its facilities and ordered the immediate removal of the patient. When the association encountered this sort of treatment, it asked for a

Congressional investigation of both the Medical Society of the District of Columbia and the American Medical Association. The A.M.A. countered immediately with a resolution urging an investigation of the Group Health Association.

This was the situation when I visited the board of trustees of the Group Health Association in Washington in April of 1938. I urged them to build their own hospital as the solution to their chief problem, and they took the matter under consideration at once.

On August 1, 1938, the United States Department of Justice charged that the American Medical Association, and its affiliate the District of Columbia Medical Society, had violated the anti-trust act by trying to prevent the Group Health Association of Washington from functioning. The accusation was made by Thurman Arnold, Assistant Attorney General, who said that the evidence would be presented to a grand jury which would seek to fix the responsibility and punish the offenders. Meanwhile, Mr. Arnold urged the A.M.A. doctors to mend their ways so that the affair could be settled without court action.

America sat up and took notice. It was one thing to bring anti-trust action against oil companies or meat packers, but quite another to do so against the august medical profession! The august medical profession, in the persons of the heads of the American Medical Association, was no less surprised. It fumed from its Chicago headquarters: "Apparently it remains to be determined whether or not the federal administration can use the laws and courts to mould the people of the United States to its belief in every phase of life and living, or whether or not fundamental principles of common justice which have prevailed in the past are to be relegated to the limbo of forgotten things."

That was certainly a typical big business reply with the anguished note of "regimentation" in every syllable. It announced the A.M.A.'s determination to fight in what may well prove the most important battle of its career, for the evidence presented by the Department of Justice and Mr.

Arnold was damning. I should like to quote from his findings at some length, because they constitute one of the most serious condemnations of the A.M.A. on record.

As examples of the restraint of trade undertaken by the medical society, the Department of Justice stated that one of the Group Health Association doctors had been expelled from the society and proceedings against another were under way. One Washington specialist faced expulsion because he had consulted with a Group Health doctor.

On hospitalization, Mr. Arnold said:

"The close relationship existing between the medical society and the principal hospitals of Washington has resulted in denial to Group Health Association physicians of access to hospitals' facilities. Not even in emergency cases have these doctors been allowed to attend their patients." The implications of such terrorism were serious, according to the indictment, because "the illegal activities of organized medicine in this instance are typical of what has occurred in other cities throughout the country whenever coöperative health groups have been formed."

The situation was made the more serious because "the medical profession has not been successful in furnishing adequate medical care to all the American people at a cost that they can afford to pay." Mr. Arnold did not blame the doctors for this condition; rather he said the situation was "the result of the low incomes of a large part of the community on the one hand, and of the increasing cost of adequate medical treatment on the other."

Drawing on government statistics, Mr. Arnold pointed out that there were 40 million Americans whose annual incomes were less than $800, and that these people frequently go without medical care:

> Infant mortality is five times higher in families with less than $500 a year than it is in families with $3,000 or more a year. Acute illness of all kinds increases as one goes down the income scale. Chronic illnesses are

seventy per cent more prevalent in relief families; non-relief families of less than $1,000 income have twice the illness disability of families of more than $1,000.

Then Mr. Arnold cited one of the strongest arguments for coöperative health associations:

> The incidence of serious illness is extremely uneven among persons of the same income. That is the reason advanced for coöperative methods of payment for medical care; by spreading the cost over the whole membership, these methods provide adequate service to all at the cost of a moderate and uniform charge to each. This type of organization is already familiar in dealing with hospital charges, and has proved highly successful. Group hospital plans on a coöperative basis are in force in over sixty cities, and cover more than 1,500,000 subscribers.

This did not necessarily imply an endorsement of coöperatives by the Department of Justice. The department, "simply takes the position that monopoly practices should not be employed to prevent what may be illuminating experience in this field."

Then Mr. Arnold closed with what is a fitting Magna Carta for the profession:

> No combination or conspiracy can be allowed to limit a doctor's freedom to arrange his practice as he chooses so long as by therapeutic standards his methods are approved and do not violate the law. Organized medicine should not be allowed to extend its necessary and proper control over standards having to do with the science and art of medicine to include control over methods of payments for service involving the economic freedom and the welfare of consumers and the legal rights of individual doctors.

Since the American Medical Association showed no signs of mending its ways, a grand jury was called in Washington to investigate it not only in the case of the Group Health Association, but also in the cases of all similar groups throughout the United States. Along with other physicians, I was summoned to Washington to testify before the grand jury on November 28, 1938. I arrived ahead of time, and had an excellent shoptalk session with colleagues from all over the country; Dr. Loos, of the Ross-Loos Clinic of Los Angeles; Dr. Stevenson of San Diego; Dr. Ogden of Little Rock, and many others.

The testimony we gave before the grand jury, with that given by the Group Health Association physicians, was sufficient to cause the grand jury to return indictments against the American Medical Association, the Medical Society of the District of Columbia, the Washington Academy of Surgery, and their officials on December 12, 1938.

That same year the Department of Justice brought a criminal suit against the American Medical Association, the District of Columbia Medical Society, two other local medical societies, and eighteen individual doctors prominent in one or more of these organizations. The district court convicted and fined the District of Columbia Medical Society and the American Medical Association. The other defendants were acquitted. After their conviction, the case was appealed by the defendants to the Supreme Court.

The unanimous decision handed down by the United States Court of Appeals for the District of Columbia is most revealing in its explanation of the economic issues involved in the Group Health Association and similar cases.

Said the Court:

> The situation which confronts appellants (A.M.A., etc.) and which they have sought to control, is not confined to the medical profession alone. Profound changes in social and economic conditions have forced members of all professional groups to make readjust-

ments. The facts that these changes may result even in depriving professional people of opportunities formerly open to them does not justify or excuse their use of criminal methods to prevent changes or to destroy new institutions. Lawyers too have seen, during recent decades, large scale change in their professional work. There was a time when lawyers worked entirely on fee or retainer in particular cases and controversies; now many of them are salaried employees on the staffs of large corporate industrial and financial organizations. . . .

There are some who regret and some who resent these changes. Over the years, as individuals and as members of professional associations, they have labored to prevent or minimize them. But they would not suggest that criminal conduct, as individuals or associations, would be proper for such a purpose.

Professions exist because the people believe they will be better served by licensing especially prepared experts to minister to their needs. The licensed monopolies which professions enjoy constitute, in themselves, severe restraints upon competition. But they are restraints which depend upon capacity and training, not special privilege. Neither do they justify concerted criminal action to prevent the people from developing new methods of serving their needs. There is sufficient historical evidence of professional inadequacy to justify occasional popular protests. . . . The people give the privilege of professional monopoly and the people may take it away.

In some instances professional groups have been charged by legislative fiat with powers and duties concerning professional education, licensure, discipline, removal of licensees from practice, and other related subjects. In such cases they act as agencies of government. Although some similar delegations of power have been made to the organized medical profession, there is no evidence of delegation of power to appellants, sufficient to authorize the conduct for which they have been convicted. In the absence thereof, professional groups must abide by the general laws just as scrupulously as any private citizen or private corporation. It is in this setting that appellants were permitted to organize, to establish standards of professional conduct, to effect agreements for self-discipline and control. There is a very real difference between the use of such self-discipline and an effort upon the part of such associations to destroy competing professional or business groups or organizations.

Except for their size, their prestige, and their otherwise commendable activities, their conduct in the present case differs not at all from that of any other extra-governmental agency which assumes power to challenge wrongdoing by taking the laws into its own hands.

Once I was off the witness stand, I remained in Washington a few days longer conferring with the doctors of Group Health Association, on one occasion addressing the employees of the Department of Agriculture at a meeting attended by the Under-Secretary and other officials of the department.

In order to illuminate the methods believed to have been employed since 1938 by organized medicine in destroying consumer plans, I may mention the fight waged against the Complete Service Bureau of San Diego. Some of these alleged methods are:

The medical society during the year 1947, and since, has attempted to poison the minds of the public against non-members of the society. It does this by publishing paid advertisements in the current editions of the San Diego telephone directory designating the members of the San Diego Medical Society among the physicians listed in the directory. The advertisement contains statements which seek to give the impression that non-members of the society are not qualified to practice medicine, do not possess professional qualifications and moral character, and do not conform to standards insuring the highest possible quality of service to the public.

"Furthermore," read the charges, "a medical-society-sponsored whispering campaign against the bureau has been in progress since 1947. The society members, nurses, employees, and members of their families frequently cause to circulate belittling and derogatory remarks about nonmembers, referring to them as quacks and their group as 'outfits' and the prepaid medical plan as a 'scheme.' "

Organized medicine does not base its objection to group practice and coöperative medicine on any evidence of professional or economic failure; on the contrary they oppose group practice because it has been successful and they fear change. Those who dominate the policies of organized medicine and who control it, constitute about 5 per cent of the doctors. They are the top-notch specialists who desire large incomes and who refuse to join groups of physicians in team work for fear their income will be materially reduced. In other words, profits come before professional duty. They aim to maintain their position in disregard of their relation to society. They are long on "professional ethics" but fall very short on applying it. They are fighting to perpetuate a vested interest. But the decision as to whether or not group practice shall supersede individual practice is not altogether the exclusive prerogative of the profession. The problem has economic and social implications as well as technical. In the long run the question will be decided by the public, for after all it is the public and not the profession that is most vitally concerned. No groups in the community should have a right which the public is bound to respect if they can be shown to be opposed to the public interest. American medicine has yet to discover the consumer—the public.

Its belated, stumbling, half-hearted approach to doing so occupied my full attention from 1946 to 1949.

Chapter 24

The Co-operative Health Federation of America

As a result of the fight made by organized medicine, letters poured into the Community Hospital from all over the nation and world asking about our plans, followed by requests that I go over the country and give lectures on our plan of service and organizational methods. Between 1938 and 1946 I lectured in nearly all the northern and western states. I also made extensive speaking tours in Texas and in Saskatchewan, Canada. These efforts resulted in the organization of similar coöperative health societies.

In 1946, through George W. Jacobson of Group Health Mutual of St. Paul, Minnesota, a call was sent to a list of coöperative health societies for a conference at Two Harbors, Minnesota. At this meeting the "Co-operative Health Federation of America" was organized, and over my objection, I was elected its first president.

The conference was attended by nearly 200 persons, representing 24 plans for solving medical and health problems coöperatively, which embraced some 200,000 persons. There were 50 official delegates and 7 fraternal delegates representing 17 states, Hawaii, Ceylon, and, in Canada, Saskatoon, Regina, Melfort, Winnipeg, and Nova Scotia. Here for the first time representatives from consumer-operated health plans with different approaches and methods of operation came together for mutual counsel and united effort. They were looking for improved ways of providing better and less expensive medical care for themselves through group action.

There were many outstanding speakers present. Among them was the inimitable Dr. M. M. Coady, head of the extension division of St. Francis Xavier University at Antigonish, Nova Scotia. Papers were presented on different phases of medical and hospital services. The following were elected to the first Board of Directors of CHFA:

Dr. Michael Shadid, president, Community Health Center, Elk City, Okla.

George W. Jacobson, secretary, Group Health Mutual, Inc., St. Paul, Minn.

Ludwig Anderson, National Co-ops, Inc., Chicago, Ill.
Cecil Crews, Consumers Co-operative Assn., Kansas City, Mo.

Dr. Elmer Richman, Labor Health Institute, St. Louis, Mo.

Winslow Carlton, Group Health Cooperative, Inc., New York, N.Y.

Harry Becker, Group Health Assn., Washington, D.C.
Addison Shoudy, Puget Sound Co-op Assn., Seattle, Wash.

James L. Monroe, Hale County Co-op Hospital, Hale Center, Texas.

E. J. Loehr, Saskatoon Mutual Medical and Hospital Plan, Saskatoon, Canada.

Charles Wilkinson, Community Health Center, Two Harbors, Minn.

The following six advisory incorporators from sympathetic organizations were given a vote on standing committees:

Nelson Cruikshank, Director of Social Insurance Activities for the A. F. of L., Washington, D.C.

James Carey, Secretary-Treasurer of the C.I.O., Washington, D.C.

Gladys Edwards, Farmers Educational and Coöperative Union of America, Denver, Colo.

Harry Culbreth, Ohio Farm Bureau Federation, Columbus, Ohio.

Dr. Dean Clark, Medical Director of the Health Insurance Plan of Greater New York, New York, N.Y.

Dr. John V. Lawrence, Group Health Assn., St. Louis, Mo.

The CHFA stands for five basic principles whose application to the health problems of the people will in its opinion bring them the greatest benefits. These principles are:

1. Prepayment—budgeting the cost of medical care.
2. Comprehensive medical and health care—preventive and curative.
3. Group medical practice.
4. Ownership and management of facilities by prepayment members.
5. No interference by laymen with the professional practice of medicine by those licensed so to do.

According to its articles of incorporation and bylaws the program and objective of CHFA are as follows:

1. To bring to all the people the advantages of the great benefits of modern medical science.
2. To represent the consumers' interests in all matters pertaining to the distribution of health and medical care.
3. To set standards for the organization and operation of consumer-sponsored health plans.
4. To help new groups to organize for the supplying of their health needs with the facilities and services necessary.
5. To carry on an intensive program of health education among the people
6. To secure and maintain the legal right of the people to organize their own health plans and to work with their doctors in their development.

As president of the Federation, I felt it my duty to devote my full time to building it up by lecturing to various groups over the country and organizing new consumer health coöperatives. To be free to do so, I resigned my position with the Community Hospital. My son, Dr. Fred Shadid, who had been with me for five years and who had shown considerable business and professional ability, was chosen to succeed me as medical director.

A year later, September 6 and 7, 1947, the annual meeting of the Federation was held at Elk City. During the year consumer health plans had expanded to include no less than 35 regular and associate members. Regular members included many of the best consumer plans and our associated members included regional coöps and labor and farm organizations, from the Atlantic to the Pacific and from Canada to Texas.

Some are rural coöperative hospitals and clinics serving sparsely settled agricultural counties on the Great Plains. Some are group health plans ministering to the needs of the people of some of the largest of our cities. Some of the member plans are insurance plans; other provide comprehensive direct health services to their members; still others combine both the insurance and the direct service methods.

Taken all together the member plans of CHFA represent the progress of a great movement—a movement among the free people of America—a movement to pool their resources and thus to bring to their families the benefits of modern medical science which otherwise would be beyond their financial reach.

During the first year of its existence CHFA engaged in the following activities:

1. Organizational mechanism and structure was agreed upon.
2. Monthly information news on health plans was published.

3. Published "Health for Millions" and many leaflets and reprints describing consumer plans. Regular news column on health established in many coöp farm and labor papers.
4. Set up special functional committees in field of professional and personnel services—education and public relations, labor, farm, and coöp contract committees, committees on legislation work, and on architecture. Through the voluntary services of these committees a tremendous amount of the ground work was laid and important conferences held.
5. CHFA assisted in organizational work on numerous plans. Throughout the year CHFA was in contact with such groups in 43 communities.
6. Legal communities of CHFA aided the Wisconsin Association of Co-operatives which spearheaded a movement in obtaining passage of a Co-op Health Enabling Act in Wisconsin and prepared a legislative manual. Testimony was given in behalf of consumer plans at hearing in Washington, D.C.
7. CHFA participated in schools and conferences with labor and farm groups.
8. A Speakers' Bureau was established and a clearing house for personnel was started.

"Meanwhile," to quote a CHFA report, "throughout the nation, CHFA's first year found some 35 new health coöperative groups forming. It found CHFA invited to participate in the Rural Health Conference of the A.M.A. And in the Pacific Northwest a pattern of health-for-the-people took shape under leadership of Group Health Co-operative of Puget Sound. . . ."

CHFA, by the time of its first birthday, found itself an organization respected in some quarters, feared in others, out of all proportion to its size and financial strength.

The organizing of the Co-operative Health Federation of America seemed to alert organized medicine to renewed efforts to check the growth of coöperative health associations. As a result many health societies that I had organized in Texas and elsewhere were destroyed by the local county medical societies. A doctor applying for a license was rejected if it were known he was to serve in a coöperative hospital. If the doctor was licensed, he was refused admission to membership in the local county medical society, and if the coöperative health society had no hospital of its own, the coöp doctor was refused hospital privileges.

In two instances, doctors in the coöp organization connived with county medical society members to destroy the coöp health society by abolishing the salary system and by making other unreasonable demands.

From 1939 to 1946 state medical associations, affiliated with the A.M.A., introduced bills in the state legislatures which would prevent anyone but physicians from forming medical insurance plans. These bills were enacted into laws in some states. These laws forbid managers and workers of an industry, members of a labor union or a farm organization, or any other group of people from forming health insurance plans with the doctors of their choice.

New Jersey was the first state to enact such legislation. This law provides, among other provisions, that all members of the Board of Trustees, the governing body, must be approved by the medical society, and further, that the plan must first be approved by not less than 51 per cent of the physicians.

Soon thereafter, Pennsylvania, California, Michigan, and Ohio followed suit. In Ohio the law promptly served to block plans which labor and rural groups were endeavoring to set up. Most of these laws were passed in the 1943 and 1945 legislative sessions when the nation's attention was focused on the war; and they were passed in states where labor and farm organizations were powerful and most likely to organize health insurance plans.

In 1947, a bill enabling the adoption of coöperative health insurance plans was introduced in the Wisconsin legislature.

In my capacity as president of the CHFA, I appeared before the committee of the legislature to testify in favor of the bill. Physicians, dentists, and pharmacists appeared to testify against it. The bill was enacted but it took all the power and influence of both labor and farm organization to do it.

For these reasons, and because national health legislation was likely to be an important issue in the new Congress, the Federation in its second annual meeting took steps to safeguard the voluntary medical care plans by advocating the following:

1. (a) That in some form or other national legislation would have to require the states to clear away restrictive laws and set up enabling acts for consumer-organized and controlled plans.
   (b) That this legislation in the states would have to open the hospitals, at least to the extent that they could not discriminate against our doctors.
   (c) That the medical societies also would have to be prevented from discriminating against our doctors.
2. That the administration be directed to foster and promote formation of plans embodying group practice and providing comprehensive service, including preventive medicine, to which end the act should provide a fund to be used for long-term loans up to 100 per cent, at low interest rates, for the use of such groups to construct and equip medical care facilities and hospitals.

The implement those objectives and obviate these discriminations against coöperative doctors, we contacted the American Medical Association, hoping against hope that the successors of Doctor Fishbein would see the light and the justice of our grievances.

A committee representing CHFA and a committee representing the A.M.A. held many meetings.

The second in the series of joint meetings between the American Medical Association and representatives of consumers of medical care took place in Chicago's Palmer House on April 29th, 1950.

Around the table were representatives of the Council on Medical Services, the Rural Health Committee, and the American Federation of Labor. the Congress of Industrial Organizations, the Farm Bureau, the Cooperative Health Federation of America, and a number of its member organizations. Representatives of the National Grange and the Machinists' Union were unable to attend but asked the CHFA to speak for them.

The three-hour meeting was marked by very frank and sometimes spirited discussion. At the outset Jerry Voohis read the statement of the National Grange and stated again, as he had in the first meeting, the two minimum essentials which the organizations representing consumers of medical care feel must be achieved if these joint meetings are to have any value to them. These are (1) the support by A.M.A. for the passage of enabling legislation in the states making clear the right of the people to organize health plans for the solution of the economic problem of paying for adequate medical care, and (2) an end to discrimination against doctors participating in such plans.

It was further pointed out that the first joint meeting (of the previous June) had passed motions to the effect that the consumers' organizations should submit to the A.M.A. in writing a statement of their problems and that the A.M.A. should, on its part, submit, also in writing, a statement of professional standards the observance of which by consumer-sponsored plans would constitute practices acceptable to A.M.A. The consumers' organization submitted their statement in November. A.M.A. had not yet done so.

There followed, at the suggestion of Dr. James McVay, chairman of the A.M.A.'s committee, a discussion of the whole question of standards. A.M.A. representatives insisted that acceptable standards must be developed before progress could be hoped for in removing barriers to the organization and conduct of consumer-sponsored plans.

CHFA spokesmen answered that upon investigation it would be found that high professional standards are now in effect in the plans which are its members, and pointed to the statement of basic policy of the CHFA as evidence of the insistence of the organization upon such standards.

The net result of the meeting was passage of a resolution, originally offered in somewhat stronger form by one of the A.M.A. representatives, which read as follows:

> It is the sense of the individuals at this meeting that we are in substantial agreement that voluntary prepayment medical care plans should be developed that will assure the public of the highest quality of medical service and that full assurance be provided for the maintenance of the quality of good medical care; and that a joint committee be appointed—three by the Council on Medical Service and three by organizations of consumers of medical care—to consider the establishment of standards in conformity with the above principles; and that such committees report back to this assembly at 10 o'clock Saturday, June 4, in Atlantic City.

The sub-committee on standards met on May 15 in Chicago and again with the assembly June 4 at Atlantic City and agreement was reached on the following 20 principles:

1. The plan shall be non-profit, paying no dividends to beneficiaries or others. All surplus earnings shall be devoted either to improving the services, to making compensation of physicians and other staff members more adequate for their responsibilities and services, to purchasing facilities and equipment, to increasing the scope of benefits, or to building adequate reserve funds. All income to the plan shall be devoted to services for beneficiaries.

2. The plan shall comply with the principles of medical ethics of the American Medical Association, which provide that it is unprofessional for a physician to dispose of his professional attainments or services to any lay body, organization, group, or individual, by whatever name called, or however organized, under terms or conditions which permit a direct profit from the fees, salary, or compensation received to accrue to the lay body or individual employing him.
3. If incorporated, the plan shall be adequately financed and organized without capital stock.
4. The plan shall be operated under an autonomous administration or trust, with segregated funds, and shall be devoted exclusively to the provision of health service.
5. Promotion, sales, organization, and administrative expense of the plan shall be kept at a minimum as judged by the accrediting body.
6. The quality of medical service shall be maintained at the highest possible level. All participating physicians shall be Doctors of Medicine duly licensed to practice medicine in any state in which the plan operates. Each physician engaged in the practice of a specialty shall be required to have adequate qualifications for that specialty. The personnel and facilities of the plan shall be adequate to insure a high quality of medical care.
7. The plan shall provide all services as set forth in the agreement with the beneficiary. When, in the opinion of the medical staff, a professional service set forth is not available because of an emergency or because of the need for highly technical procedure or for any other reason, then such service shall be provided by the plan.
8. The plan, in its agreement entered into with the beneficiary, which shall be distributed to each beneficiary, shall state clearly the services and benefits to be provided and the conditions under which they will be provided. All exclusions, limitations, waiting periods, and deductible provisions shall be clearly stated in the agreement

with beneficiary and in promotional and descriptive literature.
9. The plan shall, in its agreement with the beneficiary, state clearly the amount of dues or subscription to be paid. The amount of dues or subscription shall be adequate to provide for the benefits and services offered, and to insure proper financing of the risks involved.
10. No promotional material shall invite attention to the professional skill, qualifications, or attainments of the physicians participating in the plan.
11. Participating physicians may be compensated in any manner not contrary to the principles of medical ethics of the American Medical Association relating to contract practice.
12. Any duly licensed physician in the community who wishes to participate in the plan, who meets its professional and personnel standards, and who agrees to abide by its terms and the requirements of its beneficiaries, shall be admitted to the plan.
13. The names of all participating physicians of the plan shall be made available to the prospective beneficiary. The beneficiary shall, within reasonable geographic and professional limitations, have free choice among participating physicians.
14. There shall be no interference by the governing body with the medical staff in the practice of medicine. The traditional and confidential relationship of the physician and patient shall be preserved.
15. Adequate provision shall be made for effective participation of the medical staff in the deliberations of the governing body. It is recommended that the membership of the governing body include representatives of the medical profession.
16. All services rendered by the participating physicians, not included in the beneficiary's contract, shall be payable by the beneficiary to the participating physicians on a fee-for-service basis.

17. The method of operation of any hospital owned or under contract to the plan shall be in accordance with sound public policy.
18. The plan shall provide for like rates, benefits, terms, and conditions for all persons in the same class.
19. Investment of reserve funds shall be made in securities deemed prudent for such purpose.
20. Any plans desiring approval under these principles shall agree to such periodic reviews and to abide by such regulations as may be deemed necessary by an appropriate accrediting body of the American Medical Association in consultation with representatives of the sponsors of the plan.

Instead of assuming national responsibility in forth-right fashion for approving coöperative health plans as it did in approving the Blue Cross plan, hospitals for interneship, medical schools, and so forth, the House of Delegates of the A.M.A. transmitted the foregoing principles to its satellites (the state and local medical societies) and left it to their discretion to approve or disapprove. This was a unilateral re-interpretation of the agreement and really amounted to partial nullification of the agreement, for may societies indicated that, twenty points or no twenty points, they will not work with the coöperatives.

On account of ill health, I resigned as president of the CHFA in 1949 and was succeeded by Dr. Dean Clark, who is director of the Massachusetts General Hospital and who in collaboration with the late Mayor LaGuardia organized H.I.P., the Health Insurance Plan of Greater New York.

As for me, I collected funds from Lebanese in the United States and Brazil for a charity hospital in Lebanon, went to Lebanon to help build it, and then returned to Elk City, where the Community Hospital, thrice enlarged, stands firm. In 1945 we completed a nurses' home capable of taking care of forty-four persons. It is undoubtedly the finest and best appointed structure of its kind in the nation. In 1949 we built a beautiful clinic building which surpasses anything in the state of Oklahoma. The hospital is solvent, well staffed, and secure in the esteem of the people. And I am once more a respectable citizen, not a demon with radical ideas trying to overthrow our system. Indeed the "best people," the elite element, the bankers, the big hotel proprietor, the leading businessmen of Elk City are now enthusiastic members of the hospital association. They have discovered that the Community Hospital not only gives better care on a cost basis but that it has brought people to town from afar—people who never before traded in Elk City; and these same business people have voluntarily and liberally donated to build and equip the clinic building. They are bent on making Elk City the medical center for western Oklahoma.

We began in 1931 with a few hundred members; today there are 2,677 families holding memberships. But this does not give an accurate idea of the use made of staff and hospital. At the present time about 45 per cent of those who use our facilities are non-members, and the remaining 55 per cent are members. This means that we give service to 5,000 families. The size of the farm families being what they are in this area, we can safely say that we are giving medical care to 15,000 persons.

But Community Hospital, while successful as an institution, is much more important as a demonstration of coöperative medicine, and as a solution to the problem of medical care. This is shown by the way our example has been followed over the country and even abroad. Our idea, our principles, and our methods have been spread by word of mouth, in newspapers and magazines, and over the radio.

A recently conducted survey, made by Mr. L. S. Kleinschmidt for the Council on Medical Service of the American Medical Association, revealed the existence of 79 coöperative health associations in 27 states and the District of Columbia with a total membership of 1,100,000.

As an outcome of my lectures in Saskatchewan there are now a number of large medical coöperatives in that Canadian province, and a coöperative pharmacy in Regina, the capital of the province. In addition the government of Saskatchewan, it should be noted, has inaugurated a province-wide hospital plan whereby hospitalization is provided for the payment of five dollars a year by all adults. The province, building on a foundation of municipal-doctor schemes and union-hospital districts, is moving toward a provincial system of health services by which it is intended that every resident, regardless of income and location, will have the benefit of scientific medical and health services when needed. As Saskatchewan is now the experimental center for social and economic reforms for all Canada, it is probable that the coöperative medical associations and the provincial medical programs will be copied widely throughout the Dominion as rapidly as demonstrated and proven.

Latin American doctors and other leaders have also shown interest in our accomplishments, and are seeking to follow in our footsteps.

I have received my share of honors, from listing in *Who's Who in America* to the Order of Merit from my native Lebanon, and assorted citations, but my real recognition is embodied in the heart-warming letters I continue to receive, testifying that my crusade has not been vain.

Within the past few years, I have had two attacks of coronary thrombosis. I can no longer remain active, as formerly, in the work of lecturing, advising, and writing. These tasks must be passed on to others. No man can ask more of life than to see his constructive work endure. I have exceeded the biblical three-score years and ten; my ideas on coöperative medical care flourish tangibly at Elk City and intangibly in many hearts and many lands; I am content.

Some Notes and Reflections Fifty-Five Years Later

By Fred V. Shadid

I took over as medical director of Elk City's Community Hospital after Dad's retirement in 1946. The Co-operative Health Federation of America was formed that year, and Dr. Michael Shadid was elected as their first president. He served in that capacity until 1949 when his successor took over. During this time he traveled extensively over the United States and Canada lecturing to groups on prepaid medical care and assisting in their organization.

My father's continued remembrance of the hunger, poverty, and lack of health care in Lebanon stimulated his desire to build and equip a hospital in the town of his birth. He launched this project in 1949, traveling over the United States, Canada, and Brazil, obtaining donations from Lebanese people. He was also successful in getting the Lebanese government to agree to match all funds he raised. After three years of hard and difficult work he successfully completed a ten-bed hospital (Hospital Haramoon) with offices for three doctors in the town of 6,000 people, Judedeit-Merjayoun, where he was born. He was extremely proud of this achievement.

I left Elk City in 1953, tired and experiencing the burned-out syndrome from thirteen years of a heavy clinical and hospital practice, combined with the administrative duties of the medical director plus the legal battle of our lawsuit against the Beckham County Medical Society. Our suit was filed in August, 1950, and settled in April, 1952. I gave the Board of Directors a one-year notice of my leaving and spent six months training a member of our staff to succeed me. I moved to Oklahoma City and entered solo practice for the first time in my life.

Approximately one year after I left, friction began to develop between the Board of Directors and the clinic staff. The causes seemed to be policy questions, the division of income with the staff, and I feel, a little infiltration of local city politics. Basically, the friction was due to a lack of strong leadership.

On two occasions I made trips to Elk City and met with the staff and board without results. An impasse developed that finally caused a breakup of the staff, each went into solo practice in Elk City. By 1956 the Blue Cross plans and private health insurance substituted for Co-op medicine.

The Co-op Hospital was born in 1929, the time of drouth, dust bowl days, and the Great Depression in our nation. It filled the need for good health care at affordable prices for the people of western Oklahoma. In spite of all the obstacles and vicious opposition from organized medicine, it grew and prospered under the leadership of a dedicated, dynamic individual, Dr. Michael A. Shadid. It furthered the growth of more prepayment health plans and group practice across the nation. The Co-op Hospital and Dr. Michael Shadid has rightfully taken their places in the medical history of the United States.

In 1984, I was asked to contribute all my memorabilia of the hospital story to the Western History Collections University of Oklahoma. This library is located at 630 Parrington Oval, Norman, Oklahoma.

Index

Abodeeley, Nicholas, M.D.: 123–25
Abortion, surgery for: 79
Advertising: 108, 138–39; by pseudo-coöperative hospital, 141, 142; Shadid accused of, 166
American College of Surgeons (A.C.S.): 76, 78
American Guardian, The: 210
American Medical Association (AMA): 24, 65, 72–73; anti-coöperative views, 226, 229, 231, 241–53; influence on Resettlement Administration plan, 156–57; influence on medical insurance legislation, 259–60; joint meetings with CHFA, 260–65; report on group payment plan, 108–9; *see also* names of AMA committees, etc.
American University of Beirut: 7, 10–15, 59
Ameringer, Oscar: 101, 103, 210
Anderson, Ludwig: 255
Ansley, Bill: 223–24
Appendectomy: 141–42, 151; as profitable surgical operation, 75–76, 80
Army, rejection of unfit men: 66–67
Arnold, Fortas, and Porter (law firm): 231
Arnold, Thurman: 231, 247–52

Babcock, Lucius: 173–77
Babies, delivery of: 90, 151
Basic Science Act (Okla.): 123–24, 160, 186
Becker, Harry: 255
Beckham County Medical Society: 123, 155, 182; attacks on Shadid, 104–13; disbandment, 114–15, 121, 134; litigation

against, 226–37, 269–70; polio politics, 222–24; president opposes coöperative plan, 105–15, 118–19, 126, 163
Bird, J. W.: 214
Blake, Emerson, M.D.: 125
Bliss, Rev. Daniel: 11
Blue Cross: 90, 270
Blue Shield: 222, 230
Blue Valley Farmer (periodical): 119
Blumhagen (lawyer): 215
Branstetter, Otto: 41, 42
Brooks (doctor): 220
Browning, R. L., M.D.: 105
Bulletin (Community Hospital): 152, 166
Bureau of Coöperative Medicine: 243
Bureau of Medical Economics (AMA): 65; on coöperative medicine, 243–44
Butrus al-Bustani: 11

Cabot, Henry, M.D.: 74–75
Cabot Company: 211, 216
Calhoun, Simeon H.: 10
California Medical Association: 244–45
California Physicians' Service (insurance plan): 234–36
Campaigns, political, of Dr. Shadid: 191–208
Cancer, early stage curing of: 66, 150
Carey, James: 255
Carlton, Winslow: 255
Cheek, Tom: 119, 143, 153, 167; and state legislative fight, 178–79, 184, 187–88
CHFA: 254–67
Chicago Eye, Ear, Nose and Throat College, post-graduate study at: 40
Chiropractors: 160, 186–88
Clark, Dean, M.D.: 256, 265
Clinical Medicine (periodical): 52
Clinics, as alternatives to individual specialists: 70, 157
Clinton Hospital: 185–86
"Club practice" (England), compared to coöperative medicine: 243
Coady, M. M., M.D.: 255
Coldiron (lawyer): 215

INDEX

Cole, William E.: 128
Communist, Shadid labeled as: 194, 195, 197–98, 206
Community Health Association: 96, 153
Community Hospital (Elk City): 82, 102, 116; Beckham Medical Society attacks, 104–8; construction, 101; efforts to obtain medical personnel, 123–39; growth, 265–66; payment plans, 96, 99, 106–7, 144–46, 147; World War II staff problems, 218–21
Community Hospital News: 152, 166
"Community Hospital Service Plan, The" (folder): 106, 112
Complete Service Bureau, San Diego, Calif.: 234–36, 252–53
Contract medicine: 245–46
Cook County Graduate School of Medicine (Chicago): 134–37
Coöperative cotton gins: 60, 87
Coöperative grocery store: 48–49
Coöperative health associations: formation of, 191–92; payment plan of, 68–69
Co-operative Health Federation of America (CHFA): 254–67
Coöperative hospital bill (1940), compared to graduated land tax bill: 189–90
Coöperative hospitals organized as bogus competition: 140–44, 150–51
Coöperative medicine, physician's financial benefits in: 80–82
Co-op Health Enabling Act (Wisc.): 258, 259
Co-Op League of the United States: 243
Cost of Medical Care (AMA committee): 108–9, 111
Coughlin (anatomy instructor): 24, 26, 56
Council on Medical Education (AMA): 139, 266
Cruikshank, Nelson: 255
Culbreth, Harry: 256
Curran, John F.: 216

Daily Oklahoman (newspaper): 168–69, 174–77, 186
Danby (doctor): 43–45, 49, 50; Shadid's oil speculation with, 53–54
Davis, Lloyd W.: 138
Deaths, preventable: 66
Democrat, New Deal, Shadid as: 198
Dental Examiners, State Board of, and Community Hospital: 123, 127–29
Dentistry: under Community Hospital's discount plan, 96, 106;

flunking license applicants, 129; performed on WW II service men, 67; state legislation on, 163, 180–81
Depression (1930's): 147, 270
Deutsch, Albert: 76–77
Discount system: use by Community Hospital, 96, 106, 140, 144; use by competitors, 141
Disease prevention, neglect of: 65–69
District of Columbia Medical Society, litigation against: 246–52
"Doctor and the Public, The" (Warbasse): 80
"Doctor for the People, A" (proposed movie): 197
"Doctors' Seven Years of Conspiracy, The" (Shadid): 179
Doyle, James, M.D.: 76
Draft board, local, and Fred Shadid: 220–21
Drought (1930's): 147, 270
Dudley, Duval, and Dudley (law firm): 213
Duerkson, Henry: 209, 211, 215, 216
Dues-paying system: *see* Prepayment plan

Eckrich, J. A., M.D.: 100, 103, 116–17
Education, in *fin de siècle* Lebanon: 6–7
Edwards, Gladys: 255
Election Board, State, refusal to recount votes by: 207–8
Elk City News (newspaper): 100
Elk Sanitarium, Shadid's first hospital: 57
Enfield, O. E.: 101
Equipment, physical: for diagnosis and treatment, 71; donation by Dr. Shadid, 101
Erdman (American University preparatory school principal): 13–15, 18
Etter, Forest, M.D.: 233
Ewing, Oscar: 65
Eye doctors, kickbacks to: 79

Farmers: as members of Blue Cross plans, 90; as members of coöperative medical plan, 152, 191
Farmers' Union: free surgery for, 88–89; and pseudo-coöperative hospital, 143–44; sponsorship of Community Hospital, 153; and state legislative fight, 184; support for Shadid, 101, 173, 193
Farmers' Union Co-operative Hospital Association: 153, 154, 174, 231

Farm Security Administration (FSA), plan for medical costs: 157–60
FBI: 221
Fee-for-service system: 63–64, 67, 68–70, 87, 230; under FSA plan, 158–59
Fees: Shadid's concerns about, 36–37; sliding scale, 65; splitting, 77, 78–84
Finley, Ira M.: 124
Fishbein, Morris, M.D.: 138, 260
Foreigner, Shadid labeled as: 198, 206

Gabriel (uncle): 14, 19
Gaerhardt, Father (Elk City priest): 117
"Ghost surgery," practice of: 77
Glasser, Henry: 213–15
Glasser, Joe: 215
Glaucoma, prevention of: 66, 149–50
Goldman, Dr. Franz: 244
Graduated land tax bill (1940), compared to coöperative hospital bill: 189–90
Great American Insurance Company: 101, 122
Green, Earl: 95, 99
Group Health Association (Washington, D.C.): 74, 229, 241, 246–52
Group Health Coöperative of Puget Sound (Seattle, Wash.): 233–35
Group Health Mutual (St. Paul, Minn.): 254
Group medical care: AMA committee on, 108–9; as CHFA principle, 256; compared to solo practice, 75, 97

Hamilton, William H.: 231–32
Hansen, Fred: 175
Hawley, Paul, M.D.: 74, 76–78
Health Commissioner, Okla.: 179, 182
"Health for Millions" (CHFA publication): 258
Health Insurance Plan of Greater New York: 265
Heitholt, Harry: 209–12, 210; bequest, 209–18
Hereford, Texas: 45–46
Hershey, Gen. Lewis Blaine: 220
Hindman, Charley: 42–43
Hocker, W. E.: 99

Hollingsworth, J. I., M.D.: 163
Home Owners Loan Corporation: 246
Hospital Haramoon (Lebanon): 269
Hospitalization, cost of: 64, 90
Hospitals, and medical factionalism: 55–56; *see also* Community Hospital; Coöperative hospitals
Hotchkiss, Willis L.: 79
Hysterectomy, necessity for: 76–77

Illness, cost of: 63–65
Incomes, and medical costs: 65, 67–68
Influenza epidemic: 49–52
Insurance: 90, 222, 230, 235, 265, 270; as interposing medical control, 83; and membership in county medical association, 121; state medical plans, 259–60
International Harvester Company: 245
Internship practices: 26–27, 28
"It All Depends on Whose Ox Is Gored" (Shadid): 165–66

Jacobson, George W.: 254, 255
Jews: attitude toward in Beirut, 10–11; Shadid labeled as a, 49, 196
Johnson, Victor, M.D.: 139
Johnston, Henry: 217
John Tarleton College (Texas): 21
Jones, Margo: 196
Journal of the American Medical Association: 121, 138–39
Judaidah (Lebanon), childhood in: 3–10
Judedeit-Merjayoun (Lebanon): 269
Justice Department, U.S., and Group Health Association: 247–52

Keaton, Wells, Johnston, and Lytle (law firm): 232
Keen, W. P.: 170–71, 232
Kickbacks, in medical practice: 78–79; *see also* Fees
Kilpatrick, F. S.: 218
Kleinschmidt, L. S.: 266
Ku Klux Klan: 111

Labor unions, in coöperative medicine associations: 81
La Follette, Robert: 220

INDEX

Laird (doctor): 42
Lawrence, John V., M.D.: 256
Lawter, Zed: 119
Lebanon, Shadid in: early life, 3–15; hospital fund-raising, 265, 269
Legislature, Oklahoma, fight for coöperative medicine in: 178–90
License, dental, applicants for: 129
License, medical: attempts to suspend Dr. Shadid's, 105–15, 160, 165–77, 181; fear of loss by Dr. Eckrich, 116–17
Loehr, E. J.: 255
Longwell, W. T.: 127–28, 130
Loos, Clifford, M.D.: 244–45, 250
Los Angeles County Medical Society: 244–45
Los Angeles Department of Water and Power, group medical plan for: 244

McClintock, R. M.: 168–69, 186
McDaniel, Dr. B. O.: 176
McGregor (president, State Board of Medical Examiners): 106
McHenry (doctor): 232
McNutt, Paul: 220
McVay, James, M.D.: 261
Mangold, Lavinia and Michael: 210–11; heirs, 217
March of Dimes: 222
"March of Dollars" polio campaign: 223
Marland, Ernest W.: 178–79, 182, 186
Massingale, Sam: 192, 203, 204
Maxville, Mo., early practice in: 28–33, 35
Mayo Clinic: 70, 148
Medical costs: 63–68, 90; AMA proposed group payment plan, 109; Community Hospital's discount plan, 96, 99, 106; FSA plan, 157–60
Medical Examiners, State Board of: 105–6, 116, 185; attempt to revoke Shadid's license, 165–77; and Community Hospital, 123–26, 130
Medical factionalism: 55–56
Medical insurance: *see* Insurance
Medical legislation: 178–90
Medical practice, solo, inadequacy of: 69–75
Medical Practice Act (Okla.): 160, 163, 171, 176, 259

Medical society, county: *see* Beckham County Medical Society
Medical specialists: *see* Specialists, medical
Memberships, Community Hospital: Resettlement Administration plan, 155; sale by agents, 116; sale in Community Health Association, 96, 217
Milwaukee Medical Center: 229; low-cost medical plan, 241, 245–46
Milwaukee Trades Council: 246
Mobley, Mrs. Earnest: 223
Monroe, James L.: 255
Moreland Commission (N.Y.) (1944): 78
Murray, William H. ("Alfalfa Bill"): 119–20, 153, 161, 178, 205
Musser (judge): 215–16

Nasif al-Yaziji: 11
National Foundation for Infantile Paralysis: 221–22
National Health Insurance: 230
Nealon, Dr. J. K.: 176
Neville, Robert J.: 222
New Deal, Shadid's approval of: 198
New Jersey, law on medical insurance plans: 259
Northern Oklahoma Co-operative Hospital Association, as dummy corporation: 212–16
Nurses: applications at Community Hospital, 126–27; pay during depression years, 147

Ogden, John, M.D.: 250
Ohio medical insurance law: 259
Oil speculation, by Shadid: 53–54
Oklahoma County Dental Society: 128
Oklahoma Federation for Constitutional Rights: 205
Oklahoma State Board of Nurses: 126–27
Oklahoma state commissioner for crippled children: 222
Oklahoma State Medical Association: 169, 185; involvement in Community Hospital litigation, 229–37; *Journal*, 163, 237
Oklahoma Union Farmer (periodical): 173, 179, 190
Olesen, Robert, M.D.: 154–56
Oliver, B. F.: 175
Optical houses, kickbacks by: 79
Optometrists, kickbacks to: 79
Oracle Junction (play): 196

INDEX

Order of Merit (Lebanon), bestowed on Shadid: 267
Osborne, J. L. (secretary, State Board of Medical Examiners): 123–25, 130
Osteopathy, legislation against: 160
Otjen, W. J.: 213

Patients, solicitation of: *see* Steerage
Payments, medical: to doctors under proposed coöperative plan, 90–91; *see also* Fees; Salary, medical
"Peddler of Rags, The" (*Vici Beacon* article): 195–97
Peeler, Paul E.: 95, 97–98, 99
Pepper, Claude: 220
Phillips, Leon: 204, 213
Physicians, Dentists, Druggists, and Nurses Association: 161–62
Physicians' exchanges, and Community Hospital: 126
Polio: 221–24
Political campaigns of Dr. Shadid: 191–203, 204–8
Poor, medical service for: 67, 191–92, 201, 248–49
Porter, Harvey: 11
Post, George, M.D.: 7, 10–11
Preparatory school, American University: 12–15
Prepayment plan: 90, 92, 96; as CHFA principle, 256; copied by competing hospitals, 140–41; cost increases, 150–51; use by Community Hospital, 106–7, 144–46, 147
Preventive medicine: 65–69, 97, 149
"Principles of Coöperative Medicine" (Shadid): 228
Procurement and Assignment draft of Community Hospital doctors: 218–21
Public Health Service, U.S.: 220

Quanah, Texas: 46

Radiologist, at Community Hospital: 133–34
Ravdin, I. S., M.D.: 77
Reader's Digest (magazine): 79
Regina (Sask.), coöperative pharmacy in: 267
Registered Dentists of Oklahoma Act: 163, 180–81
Resettlement Administration, U.S.: 154–57, 180
Richman, Elmer, M.D.: 255
Roberts, Kingsley, M.D.: 243

Rochdale principle of cooperation: 99
Roosevelt, Eleanor: 220
Ross, Byrne: 164
Ross, George T., M.D.: 211
Ross-Loos Clinic, Los Angeles: 241, 244–45, 250
Run-off primary, Shadid's campaign in: 204–8
Rural Electrification associations: 192
Rural Health Conference (AMA): 258

St. Louis World's Fair: 25–26
Salary, medical: under coöperative programs, 68, 80–81, 97, 153; during depression years, 147
Samara, Rasheed, and brother: 22
San Diego Medical Society: 234–36, 252–53
Saskatchewan, Canada, medical coöperatives in: 266–67
Saulsberry, Charles: 174
Scott, Mari: 196–97
Shade, Michael A., as temporary name change for Shadid: 23–24
Shadid, Abraham (father): 4, 5
Shadid, Dr. Alex (son), medical service in World War II: 218–19
Shadid, Bessie (daughter): 40
Shadid, Deeba (sister): 3, 12, 16, 17, 19, 55
Shadid, Edna (Adeeba) (wife): 9, 21–22, 32–33
Shadid, Elias (brother): 3, 4, 12, 19, 21, 27, 55
Shadid, Ethel (daughter): 40
Shadid, Dr. Fred (son): 135, 138; litigation against county medical society, 226–37; as medical director of Community Hospital, 257, 269; and polio crisis, 221–24; wartime attempts to draft, 218–21
Shadid, George (no relationship): 129
Shadid, Kushfa (mother): 4–7, 9, 55
Shadid, Dr. Michael A.: 25, 40, 45–46, 48–49, 79, 101, 265; accused of steerage, 107–8, 114, 116, 165, 166, 171, 172; Beckham Medical Society attacks, 104–15; birth and childhood in Lebanon, 3–9; in Carter, Okla., 40, 41–54; CHFA, founding of, 254–76; on chiropractors, 186–88; coöperative started by, 87–139; education in Lebanon, 6–7, 10–15; in Elk City, Okla., 55–60; on fee-for-service system, 36–37, 63–64, 67, 68–69, 70; and the Heitholt bequest, 209–18; in influenza epi-

INDEX 281

demic, 49–52; as jewelry peddler, 17–20, 25; Lebanon trip (1928), 57–59; in Mangum, Okla., 55–56; marriage, 32–33; Maxville, Mo., early practice in, 28–33; medical license, attempts to suspend, 105–15, 160, 165–77, 181; as medical student, 23–27; name change by, 23–24; with New York cousins, 17, 19; oil speculation by, 53–54; Oklahoma, early practice in, 34–40; political campaigns, 191–203, 204–8; St. Louis Fair, guide at, 25–26; post-graduate study, 40, 45, 134–37; reputed to be Jewish, 49, 196; rumors about, 123–27; on salaries for doctors, 68, 80–81; as Socialist speaker, 41–43; on surgeons' qualifications, 72, 74, 75–77; surgery courses and practice, 56–57; tuberculosis treatment by, 47–48; and typhoid vaccine, 50–52; World War II staff problems, 218–21

Shadid, Ralph (distant cousin): 127–29

Shadid, Ruth (daughter): 33, 34; trip to Lebanon with father, 57–59

Shibley, William: 129

Shidoody, Asad: 11

Shoudy, Addison: 255

Simpson, John: 101, 103, 119, 153, 202

Simpson, William: 202

Smith, Dr. Eli: 11

Smith, Gomer: 169–71, 173–75, 213

Socialist, Shadid labeled as: 197–98, 206

Specialists, medical: applicants at Community Hospital, 131–33; competence of, 71–74; fees charged by, 64; lack of in small towns, 97

Speed, Dr. H. K.: 126, 163

Spooner (professor, Washington University): 23, 43

Standifer, O. C., M.D.: 226–28

Steerage: 105, 176; Dr. Shadid accused of, 107–8, 114, 116, 165, 166, 171, 172

Stekler, Okla., early practice in: 34–40

Stevenson (doctor): 250

Subversive activities, Shadid accused of: 205

Sugarman, M. J., M.D.: 237

Supreme Court of California, on group health plans: 234–36

Supreme Court of Washington, on restraint of competition: 233–34

Surgeons, competence of: 72, 74–77

Surgery costs: 64, 96, 99

Swain (instructor, American University): 18
Syrian Protestant College: 7, 10–15, 59

Technical Committee on Medical Care (1939): 67
Thomas, Elmer: 220
Thompson, Carl: 221–22
Thompson, J. M., M.D.: 163
Tisdale, V. C., M.D.: 228
Tonsillectomy: 142
Topley, Harve: 212–13
Trinity Hospital (Little Rock, Ark.), group medical plan: 241, 245
Tuberculosis (consumption): 47–48
Turner, Roy J.: 127
Typhoid vaccine, Shadid's use for influenze cases: 50–52

Urology, specialists in: 131, 148, 150, 157

Van Dyck, Cornelius Van Alan: 10–11
Vaughn, Harvey P.: 157
Veterans of Industry of America (VIA): 124, 184
Vici Beacon (newspaper): 195–97
"Voluntary Medical Care Insurance in the United States" (Goldman): 244
Voohis, Jerry: 261

Wails, James O.: 138
Warbasse, James P., M.D.: 68–69, 243; on doctors in coöperative medicine, 80–83
Washington, D.C., Academy of Surgery: 250
Washington University School of Medicine (St. Louis): 21, 23
Who's Who in America: 267
Wilbur, Ray Lyman, M.D.: 108–9, 111, 139
Wilkinson, Charles: 255
Williams, R. C., M.D.: 156–57
Wilson, James Howard: 211, 216
Wilson and Wilson (law firm): 211, 212, 215
Wisconsin, Co-op Health Enabling Act: 258, 259
Wisconsin Association of Co-operatives: 258
Woods, E. C.: 42–43

World Wars I and II, rejection of unfit men: 67
Worrell, Milton: 217–18
Wybrant, O. C.: 214

X-ray technician, at Community Hospital: 134
X-ray technicians, American registry of: 134